Between Extremes

Between Extremes

BRIAN KEENAN & JOHN McCARTHY

BANTAM PRESS

LONDON · NEW YORK · TORONTO · SYDNEY · AUCKLAND

TRANSWORLD PUBLISHERS
61–63 Uxbridge Road, London W5 5SA
a division of The Random House Group Ltd

RANDOM HOUSE AUSTRALIA (PTY) LTD
20 Alfred Street, Milsons Point, Sydney
New South Wales 2061, Australia

RANDOM HOUSE NEW ZEALAND
Poland Road, Glenfield, Auckland 10, New Zealand

RANDOM HOUSE SOUTH AFRICA (PTY) LTD
Endulini, 5a Jubilee Road, Parktown 2193, South Africa

Published 1999 by Bantam Press
a division of Transworld Publishers Ltd
11 13 15 17 19 20 18 16 14 12

A catalogue record for this book is available from the British Library.
ISBN 0593 042646

Typeset in 12/14 pt Goudy by Falcon Oast Graphic Art

Printed in Great Britain
by Clays Ltd, St Ives plc

For Anna and Audrey, and for Jack the Lad
who was descending to earth while we were on top of the world

In calling up images of the past, I find that the plains of Patagonia frequently cross before my eyes; yet these plains are pronounced by all wretched and useless. They can be described only by negative characters; without habitations, without water, without trees, without mountains, they support only a few dwarf plants. Why, then, and the case is not peculiar to myself, have these arid wastes taken so firm a hold of my memory? Why have not the still more level, the greener and more fertile Pampas, which are serviceable to mankind, produced an equal impression? I can scarcely analyse these feelings; but it must be partly owing to the free scope given to the imagination. The plains of Patagonia are boundless, for they are scarcely passable, and hence unknown; they bear the stamp of having thus lasted, as they are now, for ages, and there appears no limit to their duration through future time. If, as the ancients supposed, the flat earth was surrounded by an impassable breadth of water, or by deserts heated to an intolerable excess, who would not look at these last boundaries to man's knowledge with deep but ill-defined sensations?

CHARLES DARWIN
The Voyage of the Beagle (London, 1902)

Contents

Acknowledgements

Many people helped and encouraged us in fulfilling our Chilean fantasy. Our thanks go to:

Bill Scott-Kerr who, with great charm and patience, did so much to realize our accounts of our Chilean experiences. Jane Parritt, who picked up on a brief mention about Patagonia and yaks. Without her our great adventure might have remained a captive daydream. Katie Hickman and her parents, John and Jenny, who gave us much advice on where to go and what to see and introductions to their many Chilean friends. Tom Owen Edmunds, who as well as sharing his own insights on the country joined us for our time in and around Santiago and on the horse trek high into the Andes. Not only did he take many fine photographs but his companionship and good humour eased our saddle sores. Chris Parrott and Sally Rich at Journey Latin America for turning our outline plans into a feasible itinerary. Frank Murray and Noni McClure for their hospitality and generous loan of a quiet haven in Santiago. Jorge Lopez Sotomayor and Jueni Valdes Lopez, who opened up their hearts and home to us. Alfonso and Isabel Campos, for welcoming us in Patagonia and appreciating the genius of Keenan's yakic inspiration. David Ottewill for his valuable comments on John's text. A special thanks to Noleen Gernon, who traipsed around Chile on her fingertips to type up Brian's story.

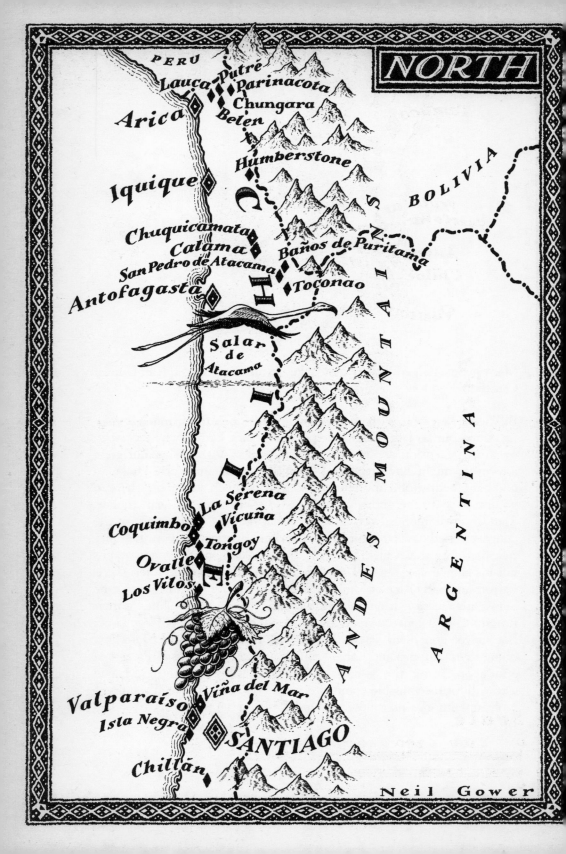

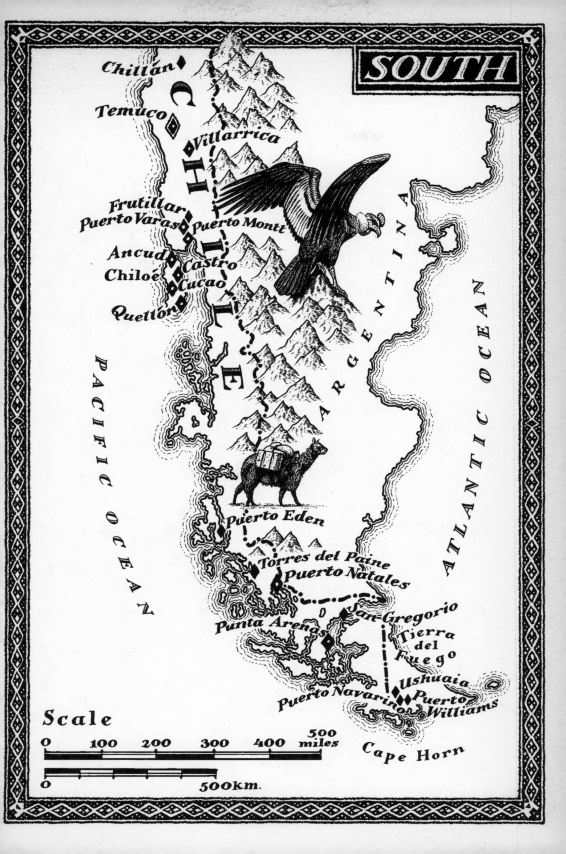

Prologue

BEIRUT, SUMMER 1990

The midday heat is intense. Sounds drift up from the street a few floors below and filter through heavy metal shutters fixed across the inside of the window. Any hint of natural light is overwhelmed by the bare electric bulb shining above the centre of our stark room.

Brian is sitting cross-legged on a thin mattress, rocking gently back and forth as he reads intently from one of the bulky volumes of our incomplete set of the *Encyclopaedia Americana*. Both his hands move methodically, ruffling and smoothing his shaggy beard.

I am lying back on my mattress which shares the same wall as Brian's, smoking a cigarette, occasionally puffing a cloud of smoke at a mosquito when it drones too close.

'Take that, you little bastard!'

'What?' asks Brian.

'Eh? Oh, nothing. Puff?'

'No thanks, I'm all smoked out.'

The mosquito buzzes over to Brian. Without looking up from his text, he snakes his hand out and snaps it shut. He holds it before him and carefully opens the fist, smiling as he sees the offending creature smeared on his fingers. Idly he flicks the remains off his hand, wipes it on the edge of the mattress and continues reading.

I turn round and, as I move, one of my legs is stopped short by the chain that runs from the ankle to a bolt in the wall.

'Bri, I've been thinking.'

'Oh God! What now, Mastermind?'

'Look, I know you think this is stupid but . . . You remember Frank Reed was released on the thirtieth of April, right?'

'Yeah. Yeah. Something like that.'

'Well, that was just two weeks after Friday the thirteenth.'

'Oh God, no, John, not that again,' Brian cuts in, snorting with a mix of irritation and amusement. 'Let me guess. I've been locked up one thousand, three hundred and twelve days, you've been locked up one thousand, three hundred and six days. If you divide that by the number of stinking holes we've been dumped in and multiply that by the number of spots on a turkey's arse, we will have the final, definitive date for our release. Am I right, my mathematical Englishman?' We are both laughing.

'Look, just because elementary figures have your dim Irish brain confused, it does not mean that I am talking bollocks!'

'OK, OK, just get on with it. I know I'm gonna have to hear about Friday the thirteenth. I'm all ears!' he says, cupping his spread hands behind his head and waggling the fingers like crazy antennae.

'We've been moved every time there's been a Friday the thirteenth. There's another one coming up in July – so something's bound to happen!'

'Sure, John, sure.'

'Well, bugger you! I'll just go home on my own then.'

The key rattles in the lock and we don our blindfolds. It is a guard, Bilal, delivering our daily ration of food.

'Hello, Brian. Hello, John. How are you?'

'OK, Bilal.'

'You hungry?' he asks.

'Yes.'

'Today very good food.' He puts down plastic plates containing felafel, hummus, chips, pitta bread and tomatoes.

'Ah, very good,' I say, peeking beneath my blindfold.

'Welcome! Welcome!' says Bilal, delighted with his treat, then he leaves.

As I cut a tomato my small plastic picnic-knife snaps.

'Bugger!'

'Just too eager to get at your eatings, eh!' says Brian. He roots through his paltry collection of belongings – a spare well-worn T-shirt, a pair of cheap white shorts in which the elasticated waist has given up the ghost, a few tissues and a sweatshirt, so faded through many, many washings that it is little more than a dishcloth.

'Ah ha! There it is!' He beams victoriously and presents me with another plastic knife, also broken but retaining an inch of usable blade.

'Thanks, Bri. At times your nefarious hoarding instincts are of real value.'

'You said it! Now don't go breaking that one. There's no more.'

After eating we lie flat, stretched out as far as the chains allow, and share a cigarette.

'I've been thinking,' I say.

'My, my, we have been busy!'

'Yeah, yeah. Anyway I'm coming round to the idea that Patagonia might be better than Peru.'

Brian looks at me intently.

'Do you think so? Really? Why?'

'Well, although those eastern slopes of the Andes appear to have the right climate for vicuña, sheep and cattle farming – and plenty of space – they are just so remote. Shipping out the wool might be tricky.'

'Mm, I see what you mean, but couldn't we use mule trains or something?'

'For God's sake, Bri. You and me riding about in the mountains? I've been on a horse twice and fell off once, and what about you and Billy?'

'Ahh, fuck Billy. Butch Cassidy and the Sundance Kid. That'll be us.'

'Well maybe, but Patagonia is flat.'

'But it's pretty remote too.'

'OK, but the city there, Punta Arenas, has a serious port – even an airport. There is one drawback with Patagonia though.'

'Howling winds?'

'No. The Welsh.'

'The Welsh. What's wrong with them?'

'After four years of the Celtic fringe I'm not sure I could take any more.'

'Racist Brit bastard. The Welsh are only in the Argentine part of Patagonia. The Chilean bit's got Scots and English.'

'English. Excellent! Chilean Patagonia it has to be. No Irish?'

'Well, I don't know . . . but don't forget Bernardo.'

'Who?'

'Bernardo O'Higgins, the Great Liberator – son of an Irishman, set Chile free from the yoke of Imperial Spain, established a—'

'OK, OK! So I'd forgotten bloody Bernardo. Still, I reckon Patagonia makes sense. Plenty of space and no one to come bothering us.'

'What about Pinochet?'

'Don't you remember that *Time* magazine we got a couple of years ago? Said he'd had a plebiscite and was going to hand power back to the civilians.'

'Oh yeah. Yes, so that should be all right then.'

We spend the afternoon and evening reading, occasionally swapping notes and sharing a cigarette. Bilal reappears with some black tea and pitta sandwiches containing cheese and olives. Then we are left in peace, unlikely to be disturbed again before morning. But we do not relax totally for fear of being too mentally vulnerable should there be a sudden jolt of activity, with guards stomping everywhere before carting us out, bound and gagged as well as blindfolded, and heaving us into the boot of a car for an uncomfortable drive to yet another location.

I am suddenly conscious of Brian tensing.

'What is it?' I ask urgently. 'You all right? Did you hear something?'

'No. No, I'm fine. Listen to this: "Yak. A wild and domesticated ox, with a long shaggy coat of silken hair used in weaving." Big beasts. They'd be ideal for Patagonia.'

This last, triumphant phrase echoes in the sudden silence of a power cut. Within a second a guard raps on the door and hisses for quiet.

'All right! All right!' mutters Brian and starts going through his belongings again. He turns to me in the darkness.

'Got the matches?'

'Here,' I whisper, striking one and reaching to light the candle in his hand. He sets the candle down and once the flame has strengthened pulls the volume up close to him.

'I thought yaks came from Mongolia or somewhere.'

'Aye, Tibet it says here. Listen:

> YAK: an animal (*Bos grunniens*) of the Bovidae family, distributed in the high bleak plateaus and mountains of Central Asia. It is found in Tibet, Kansu (northwest China), and the Chang Chenmo Valley of Ladakh (eastern Kashmir). It ranges from the lower valleys to 20,000-foot levels, feeding on coarse grasses. The wild yak moves in winter from the snow-covered slopes to the valleys.
>
> The yak is exceptionally well adapted to endurance of cold and shows superb stamina, which makes it an excellent animal for carrying people and other burdens. Its numbers are decreasing, although it once was as abundant as the American bison. Old bulls wander about in twos or threes, but females and calves herd together for protection.'

'How would we get them to Patagonia?'

'Easy. When we get out of here, we'll just write to the People's Republic of China and the Dalai Lama and say we want some yaks, and they'll send us half a dozen cows and a few bulls. We spend a few years breeding them and increasing our herd size . . .'

'OK, then what?'

'Listen to this:

> The domesticated forms, although used principally for transportation, are valued also for their meat. This is of excellent quality, and calf meat is especially tasty. The cows provide quantities of rich milk. The Tibetans also extract good yields of butter, which they use to flavour their tea or to burn in religious shrines. The long hair of the yak is made into ropes, while hides

with hair are used as coverings for tents. The tails are sometimes dyed bright red and sold as flyflappers in the cities of India.'

'So?'

'So then we set up "Paddygonia Enterprises Inc.", that's P-a-d-d-y-gonia, and we corner the world market in yak products. Imagine it, we'll be shipping out tons of yak yoghurt and butter. Yak steaks will be the speciality of every top restaurant in the world. Then there's yak burgers, yak sausages . . . And I haven't even started on the hide and wool yet. Think of it – we could be millionaires.'

'I'm convinced, but what about the flyflappers?'

'Fuck the flyflappers . . . we could sell them as a fashion accessory.'

We look at each other, pondering the possibilities, silently sharing the realization that one day we must go there. But there's no denying our present situation. Whatever our dreams, Patagonia might as well be a million miles away. For the moment at least, we are not going anywhere.

Part One

Arica

•

Atacama

•

Santiago

Chapter One

≡Ⅲ≡

A gentle shaking wakes me. Brian is leaning across to point out of the window: 'There they are. The Andes!'

From our bird's eye perspective the first ridges and valleys look rusty and dusty, the hide of an elephant close up. Then we are among snow-capped peaks for a minute or two before starting our descent on the other side. Above us, clear blue sky, and from the plane's wing-tip a small vapour trail streams, an effete cigar whiff compared to the monstrous clouds that swirl like steam from a boiling cauldron.

As quickly as they appear, the mountains vanish and we make our final approach to the capital, Santiago de Chile. The land is flat and wide with roads, irrigation ditches and fields as neatly laid out as any in Europe except here they are on a vast scale. There are no houses, as though the place has been planned, basic development started and no one has taken up the estate agent's offer.

Chile's physical boundaries – the Andes in the east, the Pacific to the west, desert in the north and the ice of Antarctica to the south – create a natural island. Certainly these borders, before the advent of big ships and aircraft, meant that only the most determined came here. Although Magellan discovered in 1520 the channel from the Atlantic to the Pacific that now bears his name, it was not until 1536 that the first Europeans entered Chile.

Led by the Spanish conquistador Diego de Almagro – who with Francisco Pizarro had conquered the Incas in Peru – a force of four hundred men made their way over the Andes into Chile. The expedition was a disaster and many died or suffered cruelly in the harsh, cold, mountainous conditions. Looking down from the plane, I wonder at the ambition of people like Almagro. Had they known what lay ahead, would they have persevered?

I know that we are heading for an arid region, indeed one of the driest places on earth, the Atacama Desert, but I was expecting the transition from the green plains around Santiago, in Chile's lush heartland, to the brown hills and valleys of the north, to be more gentle. Yet, almost as soon as we have changed planes and left the capital for Arica, green becomes nothing but a memory. The scene is utterly lifeless, scalded and scorched, with slivers of road wandering here and there. The mountains below stretch away to my left where I can see the shoreline and the Pacific breakers rolling in.

For a long while we follow the coast, a seemingly endless succession of wide bays and small coves. Low cloud hugs the shoreline, blurring the distinction between land and water. Mostly, though, the ground looks quite barren, with no settlements, no boats and just the occasional track. I feel a sudden, unexpected respect for this uncompromising landscape.

The coastal range looks like a giant skeleton picked bare by the vultures of sand and wind. The absence of even a hint of water, let alone anything green, conjures in my mind an image of a colonist, hopeful of founding a great estate, being defeated by nature and gradually going insane. In his dotage, believing that his slice of nowhere is really bountiful earth after all, he carefully plots it out and farms stones.

Nearing the start of our Chilean journey, we fly along a narrow coastal strip of dull brown earth. A road, glistening and wandering like a filament of treacle, spins along near the sea, the few vehicles on it like beetles scuttling for safety. The sun beats down a hot warning. As we descend, and the plane's shadow shrinks to a tiny, toy size, a small terminal building shimmers in the heat. This is Arica, the real start of our Chilean experience. I am excited yet tired and, now we are here, a little apprehensive.

'We need an oasis, John.'
'You're not wrong there, Bri.'

∧∧∧

The flight into Arica airport should have filled me with some kind of anticipation or even excitement but for some reason that wasn't the case. I spent most of the journey intrigued by a woman passenger sitting to the left of me. Her features were classically South American. Her skin and hair seemed to be shellacked. Her face and arms were a tone brighter than milk chocolate and her hair, pulled back tightly from her face, was so lustrous that you couldn't define its separate strands. I tried to make conversation but failed miserably, my Spanish being almost non-existent. I watched her glance towards John, who had a book on his knee, Isabel Allende's novel *The House of the Spirits*. She looked closely and not inconspicuously at it.

John noticed her curiosity and smiled. She smiled back and leaned across, pointing at the book and saying simply, 'This is a very good book.' Unfortunately her English was as poor as my Spanish and she could add little to her statement. I knew the story and could imagine what she meant by its being a good book, but I would have loved to be able to talk to her about it. Would her native perspective be very different from my alien one? But that was one of the reasons I came to Chile, to find my own particular House of Spirits.

Like many encounters, this one was all too brief and as swiftly as the small aircraft landed she was gone with a polite smile of acknowledgement. As we took down our belongings from the luggage racks I glanced again at Isabel Allende's novel as it lay on the aircraft seat. Looking at the face of the woman on the book cover, I was momentarily struck by the fact that it could almost have been the face of the woman who had just left. It was one of those quirky moments you try to brush off but it lingers with you. To a weary traveller in a strange land, coincidence takes on a curious significance.

Whatever I was beginning to make of this seemingly ghostly encounter was soon dispelled as we descended the aircraft steps to the tarmac. I looked about me. In the hot sun the landscape shimmered, bleached and bone white. It was barren, desolate and empty. Even the sea on one side could not relieve it. For a moment I wondered, what in the name of Christ are we going into? But my musings were noisily interrupted. Steaming towards us was an open-topped blue tractor of a dubious vintage with two very badly buckled front wheels. It lurched from side to side with all the grace of a demented bull. It looked like a mechanical animal puffing huge draughts of black smoke into the white-hot sky. When I considered it, I realized that no other kind of creature could survive in this landscape. It belonged here, buckled and huffing, roaring with a parched groan.

As we made for the shade of the airport terminal we were con-fronted by a gaggle of passengers milling about. Everywhere men, women and children were carrying bags of goods purchased in the tax-free shop. The scene had the feel of a Sunday school outing. I looked back towards the aircraft, hoping to catch a glimpse of the spirit woman once more.

Instead I saw a huge and very gaudy lampshade marching jerkily by. It was being carried by a small child who had hoisted it over his head so that only his legs protruded from under it. Behind the lampshade in single file came the rest of his family, each of them loaded down with colourful bags or boxes. They looked for all the world like a column of ants in clown costume parading across the tarmac. It was the only colourful relief from the bleakness of this place.

But it was too hot to stand looking for the living embodiment of a book cover. We quickly collected our luggage and cleared the terminal.

≡ⅲ≡

The sign says 'Arica International Airport'. For the size of the place, this seems a joke, but it is just a couple of miles to the Peruvian border and half of Bolivia's trade passes through Arica. I see a signpost, 'Arica 16 km: Santiago 2058 km', and I think, Christ, we've just come from there, and now we've got to go all the way back. We have just touched down in a place of dreams and I am twitchy and cross. I look at Brian who, though I know he must be tired too, looks in good spirits. The bastard.

∼∧∼

The drive from the airport to Arica did little to dispel the feeling of emptiness of this place. Everywhere about me, desert scrubland rolled down into the boiling sea. Here were two salty wastes meeting on this bitter coastline. One hot and burning, the other liquid and coolly inviting.

Arica itself was something of a curiosity, clinging desperately to that defining line between the desert and the ocean. I had imagined Arica to be like any frontier town, small and seedy and existing simply because it was just that, a marker delineating the border between Chile and Bolivia. A place where perhaps history had passed by and people survived because mankind, like animals, must have territories and borders and needs places like this to mark out the defining lines.

But Arica has a history. During the Inca period, it was the terminus of an important trade route. Even then the Indian peoples exchanged corn, fish and maize for potatoes, wool and whatever other produce might arrive there. With the Spanish colonization this small trading port was upgraded to the status of a city in 1545. But more importantly, the discovery of a huge and fabulously wealthy silver mine near Potosí, in present day Bolivia, greatly increased the size and importance of Arica. It is difficult, but intriguing nonetheless, to imagine that by 1611 the town and the area surrounding Potosí was one of the most densely inhabited cities in the whole of the western hemisphere, and Arica was the equivalent of some Los Angeles suburb.

I thought how McCarthy and I had marked out territories for ourselves, both literal and metaphorical, during our long sojourn in Lebanon. The lunacy of dividing up the planet in some squalid basement in Beirut suddenly struck me. For years we had survived on dreams and now here we were entering the reality of them.

Most people suggest one should leave dreams where they belong, back in the never-never. But here we were, dreamers to the end, pursuing the never-never like Don Quixote and Sancho

Panza. Perhaps we both needed our heads examined or perhaps, as my mother always used to say, 'Be careful what you want because if you want it hard enough you will get it.' As the bus chugged through the town traffic into the heart of Arica, I could still hear McCarthy's voice defiantly stating, 'You can't have the Caribbean, that's mine, and I'm gonna roof it!'

Our hotel was a stucco construction, a kind of mock-Spanish adobe. It was surprisingly lavish for a nondescript desert town. Having registered and had our bags taken to our room, we were offered a pisco sour, a local brandy-type spirit mixed with sugar and lemon juice. Two of these were more than sufficient.

≡|||≡

Sitting at the poolside bar of the Hotel Arica, a fine spot with the Pacific breakers creaming in a hundred yards away, things seem less stressful as we chat with Karlen, our guide for the next few days.

'So you are going to see all of Chile?' she asks.

'We hope so,' I reply.

'Why Chile especially?'

I explain briefly about Lebanon and the dreams and plans we had then.

'When did this happen?' she asks.

'Well, it's more than ten years ago now that we were taken,' says Bri.

'Ten years?' she asks, looking perplexedly from one to the other of us. She muses for a moment then goes on, 'Well, I hope Chile is as good as you dreamed!'

We talk through our plans to spend the next few days around Arica, learning that our guide tomorrow will be a woman called Katia.

It begins to sink in that we have two months of this, and that, though we are tired now, it might not be so bad after all. We are here and settled and all the months of planning are about to pay off. We have spoken much on the phone about the details of the trip but haven't actually seen each other for quite a while – what with Bri being in Dublin and me in England.

I felt the same thrill as always when we met at Heathrow. Hugging Brian's solid frame inevitably lifts my spirits in antici-pation of laughter, affection and discussion of any number of topics and the likelihood of intense debate. Yet since Beirut we have only ever met for short periods, at most two or three days. Now we are committed to months on the road together, dealing with unknown problems, sharing brand new experiences. Since Lebanon our relationship has moved on, becoming more relaxed yet not losing its intensity. The captive days are far enough behind us now not to dominate, happily wrapped up as we are in our separate lives.

I wonder to what degree, if any, we may have lost the ability to read each other's feelings and react in tandem to situations without the need for explicit communication. But such musings will resolve themselves in the days ahead so for the moment I put them aside.

Given the fact that we are very evidently in a desert it comes as no surprise that the bathroom is plastered with signs urging minimal consumption of water. I rinse some socks and myself in the feeble shower, then dress and go for a drink on the terrace while Brian freshens up.

I had a shower and made the obligatory phone call home. Then I sat and read, but my mind was too preoccupied to be attentive. Instead I watched the desert sparrows flit to and from the balcony. For some time I sat trying to resolve with myself what this was the beginning of. There were three thousand miles in front of us, always heading further south, from the foothills of Bolivia and Peru to the wastes of Tierra del Fuego. It was a dizzying thought. Contemplation of this journey might have filled up many months of our captivity but the actuality of it was another thing. I looked around the room and then out into the vista from the balcony to confirm the reality.

The hotel had left some food for us, fruit, biscuits and some local cake. I wasn't hungry, so I brought the biscuits and cake out to the balcony and fed the desert sparrows which darted in and out of the eaves of our hotel.

When I joined John on the terrace, I wasn't surprised to find that he had dressed for dinner. I recalled the day John arrived at Lyneham air force base after being released from his captivity. As I stood watching him descend from the aircraft, I remember remarking quietly to myself, 'Well, he would have to look like a film star, wouldn't he!' The memory, combined with his immaculate appearance, now confirmed who was to be Don Quixote and who was to be Sancho Panza on this trip.

Thanks to the combination of our own weariness and excitement and the strangeness of the place, our conversation over dinner was inconsequential, circling around the fact of us being here and the reason for it. Could anyone believe where this trip had its origins, when two half-naked men, blindfolded and chained to a wall, discussed with fevered enthusiasm the possibility of setting up a yak farm in Patagonia?

We discussed the various travel books we had read as if trying to fit ourselves into the appropriate mould. John has a particular fondness for travel writing and is much more widely read on the subject than I. I felt somewhat out of place. As we discussed what travel writing should be I remember remarking that the travel writer has to engage the reader with a new and imagined present. He has to convey the essence of an incident or a place rather than the fact of it. The history of the continent we were in and indeed the history of Arica, as we were to learn, had shown how the facts of history were transcendent.

John seemed to be listening intensely but was obviously in no mood for such academic debate. In a broad Belfast accent he mocked my words with a taunt: 'Ah, would you ever go and give my head peace.' We both laughed and decided to retire to the patio near the pool.

Arica is a holiday resort for wealthy Bolivians and there were some people still swimming in the pool or sitting, like ourselves, to enjoy the evening. We were intrigued by the faces of our fellow guests and tried to discern the signs of Indian, colonial Spanish or other European ancestry in the people about us. There is something distinctly lovely in faces that display a mixture of bloodlines. They have a beauty that is their own.

We looked out over the pool to the sea beyond. It was becoming dusk and for what seemed more than an hour we watched as a lone trawler to-and-fro'd across the horizon as if sucking up the very innards of the ocean.

That night I lay on my bed listening to the monotonous drone of the fishing boats and in the subsequent hours those ships roared through my sleep. For a while I lay awake thinking of the faces in the hotel and I remembered something of what D. H. Lawrence had said in his dismissal of what he called a 'Dead Europe'. He spoke of the 'passion' of Catholic countries where women had not lost their identity in the gender-bending emotional and socio-logical war of the sexes. Lawrence's own sexual confusions were no panacea. I remembered looking at his paintings in the desert of New Mexico and I thought, Here I am also in a desert but a lot less sure of myself. I was far from home and feeling lonely, my thoughts maudlin, and I suspect trying to find a first foothold for our oncoming expedition.

≡III≡

I wake abruptly at five. One of my earplugs has come adrift and the Keenan nasal buzz-saw is droning at full throttle.

'Shut up!' I bark, switching on a light.

Brian pops up from the horizontal saying, 'Is it time to get up already? I haven't slept with that ship making all that row out there.'

I ignore him. Brian's snoring and this subsequent reaction is a throwback, and while irritating and recalling broader frustrations from the past, it is also reassuring.

We go back to sleep and then, on reawaking, I try to make sense of my bags and belongings. Whichever way you look at it, my main bag is not sufficiently large for the amount of gear I have with me.

'Do you not think maybe you've got too many things?' asks Brian, lying on his bed as I re-sort various bits of kit into piles. 'What are they? Swimming trunks?'

'No. Cycling shorts.'

'Cycling shorts!' he snorts, jumping up and rifling through my bag. 'Don't tell me you've got a fold-up bike in there too!'

I cannot help laughing with him but have to explain, 'No, smart-arse. Anna gave me them for the horse trek in the mountains.'

'Oh well, that seems pretty sensible, I suppose. Good on her.' Then he starts laughing anew.

'What now?'

'I was just thinking that you'd have been better off if we'd gone straight to Tibet to check out the yaks' – his voice becoming high and throaty as he revels in his joke – 'then you could have had a sherpa to lug all that gear for you!'

The motto of Chile is 'By reason or by force' which I suppose means, 'if you don't agree with us we will make you'. And that in itself could be an adequate definition of colonialism of any description.

In Arica there is a long wall facing the sea. Someone had painted a mural outlining that colonial history. Here were images of the native Indian culture, the Spanish colonial conquest and through to the present day, including what is called 'the War of the Pacific' in which Arica was taken from Peru and became Chilean national territory. But there was one glaring omission. There is nothing to denote the events of the Pinochet regime, one of the most ruthlessly fascist governments in the history of South America.

Near the harbour were the beached remains of a shipwreck which looked oddly like a gingerbread cake. Beside it, a Spanish fortress sat crumbling on a promontory into the sea, circled by and infested with what the locals call TVs or turkey vultures. The gingerbread shipwreck and the turkey vultures nestling in the ruins of Spanish colonialism seemed to be an apt comment on the history of this place.

Overlooking the town was a hill, El Morro, on which stood an old fort housing the Arms Museum dedicated to the War of the Pacific and the taking of Arica from Peru in 1880. There remains to this day some dispute between Peru and Chile about the rightful status of Arica. This was interestingly summed up on that hill.

Just off from the museum was a plinth-like structure, something like a miniature Mayan temple. Our guide Katia told me it is awaiting the erection of the Christ figure when all the political problems are solved. This confusion of faith with politics is one I still fail to understand. But it remains a means which every right wing and arch conservative organization has used to subjugate the minds and imaginations of their people. I speak with some authority, having been on the receiving end of minds poisoned by such thinking.

≡Ⅲ≡

Katia is quietly spoken with fluent English and an engaging giggle. 'Local legend says that the fifty-five Chilean heroes prepared for their final attack by drinking strong liquor fortified with gunpowder,' she tells us and Bri mimes pouring a drink and handing me a glass.

'Here, John, this should knock your head off!'

Laughing, Katia leads us underground to a moving exhibition of photographs of the army of the time and a plaque to the dead draped with a flag. The sombre effect is undermined by the ludicrous martial music that belts out from tinny loudspeakers.

From the cool of the museum we emerge into the blinding heat. El Morro has little enough scrubby vegetation, but inland the terrain is balder still. It seems a very alien environment.

'How many people live here, Katia?' I ask.

'Around a hundred and seventy thousand people.'

'But what do they all do?'

'The main local industries are fishing, motor car plants, Wrangler jeans factory and tourism—'

'Tourism!' interjects Brian, rifling through my pockets and taking out cigarettes and lighter. 'I don't want to be rude, Arica seems a nice place, but who wants to spend their holidays with that appalling stench?'

He lights up and puffs furiously – unusual for him as he smokes only occasionally. He is right about the smell: it is so thick you feel you could touch it, cut it with a knife. With the heat and humidity the effect is suffocating and my head feels as though it has been submerged in a bowl of warm, rancid glue.

'What is it?' I ask, lighting my own cigarette.

'The fishmeal factories,' she replies, declining a proffered cigarette and adding through giggles, 'Sometimes money does not smell well, eh?'

∿∿

Descending the hill towards the centre of Arica one had to pass through a shanty town. The whole of this rudimentary community was pockmarked with tiny Methodist, Mormon and Seventh Day Adventist churches. These buildings were not much bigger than some of the appalling shanty homes, indeed, some of them may well have housed a family before becoming a structure of faith. In the middle of all this reformist zeal there was a small but robust Catholic chapel with a stubby steeple. It stood defiantly, declaring that it alone was at the very centre of people's suffering.

Back in the town, standing in stark contrast to these small churches was the church of San Marco or the Iron Cathedral of Eiffel. As its name declares, the church was designed and built by the same gentleman who constructed the great iron tower in Paris. It was built entirely in prefabricated iron. Even the walls and ceilings were lined with stamped, moulded iron plates. Only the door was made of wood. As this is a desert climate and it has not rained here in the memory of the oldest inhabitants, the builders of this cathedral were assured that it would never rust or decay. Entering it, one felt immediately its coldness, its impersonality and even its sterility. Metal is not the medium of passion, and in this hulk of a God house I could feel no movement of the spirit. Only standing in the patio of the grotto at the side of the church did I have any sense of religion, as I watched one little bird hop and dance around a bent old woman as she moved about sweeping leaves.

Although I rejected the whole notion of an iron church, I was nevertheless intrigued as to why Gustave Eiffel should have bothered to design and ship one out in prefabricated sections to a remote corner of South America. Did he imagine that in this new continent he could eclipse the majesty of those medieval cathedrals and churches that litter Europe? Did he perhaps see himself as a visionary in iron? He had also designed the little Customs House, the Aduana, which now staged exhibitions. Whatever his motivation, I was completely unmoved by his cathedral. I wanted to be where living people were.

We walked on quickly towards the harbour where big, skulking pelicans pushed and jostled among the boulders on which it was built. I remembered seeing such birds in fairytale picture books but these were an ugly and brutal travesty of my childhood imagination. Everywhere about me was the putrid smell of fish processing. My stomach was rising to my throat and I wanted to be away from the place fast. Walking back towards the town I was thinking, was this the essential dichotomy of Arica, the empty, fusty-smelling iron church in a desert city that reeked only of fish?

Back in the town proper I was glad to be confronted by the deep reds, yellow and violet of hibiscus bushes and the soft reddish blush of lobelia flowers. I lingered by them for a while, but it was a mistake. We were quickly surrounded by some gypsy women and their children. They hobbled after us, pulling at our arms and pleading, proffering their hungry babies. We ignored them and walked on in silence. They persisted, then after some moments gave up, making some remark, no doubt, cursing the gringos. I said nothing to John but I remembered feeding the desert finches on my balcony and I remembered the little bird at the cathedral. I hate this *mea culpa* thing that wells up in me. Rather than say anything of how I was feeling, I stopped and took a close-up shot of a clutch of hibiscus flowers.

≡ꛈꛈ≡

A beggar woman comes towards us, muttering and pulling at our sleeves. 'Gypsies are the same everywhere, I think,' says Katia. Her comment strikes a strange chord. Although we are on the other side of the world, surrounded by deserts and faces with high cheekbones suggesting Indian ancestry, where everyone speaks Spanish, a language I hardly know, I am surprised at the lack of culture shock. Everything is new to me but seems familiar.

In Colon Square there is a monument erected in 1991 by the local Socialist Party to commemorate its members killed in General Pinochet's 1973 coup. Brian goes over to take a photograph of this and I say to Katia, 'I've read that the Socialists were very strong in the north. There must have been big celebrations in '88 when Pinochet handed over to a civilian government.'

She looks blankly at me, muttering something about 'the military period' and changes the subject. This comes as a shock. I wander off a little and take a photo of the square. Brian comes up and, seeing my perplexed expression, asks, 'Something bothering you?'

'No, no, just thinking. I'll tell you later.'

Hidden away among all the brown earth and rock Arica has two fertile valleys: the Lluta and the Azapa. Katia takes us to visit the archaeological museum of the University of Tarapaca, the name of the province we are in. It is very hot and our surroundings make us thirsty. On the way we pass shanties built of packing cases with burned-out trucks and skinny dogs in the yard. The course of the river is little more than piles of stones. There are smallholdings, oases of olive and fruit trees and corn. It looks a hard life with the desert reaching right up to the back door. Katia, once again her effusive self, tells us, 'They are expanding the cultivated area with Drip Watering Schemes. The land looks dead now but some green will come up.'

Further up the valley, beyond even these spartan outposts, we get a mysterious sense of the people who were living here centuries ago. High up on the hillsides you spot what could be a pattern; you almost dismiss it before you realize it is a definite form. They are geoglyphs, figures either carved in the rock or marked out by large stones.

The most exotic geoglyph was Cerro Sagrado, 'Sacred Mountain'. The images of a pregnant woman, a phallus, monkeys, serpents and lizards are all clearly visible high on the bluffs above us. We stand looking in silence, a small group in a vast area, the only sounds the wind and an occasional bird cry. I feel a strange mix of the familiarity and the fear that such ancient monuments often inspire. You can imagine walking beside a trader from the mountains six hundred years ago, looking up and seeing Cerro Sagrado and knowing we are near the coast and at our journey's end. Then you realize that that world was quite alien, and mysterious; that that site was not Cerro Sagrado to the trader, for he spoke another language, had never heard a word of Spanish and had no concept of Europe. He lived in another world as well as another time. Here is culture shock after all.

〰〰

I was half listening and half sleeping when mention of the word 'geoglyphs' woke me. One can only wonder at the energy and imagination that it took to construct these images. The people who created these things would have had to stand at a distance from the hill, and there, in their mind's eye, design the outline of the shape they sought to build, then trudge three, four miles up the hill, spend weeks clearing the rubble and create with perfect configuration that creature of their imagination or that animal of their reality. The further we travelled into the hills the more we saw of these visual messages from a people and a civilization long since disappeared. Everywhere were representations of llamas and alpacas. On one particular hill some artistic genius had described the outline of a huge lizard that bore no resemblance to the gekkos that constantly stirred at the edge of the road. And beside the lizard, the outline of what was obviously a monkey. Yet there were no monkeys in Chile, so the image demonstrated the huge distances that the Inca civilization had spread itself from central Peru. I asked Katia about the lizard. Was it a native creature of Chile? She told me that the lizard was only representative, a symbol of water.

Around the images of the lizard, the monkey and the other animals were figures of hugely pregnant women and tumescent men. The hill was a holy place, our guides explained, and all the images together represented the circle of birth and death and rebirth.

On another hill we had pointed out to us the images of men dancing to a shaman playing his pipes. I was drawn to this figure. I thought of our own dancing days in those tiny sweaty cells in

Lebanon. Like that shaman on the hill, I too believe that dancing is divine. It is the great liberator.

I was captivated by these etched images and their stone-constructed counterparts. The energy of these vitally alive representations made the airless tomb of Eiffel's iron church even more alien than I had first felt.

I looked back at the pregnant women and the dancing men and remembered my lamentation on our arrival about D. H. Lawrence, Catholic passion and the beauty of ethnic women. Somehow these ritual figures were not simply stone effigies.

My wife of a few years was at home carrying our first child and I was desperately missing her. This wasn't just mawkish sentiment. The dancers on the hill made my loneliness back at the hotel seem foolish and adolescent. They were mocking me yet simultaneously giving me passage into the landscape. Several thousands of years after they were built they still served their original purpose, as a guide for travellers and a place for the spirit.

≡Ⅲ≡

We continue to the archaeological museum along a very bumpy road. The buildings there form a tranquil oasis. We look at the huddled mummies dating from the Chinchorro culture; they are believed to pre-date those in Egypt. There is also a good exhibition of ancient artefacts demonstrating the lives and links between the hunter fishermen of the coast area and the farmers of the Altiplano. I knew that horses were unknown before the Spanish but had not realized that knives were similarly absent. This seems highly unlikely but Katia confirms it.

'These people were obviously good hunters,' I say to Bri, 'so how did they manage that without a cutting edge? With drugs or hypnotism?' I squat down and squint up at him as if at a bird in a tree, 'Hey you, bird! Listen to me: you are getting very sleepy . . .'

Brian turns to our guide. 'You see what I have to put up with, Katia. Mad dogs and Englishmen!'

'Ah, yes!' she replies. 'Of course, *vaca loco*, mad cow disease. They all have it?'

'Every last one!' Brian confirms.

I was struck by a group of mummies, which had been carbon-dated as being eight thousand years older than the mummies of Egypt. Yet this amazing fact could not dispel the poignancy of this dead tableau. Mother, father and children had been buried sitting in an upright position with all the accoutrements of their household. At first I could hardly bear to look in on this family, and one particular relic made the whole scene even more moving. It was a small box a little larger than a snuffbox. It contained the foetus of a stillborn infant. It was a powerful testament of life and of life after death. Even this stillborn child was assured of an existence in the afterworld. This was real passion, more meaningful than D. H. Lawrence's egotistical ramblings about it.

While I was busy with all this thinking, John was intent upon his own jigsaw. He has an insatiable curiosity about things. I'm sure if I ever possess a cat I will name the creature McCarthy after my travelling companion. While John was extracting information from our guides, I sat silently asking my own questions, trying to fathom what specifically had brought us here. The idea of the yak farm was certainly a means but were there other things compelling me?

All travel is, after all, a journey in time and in mind. Like many people I believe that physical landscapes are a mirror of, or perhaps a key into, our inner landscape. It wasn't simply chance or good luck that brought us to Chile. The silent messages from the images on the hillside and those unearthed from the desert had assured me of that.

I began to wonder was there something else, something more that lay dormant in me, and only by coming here might I recognize it?

I had brought with me the collected poems of Pablo Neruda, the fabulous Chilean Nobel prizewinner. Curiously it was the first gift I was given when I returned from Lebanon. Was that just a coincidence too? In any case I had chosen Neruda for my spirit guide, though if anyone was to ask me I wasn't sure why.

I also wanted to know if there was any resonance in this real landscape for the imaginary landscape I had concocted while incarcerated. Neruda's intoxicating verse somehow seemed a familiar echo of that thinking so long ago. Why, I began asking myself; and would being here answer my questions?

'My country has the shape of a great albatross with its wings outspread,' wrote Neruda in 1972. The association of the land with the albatross is an intriguing one, for it carries with it notions of destiny. The fact that we were here was for me more to do with a fixed destiny than an act of chance. Our three-thousand-mile journey between extremes of Chile's land mass was our own albatross flight.

≡Ⅲ≡

We drive back to Arica at lunchtime. Katia cannot stay but drops us off at a covered market where we have delicious *ceviche* (raw fish) and a beer.

'It was odd the way Katia clammed up in the square when I asked her about the Socialists and Pinochet.'

'Was that what was bothering you then?' Brian asks.

'Yeah. She just didn't want to know, sort of closed it off with that phrase "the military period". I'd have thought people would have been happy to talk – there can't be any real threat of oppression now, surely.'

'No. She must have grown up during the Pinochet years. Maybe her family supported him, or maybe the Chileans just can't deal with what happened.'

'What they let happen to themselves?'

'Perhaps. We'll see what other folk think. Maybe Katia doesn't care about politics or reckons it's not right to talk to us gringos about it.'

We lapse into silence, eating and sipping. The market is strangely proportioned, the roof high above – as you would expect – but everything at ground level, while being the right height, seems to have been constricted in width and depth. The narrow, cluttered passageways bustle with people selling all manner of things. About three feet from our little table is a kiosk of esoterica:

candles, incense, maté tea, herbs and many mysterious packages. It looks wildly superstitious but is doing a brisk trade. The man behind the counter has an aquiline nose and thick spectacles. He looks other-worldly in his drab black trousers and nondescript shirt – not evil but, half closing my eyes, I can visualize his tall skinny frame draped in a dark cloak. The place is noisy, fun and friendly; it just feels as if you are eating in a hall of distorting mirrors.

〰〰

Everything from alabaster saints, special potions and curses to ready-made prayers, dried animal parts and God knows what else was there. This kiosk unreservedly served every religious inclination imaginable. The owner seemed to have plenty of customers and listened priest-like as they explained their needs to him. He had something in his tiny shop no matter what they requested. I was slowly beginning to understand why the iron cathedral was empty and why the statue of Christ might take longer to be erected than anyone could have imagined.

Back at the hotel that evening I slept fitfully as I usually do in strange bedrooms. The noise of those infernal fishing boats toing-and-froing across the ocean outside the window, combined with the ever-present odour of fish, did not help. The next morning I was too tired to do anything but sit and consider the journey in front of us. We were headed into the Altiplano towards Lago Chungara, one of the highest lakes in the world, some five thousand metres above sea level. The thought of this place encouraged me. At least there we would be well away from this insidious stench of fish.

As we finished breakfast the waiter informed us that our two guides were waiting. There was little more to do but head for the hills. We collected our baggage and loaded it on to the four-wheel drive. Karlen, who had met us at the airport, was in her middle to late twenties and was studying law at university. Her companion, Eduardo, a man in his late thirties, had come to live in Arica to get away from the smog and unhealthy conditions in Santiago. I couldn't really imagine anyone choosing to live in Arica, but for our guide it was not a matter of choice: rather doctor's orders. The air in this area was good for him, he told me. I might not live there, but I had breathed in enough fishy air to have doubts about the veracity of his remark.

Chapter Two

≡⦀≡

Heading inland from Arica, a dirt road runs up and down, sweeping across high ridges between mighty valleys. We stop on a salt flat, the sandy-looking surface firm and crisp to walk on. My spirits tingle in such space and solitude. Taking off my hat to feel the sun on my face and the breeze in my hair I stretch out my arms, welcoming a sense of great freedom.

This is what I wanted back in Lebanon, wilderness untainted by man. A place where there were no guards to hiss and make you whisper, where you could shout and bellow and the world would remain mute and uncomplaining. Yet suddenly I feel uncertain. This is not a landscape you could trust. The crust of salt that extends to the horizon feels as treacherous as ice on a pond and although I marvel that the crystals sparkling in the sun create a shimmering mirage that absorbs our car parked a mile away, I shiver in the morning's heat. I turn to look for Brian. He has disappeared! Crusoe-like I follow his footprints and come to the edge of another vast valley. A little way down its rocky side, I find him poking at something on the ground – skeletons.

'What are they?'

'Sheep, or could be a llama, I suppose,' he replies.

His face has that closed-down, pensive look I know so well. When we first met that look would make me feel excluded, as if I had done something to offend him. But I soon learned that it was his way of concentrating; though his eyes remain open he is looking inward, studying vistas and images in his mind's eye. He is away in his own place, making sense of something, putting it into a context that he may want to share later. From under the brim of his straw hat, he looks around searching for an answer – perhaps unsure of the question that nags him. As he looks up and out across this great valley, to the valleys and hills beyond, his face remains inscrutable. Here is nature on the massive scale we had dreamed of, yet I sense that, as for me, the thoughts and feelings it inspires in him are by no means clear cut or simple.

Before we entered the mountains proper, we crossed a high desert plain. I enjoy open spaces and remote places, the solitary in me calls out to them. But emptiness disturbs me. It makes me uneasy. I love silence, but even more I like to hear it filling up with first sounds that put a sense of imminence to the day. Here emptiness was complemented only by absence. It did not encourage me for the days ahead. We have an expression where I come from for such places: 'There is a desperate want in them.'

We stopped briefly to stretch our legs and take some fresh air. For mile after mile after mile, the empty desert's edge surrounded us. As we left our jeep and started to walk into it, I was surprised at my reaction. I was walking on a hard salty surface. On its immense flat expanse it seemed as if you could see for ever, as if we were standing on an enormous pie-crust. Even the mountains shading out of the distance had curious indents as if they had been delicately shaped with a pastry spoon.

'It's not what I expected,' John commented.

'Nor me, but remember what I told you years ago: hope for everything, and expect nothing. And there's any amount of nothing here.'

We stood for a moment turning slowly and taking in the emptiness. John said something to me about the silence of things. I simply insisted on stamping my foot. I was amazed that, with all the force of my feet and legs, I couldn't break the salt crust on which I was standing. I saw John look at me as if there was something wrong with my head. Then he said simply, 'Well, there's certainly nothing here.'

'I've never seen so much nothing in all my life,' I replied.

We returned to the jeep and climbed aboard. As we drove on further into the hills we were both silently contemplating the fact that we had to cross six hundred miles of the most utter wilderness in the days to come. I was about to comment on this to John when my eyes were attracted to something far out towards the horizon of this great salt plain, something shimmering and fluid. Could it be lights in the distance? Or perhaps light glancing off the bodywork of a car or truck travelling towards us, but some fifty miles away. And again I thought perhaps it was a rainstorm somewhere and the sunlight was shimmering in the downpour. Then I realized the idiocy of my thinking. This was one of the world's perfect deserts. Perfect in the sense that in some parts of it there had never ever been any rain.

I pointed off to the horizon and asked Karlen and Eduardo, 'What's that?'

They looked where I was pointing, then at each other and said, 'What?'

I repeated again, 'There, that bright light, it seems to be moving.'

Again they looked at each other. There was no point in looking at what I was looking at.

Smiling, Karlen explained, 'It is the sun glinting off the silica that is strewn across the desert.' I sat back feeling a little foolish and deflated. As we drove on for a few more hours, these desert lights seemed to change. On occasion they looked like small encampments glowing in darkness. I was slowly beginning to understand what the word 'mirage' really meant. I decided to pay little more attention to them, for, like any mirage, they had the capacity to become hypnotic.

≡Ⅲ≡

There is a relaxed atmosphere as we drive along, getting to know our guides. Tall and thin, wearing a black stetson above a craggy, weatherbeaten face that is often wreathed in smiles, Eduardo has some English and drives tourists around in his jeep. Karlen, we learn, was born in 1974 and works as a tour guide to earn money to put herself through college. She wants to be a lawyer. We fall silent for a while as Eduardo steers the jeep over the often rutted and sometimes very treacherous roads. Brian dozes next to me in the back. Karlen turns and nods at Brian, smiling. 'He is very tired?'

'No,' I say, grinning, 'just very old.'

Her eyes flash understanding and she switches to Spanish for a quiet conversation with Eduardo. I notice that he is looking quizzically at Brian and me through the rear-view mirror and shaking his head. Karlen turns round, speaking quietly.

'You say it was more than ten years ago that you were kidnapped?'

'That's right,' I say, 'in 1986.'

She and Eduardo exchange glances.

'How old are you?' Karlen asks me.

'I'm forty,' I say, feeling confused myself now.

'No!' she exclaims, saying '*cuarenta*' quickly to her colleague.

Eduardo slows the car and starts laughing, his English suddenly more accomplished.

'You are Dorian Gray, or you drink the blood of virgins!' He laughs uproariously and I turn pink with embarrassment. Eduardo goes on, 'Karlen, she tell me we are taking a father and son for this trip!' Brian is suddenly wide awake, his face an owl-like expression of amazement.

'Karlen thinks you are twenty years maybe, John. She say, how can Lebanon men, even terror men, take a child of ten for prison?'

Karlen remains dubious until I show her my passport. As I put it back in a pocket I cannot resist turning to Brian.

'You know, these people are very perceptive and sensitive. I think we'll get on very well. Don't you, Old Timer?'

He glowers at me for a moment before performing a favourite mime he uses when he thinks I am talking nonsense. He puts his hands down by his chest and starts rotating them up to his mouth as if controlling a massive tongue.

'Roll it up and put it away, John!'

~~~

If I was beginning to feel that the desert was yielding up some of its secrets and becoming less frighteningly empty, I had yet a thing or two to learn. Climbing a steep incline in a narrow road and turning on to a short but level expanse, we pressed ahead. The road seemed to disappear between two huge boulders at either side. Suddenly Eduardo braked and pulled over, pointing to a small shelf at the side of one of the boulders. 'Come,' he insisted and we both climbed out of the jeep. Where he had pointed there was a small, crudely constructed grotto, the like of which I had not seen before. A single cross inside was made from the tied-together roots of some long-dead shrub. On it, several small, weird posies of flowers had been bound with gaudy ribbon. Nearby I spotted the remains of a transistor radio. There, a single green plant in a brown plastic pot, like something you would buy in a supermarket, was still thriving. The place had the look of a rubbish tip. Plastic cups, plastic knives and forks were littered about. There was the headless body of a small plastic doll and other doll-like things which looked as if they had been made from the rags of old clothing. Several small illustrations of the Virgin Mary were framed in cheap plastic, and an equally cheap set of rosary beads was draped over the cross. At the foot of the shrine were a few Mass cards in Spanish with the faces of long-dead saints staring out of them. Other miscellaneous items were scattered about, the significance of which I couldn't fathom.

But the most arresting memorial was a piece of cardboard on which something had been written in red felt-tip pen. The handwriting was big and awkward. I asked Eduardo to translate. He explained that it was a warning and a curse: '"Anyone who moves anything will be haunted by the ghosts of the dead and many very, very bad things will happen to them,"' he quoted to us. It had been printed in red, I was told, to make it look as though it had been written in blood.

When I asked our guides if they believed in the curse, Eduardo lowered his eyes in a silent gesture of acknowledgement. Then he went back to the jeep and returned with an empty bottle and the huge plastic container in which we carried our own spare water.

He filled the bottle and deposited it near the cross before pouring lavish amounts of water on to the plant. I completely understood what he was doing but when I asked him for whom he was leaving the bottle of water, he simply said, 'Whoever needs.'

'Even the ghosts?'

'They must drink also.'

As we prepared to drive off I thought of that little, crudely constructed memorial. It seemed to me that whoever had died here must have been a child. Though how or why it had died I could only speculate and at this moment I didn't feel the need of an answer. Instead I wanted my spirit guide to leave a gift for the child ghost who must be dreadfully lonely waiting for people to come along this forgotten desert road and leave her some presents. I read these lines for Neruda to take to her:

> The harsh noon of the great sands
> has arrived:
> The world is naked,
> broad, sterile, and clean to the farthest
> sandy frontiers:
> listen to the brittle sound
> of the live salt, alone in the salt marshes:
> the sun shatters its crystals in the empty
> expanse and the earth rattles with the
> moaning salt's dry and muffled sound.

The monotony and the barrenness of these places dry up the soul a little. In a curious way, I was glad of the respite of that little memorial. In its own way, it refreshed the soul. Perhaps that's why I asked Neruda to take those words of his. Consolation is about sharing loneliness and making it bearable.

≡Ⅲ≡

We are surprised and amused to see a road sign in the middle of nowhere, pointing in various directions with many place names. It seems that there are a fair few little settlements out here in the wilds. Political parties have painted slogans on the rocks. These latter-day geoglyphs really do seem ridiculous – talk about marginal constituencies.

At around a thousand metres, bedraggled, thin cacti appear and, as we rise higher and the temperature drops, they become profuse, increasing in size and strength to cover the valley sides. Microclimates proliferate: there are lush little valleys with fiercely running streams, much greenery and giant eucalyptus trees, along-side barren mountain areas.

We have a picnic lunch by the old church at Tignamar. The church, thatched with pampas grass, is all that remains of the village apart from some desolate little mud-brick structures, once family homes. Higher up the hill is a newer village but we stay beside the stream that roars over the stones of its wide bed.

'In 1973 there was a terrible flood,' Karlen explains. 'It swept away the old village.'

Thinking of that larger, political flood, the *coup d'état* led by General Pinochet that swept over the whole country in the same year, I ask Karlen about the 'military period'. Since my disappointing exchange with Katia I had done some more reading. The far north, El Norte Grande, home to Chile's great nitrate and copper mines, had long been the centre of radical leftist politics. Much of the support for the Marxist government of President Salvador Allende, whom Pinochet ousted, had come from this region.

'You were born a year after the coup, Karlen. What was it like growing up under the dictatorship?'

'It was better than if Chile had gone like Cuba,' she replies abruptly.

'But what about the oppression, the torture – all the people who were "disappeared"?'

'With Communism we would all have been poor.' She speaks in a monotone as if brainwashed on the subject, unable, or unwilling, to accept that, unlike Cuba, the Chileans had voted to have a Marxist government.

'The people could have elected another government without denying themselves freedom for a decade and a half,' I argue. 'Surely everyone thinks that now?'

'Pinochet brought prosperity and stability – the Communists

were destroying everything. My father says we nearly starved,' she says in the same monotone. 'There was no choice.'

'There is always choice,' barks Brian. Eyes flashing he says to her, 'You want to be a lawyer?' Karlen nods. 'Well, doesn't the word justice mean anything to you?'

Impervious to Brian's angry tone she states, 'The Communists were not just.'

Brian shakes his head in exasperation and walks off to the stream.

I turn to Eduardo: 'What do you think?'

'All politics is no good.'

∿∿

We had finished lunch and were about to leave when Eduardo stood up and walked some distance, then threw down some bread and cheese and the remains of his half-eaten peach at his feet. From where she was sitting, Karlen did the same thing, casting some bread and cheese to the ground around her. She noticed my curiosity and said, 'Something for Patcha Mama.' She told me this was the great earth mother and we should always be kind to her for she had, after all, given us this food. I did likewise. As I cast away the remains of my lunch, I was taken by the notion from the mists of my own Irish history, that as St Patrick and those first Christians found when they attempted to convert the pagan Irish, they too would not accept Christ without Mary. The pre-Christian Irish had their own 'Mama' like many peoples throughout the world. They could not accept the convoluted paternalism of this new religion without a Patcha Mama.

≡⦀≡

As we drive ever higher during the afternoon, the dull brown valley sides are now often streaked with mineral content. At times there are great swathes of colour and as we move from one small valley to the next the hue turns from green to yellow to blue and red. From a bird's eye view this place must look like a terrestrial rainbow.

Some areas have many caves scoured out of the limestone rock by water erosion. I try climbing up to one that has clearly a man-made wall across it. As I scramble my legs begin to feel heavy, then wobbly and I start to doubt my balance. I give up at a steep scree but am filled with archaeological fervour, thinking of the ancients who lived here hunting and trading – and building walls round caves – as much as nine thousand years ago. I look around the valley with its steep sides and many caves, hoping to make a discovery, to find something special that no one has seen or touched for thousands of years – a mummy perhaps. Below me Eduardo and Karlen are looking among the small rocks at the road's edge. Karlen straightens and waves me down. She gives me a little shard of patterned pottery. Although it is a common enough find, I am delighted with the discovery.

Brian is asleep in the back of the jeep. I am surprised at this. Although I have not been able to resist encouraging Karlen and Eduardo in their growing belief that Bri does little beyond dozing, telling them about the times when he would be snoring despite great ructions beyond the door of a cell and then claim, fiercely, the next morning that he had not slept a wink, I am surprised that he is so tired today. Normally he likes to look around for old bits and pieces up for the asking – what he calls 'honest pruck'.

The skies cloud over and the air fills with a misty rain, giving the occasional villages a surly atmosphere. We come across them suddenly, turning a hairpin bend to see a narrow valley with a stream bustling through it and above us a narrow cleft laid out in terraces, a couple of raggedy horses grazing by the road and then the small village itself. Many of these date back to pre-Columbian times, when this region was the home of the Aymara people.

Since the colonial era there have been concerted efforts to destroy the old indigenous cultures and to create a homogeneous Chilean identity. Yet Karlen shows us examples of the inevitable compromise between the existing beliefs of the native population and the Christian tradition of the conquistadors.

'Around the doors you see carvings like totem poles including images of nature's gods as well as angels,' she tells us as we stand in the deserted square of Belén before a whitewashed church. 'Also, for the old religion, fertility was very important. In the churches of these high villages, the bell tower, as a phallic symbol, is kept separate from the "female" body of the church.'

In case we do not grasp this idea, Eduardo points at the main building then forms a large circle with both hands which he positions over his groin. Next he points at the bell tower before clasping a hand above the elbow of the other arm and raising its forearm rigid, fist clenched in the universal sign of virility.

'Thank you, Eduardo,' sighs Karlen, eyes rolling heavenward.

These small villages are neat and often organized on a grid system. Yet with the cool misty air about us they seem quite eerie. We wander around the side streets, mainly just dirt tracks with little streams meandering down the middle, where most of the houses are boarded up. Karlen tells us the familiar tale of remote communities the world over. Most young people have moved to the big cities, on the coast and further south, for education and work. But families do spend time in the villages tending the terraces and then sell their produce in Arica and it seems there has been an upsurge of interest in Aymara culture among the young. They meet in Arica to speak their language, play their music and eat traditional meals. As it is the villages are ghostly and remote and we walk around in that hushed way, as if in a church. It is a shock and a relief to turn a corner and hear the chattering of neighbours at the open front door of one of the houses.

The sense of gloom and decline is emphasized outside Belén where there is a cemetery surrounded by a high wall with a massive eucalyptus tree, dead and skeletal, towering above it. It is an image from Armageddon.

We drive on through the afternoon over narrow, rutted tracks in the thick fog called *camanchaca*. Our horizons expand a little when we pull in at a truck stop. We are now on the main road from Bolivia down to Arica and many huge lorries loom out of the fog.

Brian has appeared to sleep for most of the afternoon. Not a bad idea given the dullness beyond the windscreen, but we other three keep giggling about his 'advanced years' and his need for rest. I become aware of a beady eye glinting at me.

'I am not asleep – just resting my eyes.'

We are aware that altitude sickness can be unpleasant and Brian is taking no chances; we still have a long way to climb so he is keeping his breathing regular, like the wily old timer he is, rather than getting puffed as I have done looking for ancient remains.

Eduardo leads us into the café for some maté tea which he says is good for altitude sickness.

'And it will keep the old man awake,' he adds, doubling up. The place is very basic but it is clean and the family who own it give us a warm welcome. We have bread and cheese with our tea as we look at Tourist Board photographs of the great Chilean beach resort of Viña del Mar and the spectacular views of water and snow-capped volcanoes bright in the sunshine of the Lake District far to the south, the only points of colour in the otherwise drab room.

~~~

When we reached the truck stop, the light was fading fast and the evening was becoming bitter cold. The place was as spartan as one would expect in this region and we desperately needed something hot.

Maté is not a drink native to Chile, but it is common enough in Bolivia and Peru and we were near to those borders. I had not tasted it before and was curious. It is simply a brew of boiling water and thick green leaves. When the large steaming bowl was set in front of me, I mashed up the leaves in it and tried to smell what I was about to drink. Eduardo told me it was necessary to let it infuse. I was given a few straws but thought it a little childish at my age to be sucking tea through a straw, so while the others chatted, I sat and waited. We were brought a large plateful of chocolate digestive biscuits. McCarthy laughed at this small surprise and quickly began demolishing them. I had ventured into the maté. It tasted quite innocuous and so, as I drank, I chewed the leaves. I ordered another as I was sure I would not be tasting any more for the rest of our journey. Karlen and Eduardo looked at me incredulously.

'What are you doing?'

I joked that I was still hungry.

'But this is very strong tea,' they said, 'you must not chew the leaves.' I thought I had heard Eduardo telling me that these were coca leaves and I shrugged my shoulders.

John roared with laughter. 'No, you blithering imbecile, not *coca* leaves, *loco* leaves.' L-o-c-o, he spelled out, grinning wildly. When he had finished, he informed me that if I persisted I would go crazy. I wondered whether the guides were having some fun with us and I continued chewing, rolling my eyes in mock dementia.

That evening we were due to stay in the outskirts of the town of Putré. The hotel, if you could call it that, had originally been built to accommodate migratory miners. It was more or less a series of one-room cabins set off from the main building, where one could eat and watch television in a communal room. John jokingly warned our guides that if they wanted to sleep that night they should take cabins well away from the mad Irishman. When they questioned him as to why, he informed them that he would tell them in the morning – 'if they slept'. We quickly unpacked our bags and took a very brief and very cold shower. The absence of any mining in the area and the scarcity of people passing through meant that there was no perceived need to heat any water. To underline his own advice, John had taken a room some distance from mine.

After half an hour or so we all gathered in the dining room for our supper. There was no menu and only one basic dish of potatoes and vegetables and a choice of meats. The hotel cats were probably better fed that evening than they had been in several years.

Perhaps because this part of our journey was coming to an end we were relaxed and in good form. We cracked some jokes about the impossibility of eating the meat, which had the texture of well-tanned yak hide. Our guides were intrigued by our yak farm idea. We began explaining the project as simply and as briefly as we could without labouring the subject of our captivity in Lebanon.

I was becoming a little light-headed and giddy. I thought it had to do with a combination of thin air, my own tiredness and the wine we had been drinking at lunch with Patcha Mama.

We were also discussing the various ceremonies and festivals that take place in these villages. The conversation triggered a lunatic train of thought in me. I began to explain that for many years after we had established our yak farm in the area, these villages would have a new festival day dedicated to the yak. With elaborate descriptions I painted the picture of these nomadic herders coming for miles and miles through the mountains to the ceremonial village on the blessed Day of the Yak. And how, many years later, a wizened, grey-bearded village elder, a rough-cut St Francis of Assisi, would tell the village children of the two strangers with their great lumbering beasts. A folklore would develop around the story of these gringos. In every adobe cabin in every village there would be old sepia photographs of McCarthy and Keenan pinned to the wall and above these images would be posies of bright mountain flowers.

I was concocting the story as I spoke, encouraged by the stunned faces of the guides. McCarthy was clearly enjoying the fantasy I was unfolding, and was soon laughing with me. As my elaborations grew so did my laughter. The lunacy was catching.

Prayers would be offered up for the repose of the souls of Keenan and McCarthy. At supper, bottles of red wine would be hoisted up to these two men. Everyone would carry a miraculous medal with our faces on one side and the head of the bull yak on the other. The after-effects of the maté were producing scenarios that drew even more strange looks from our guides, but threw McCarthy into outrageous guffaws.

When we arrived back at our cabins I was too exhausted to do anything other than flop on to the bed. We had been warned by our guides that the thin air in these regions sometimes made sleeping difficult if one wasn't used to it. They added that it also had the effect of producing strange or disturbing dreams. I felt so weary that I was heedless of their advice, convinced that nothing would affect my sleeping.

I looked around the tiny room, and thought about the miserable lives of the miners who had nothing more to do at the end of a day's labour than sleep or read a newspaper. I undressed and rolled into the bed as if I myself had dug up half the mountain that morning.

I don't know when I slept or for how long or if during that time I had even dreamed, but some time in the middle of the night I was suddenly awake, panicking and gasping for breath. One moment I was asleep and the next I was sitting bolt upright on my bed and taking short gasps of breath as though there was no air in the room. It took me some moments to compose myself and return to a normal pattern of breathing. The effects of what had happened to me were something similar to a miniature seizure. I quickly assured myself that I was not at the edge of coronary collapse. But I also convinced myself that if this was the result of living in high altitudes then the Indians, the miners and whoever wanted it, could keep it.

I burst out laughing. I imagined myself galloping across these hills, got up like some pioneer mountain-man. Dressed up all in leather and sheepskin but on my back I had strapped a gleaming tank of oxygen! Clamped across my face was not a colourful scarf but a breathing mask. As suddenly as I had begun, I stopped laughing. I felt myself losing control of my breathing again. I began panting like a woman in labour.

However I got through the night, it left its mark. The next morning I had deep, dark rings around my eyes. I washed and dressed hoping that breakfast would be an improvement on the evening's meal. The water was still freezing cold. I shuddered as it stung my skin. It was becoming obvious that I was not mountain-man material.

When I entered the dining room our guides and John were already perched at the table. Having greedily gulped down the steaming coffee to warm myself, I mentioned to John and our companions that I had had a poor night's sleep. He replied that he too had found difficulty sleeping and had woken gasping for air. And then he wheeled in his chair and said, 'It's all your fault anyway.'

'Me?' I exclaimed.

'Well, the amount of air you filter through your nostrils every night, it's no wonder there was no air in your room, or anybody else's for that matter!' John paused and, turning to our guides, asked solicitously, 'And did you two sleep well last night?'

They hesitated for a moment before Eduardo said, 'Well,

not really, I seem to hear many volcanoes in the night.'

Karlen quickly agreed. 'Yes, me too, all through the night, volcanoes and earthquakes.'

I didn't know whether to laugh or feel embarrassed, as John rounded on me again: 'See, I can't take you anywhere.'

≡Ⅲ≡

The next morning the air is thick with *camanchaca* as we enter the Lauca National Park. The main road takes you past the world's highest military base at 4,350 metres. Although there is some ill feeling towards Chile from Bolivia and Peru because of the lands taken in the War of the Pacific it seems overcautious to have a military presence here, rather than merely a customs post.

'Really they are more interested in the drug running than invasion,' Karlen explains.

'Given the fog,' I say, 'I'd have thought even the most incompetent smuggler could simply walk past the gate, with kilos of whatever, in broad daylight.'

Just inside the park we see some vicuñas and the curious little rabbit-like vizcachas with their long tails and ears which sit on rocks. The Aymara herders keep their flocks of llama and alpaca in this region. These domesticated beasts, which, with the guanacos and vicuñas, are South American members of the camel family, like to feed on the *bofedales*, the swampy pastures. They provide a strange sight, with their long necks and shaggy coats, some adorned with ribbons, as they munch the wiry, dark green grass in the muted, foggy atmosphere.

Eduardo stops to talk to an old herder who is wearing light trousers, a thin jersey, sandals but no socks, and a sou'wester over a baseball cap. The whole ensemble is topped off with a sheet of polythene wrapped around his shoulders. He says it is the lambing season. Most herders have around a hundred head and keep them penned in stone folds at night. A friend comes up carrying what looks like a small piece of sponge. It is in fact rock hard and Karlen explains that this is *llareta* which, when dead, as is this piece, can be used as fuel. It grows at a millimetre a year which seems like a hell of a long time to wait for a bit of warmth. The men though, in their light clothing, seem oblivious to the murky conditions and their faces, weathered to a deep mahogany, are constantly smiling.

As we climb still higher there are patches of snow on the ground but it is impossible to maintain a sense of perspective because of the fog. Now we are on a good road we seem to drive for miles without seeing any other traffic, often climbing up a rise that suggests we will disappear into the clouds and find something new, only to discover another stretch of snow-skirted tarmac ahead.

Brian and I exchange glances. Having spent so much time together we are pretty adept at following each other's thoughts, a skill honed in situations where, blindfolded, we might be dealing with a hostile guard and every nuance of conversation could be important. We learned to read as much from each other's pauses as from the spoken words. The need for cautious communication was also useful when dealing with our own disputes and those of other hostages. Generally we can read each other well though there are times when we get things wildly wrong. This is not one of them.

'This is beginning to get rather dull,' I observe and Brian just grins and gives me a 'you said it, pal' wink. The captive imagination had not conjured the Andes in this way: anxious, heavy breathing in a bank of fog.

Then, as if stage-managed by a great impresario, the clouds part slowly to give us spectacular views of Parinacota, 6,342 metres high, the snow-covered volcano beyond the sun-bright waters of Lake Chungara.

It takes whole minutes for the view to be revealed. I find myself trying to guess how the mountain will appear as, almost coyly, it sheds its cape. Down by the lakeshore one can really appreciate the scale and majesty of the place. It is vast, peaceful and there are no other humans in sight. I stand there pondering the wonder of it all when I become aware of the sound of derisory laughter. Looking around to find the source I realize I am being mocked by birds. Checking in my guidebook I discover that Chungara is home to the *Fulica gigantea* – the giant coot.

We take a drive with Jorge, a ranger for Chile's Corporacion

Nacional Forestal (CONAF). As we go along he points out vicuñas. Karlen translates for us. 'They are smaller than their guanaco relations and have very fine wool. Once they were all owned by the Inca kings. They were almost hunted to extinction, but now they are protected by CONAF and are doing very well. Jorge says that they may provide additional income for the Aymara herders.'

An eagle swoops from high above us down low as if to mock the ungainly scuttlings of the rheas, cousins to the ostrich.

We reach our destination, the thermal springs at Chirigualla. The water from them bubbles up green, yellow and white over the rocky stream bed. The air close by is clammy with steam and thick with the smell of sulphur. I go up to where Jorge squats next to the main thermal pool, wanting to feel the water. I feel it all too much as one leg goes in up to the knee: the rock I thought I was stepping on is nothing more than a platform of mineral scum. Strange place, this Lauca: plants that look soft but are as hard as rocks, and rock-like objects as soft as soggy papier mâché.

Now it is Brian's turn to laugh with our guides. 'Watch out, John boy, or you'll be putting your foot in it!'

I slept until we reached the village of Parinacota. It is one of several ceremonial villages located in the area. It dates back to pre-conquest times and has belonged to the Aymara tribe since then. It is ceremonial in the sense that it is not a permanently inhabited village. These people are still nomads and permanent settlement is not part of their way of life. They live with their animals and go wherever they go. But they return to this village for certain specific religious or other tribal meetings. Though the village is empty apart from these ceremonial occasions it doesn't have the feel of a ghost town. It is so well kept. At any moment one expects someone to open the door of one of the small adobe homes, or a shepherd to come wandering around a corner with a flock of sheep or goats, or to see the priest scurrying across the courtyard to ring the bell and call his parishioners to prayer.

The church itself sits at the very centre of the village and undoubtedly is the hub of all life here. It is an exquisite and magnificent example of its kind, enclosed by a clay stucco stone wall with three arched doors and capped in pink volcanic rock. The massive bell tower is attached to one corner of the church perimeter. The original church dates from the early seventeenth century and had been partly rebuilt in 1789. It still retains its traditional thatched roof and even the wall surrounding the church grounds is topped with thatch. Once again, the bell tower or steeple was deliberately set separately from the church structure itself. I liked this male/female division. Indirectly it spoke of sexuality and of fecundity and procreation, and this tiny little church high in these cold northern hills was more eloquent than any church I have been in before or since. There was something simple yet immensely more passionate here than in any cathedral of any great city or empire in the world.

As I stood looking, I thought that the little church and the landscape it sat in would have been a colourist's fantasy. The massive sky overhead seemed to have so many shades of blue. The clouds were either incredibly white or tinged with grey-blue and a kind of feeble purple and pink. The landscape beyond the village was one of rolling hills and great mountains in the distance. Here were browns and greens and greys. It could have been a scene from the Scottish Highlands. But the church itself animated the scene. The walls enclosing it were losing their whitewash, revealing the curious pinks and beige of the volcanic stone from which they were built. The arched doorway of the church was a soft powder blue with side pillars and lintel decorated in strong red and bright primrose.

Inside, at first glance, one thought oneself in a barn. For here was no vaulted ceiling or flying buttresses, only tree-branch rafters covered in cobwebs and thatch. The whitewash was peeling in here also, and everywhere the villagers had embossed the walls with a naive decoration in green and gold. No barn could have been so lovingly painted. I was attracted by the images of the Virgin and the saints. They were unlike those statues one normally finds in churches. Here each of them was dressed in real clothes which had been specially sewn for them and they were more like dolls than objects of veneration. The altar itself was smothered in lavish heavy lace and damask; bunting was everywhere, giving the place the atmosphere of a carnival about to begin. It might have been a hoopla stall.

The little Indian caretaker who had come with the key to let us in was silent and unintrusive as we slowly walked around. I noticed that he was dressed in a suit. It was a little too big for him and probably twenty-five years older than he was. But I was impressed by him. In this back of beyond he had deliberately dressed in his Sunday best to open the church for us gringos. He led us excitedly to the back of the church and revealed an old sea chest. When he opened it we were shown the boots and clothes and the sword of what must have been one of the very first Spanish settlers in this area. Everything was covered in a heavy layer of dust. The smell of age as the old caretaker opened the chest was all too evident. I wondered how long he would still have these relics to show to the very occasional stranger.

As John and I wandered about independently, our caretaker sat quietly on one of the long benches that lined the walls. There were no rows of pews in the body of the church. I suspected that these people's religion was of the severe form, and that those who intended to worship in church would feel it blasphemous to sit on their backsides in such a holy place. For them it was only right and proper to stand before their God with their heads bowed, or else to kneel on the hard rock floor.

But the real masterpieces of this church were the surrealistic murals that lined the walls. I fell in love with them immediately as my eyes hungrily took in the images that these peasant people had painted to adorn their place of worship. In these pictures was the spirit of Hieronymus Bosch, and here too were the dark intimations of Goya and the enthusiasm of Salvador Dali. Here was magic and realism sitting side by side and telling the Christian story with an excited kind of lyricism I had not encountered before. Social commentary, theology, nomadic imagination, and the primitive blasphemy of colour and concept were blazing through these unique masterpieces. This small, empty church didn't need communicants; it was already full to bursting.

There was little else to see in this locked-up village. And I watched as the little immaculate caretaker took the huge key from his pocket and carefully closed the church doors. I still wonder if he knows the value of those paintings. I hardly know myself. In comparison to the many monotonous Stations of the Cross that I have viewed in hundreds of other places of worship, these simple iconoclastic murals depicting Christ's suffering were priceless beyond measure. When we drove off our guide was explaining something about the murals that I had not fully grasped. In one of these paintings the soldiers who were escorting Christ to his crucifixion at Golgotha were all dressed in the uniform of the Spanish conquistadors. Was that perhaps why the little caretaker had eagerly shown us the uniform in the old sea chest? Did he think that he had a holy relic in his church – the uniform of one of those who had driven Christ to his crucifixion?

Another question was beginning to intrigue me. How was it that those who had brought the faith of Christianity to these remote hills and these tribal people were later seen by those same people as the betrayers of Christ and thus of Christianity? I am sure the men of the Inquisition would not have viewed these blasphemous paintings on this remote church wall lightly. But then Chile was never the golden treasure chest that Mexico and Peru had been for the Spanish Empire. Why would the church of the empire worry about the muddled thinking of some backward Indian imagination in this forgotten landscape?

As our jeep bumped over the rough-hewn highway John and I chatted enthusiastically about the village we had left. The whole notion of a ceremonial village was fascinating. It was curious to think of a complete village that existed purely for the purpose of ritual. These Indian people lived in a vast changing landscape. They understood it and adapted to it. They came together only to worship and celebrate. So for a few days in every year the little village of Parinacota, like a few other villages on this northern frontier, would be buzzing with life. The people would be telling their stories, sharing their hardships and their humour; some would take wives and others husbands, children would be baptized, families would bury their dead and then disappear into that wilderness until the next festive occasion. I loved the whole idea of a village which functioned only as a place of ritual, and where life was lived elsewhere. I could see how this would bind these people together intimately, so that perhaps they truly felt themselves one tribe and one family and one people. Whatever that sense of a place with a desperate want in it that I had first encountered at the edge of the desert, Parinacota was an epiphany that obliterated the feeling, like a small candle burning in a dark place.

≡Ⅲ≡

We lunch in Putré, the main town in the area. The restaurant looks closed and tiny from the outside but proves to be large and quite full. Soap operas, *novellas* in Spanish, play at full volume on the TV. Nobody seems to be watching them and they are an unwarranted disturbance in a town whose name means 'the water that whispers'.

We stop for a coffee in the middle of nowhere as we descend once more into the desert regions. A few buildings around an old railway carriage are run as a café by hippy owners, one of whom, a qualified doctor, tells us that the carriage had originally worked on a railway serving the nitrate mines at Iquique. Built in England it had ended up here to be used as a laboratory for the gold mines in Lauca. I like this woman. Her gentle nature, sweet face and soft complexion belie the harsh environment. But I am surprised with her reply when I ask why she lives in this remote encampment with two children.

'Before I lived in the world, now I live in the earth.'

It seems a little trite, but perhaps too many tourists have asked the same question. She wishes us 'a nice life in the world' as we leave.

The cool and damp of the *camanchaca* are now a fading memory. The world is again burning, blinding hot and the cross-like cacti dotted over the hillsides suggest a mass crucifixion. I wonder how people can stay here: what are they avoiding or discovering? When we pass a modern-day geoglyph with the message '*Christo Viene*', Christ comes, it strikes me as a somewhat forlorn hope.

When you think you have seen all the barren mountain landscape imaginable and have been descending for hours, there is the big one, a sheer drop of eight hundred metres to the Lluta valley, Arica's other garden. After the sights of the past two days, the terrain of this green, fertile and flat valley, even with its vast walls of light brown cliff that had seemed so alien, is now positively normal, homely and welcoming.

'You can't get sunburnt through a window, can you?' I ask.

'No,' says Brian, 'you just get exceptionally hot.'

I had planned to get us seats on the shady side of the bus to Iquique. But confusion over where the sun would be in relation to our route and forgetting the rather basic fact that the driver was on the left-hand side of the vehicle meant that I had cocked up. We are sitting behind the curtained driver's compartment with the sun beating in on us. I am fuming; angry with myself for not working things out correctly and annoyed with Bri for being so blasé. Now he settles back in his seat, doubtless preparing for more sleep. Chin on chest he turns to me, 'With all those guidebooks and that little compass of yours I'd have thought you could work out where the sun is.'

'At least I was thinking about it!' I hiss through clenched teeth.

'Temper, temper!' he says, snuggling down further. I drum my fingers on the armrest in righteous rage. We both like to get things right and both find it hard to resist the 'I told you so' attitude when one proves the other wrong. It balances out but, with this long journey ahead and the constant need to be organized, I wish Bri would take more interest in the nitty-gritty of getting about. The whole process of getting our tickets had been dauntingly bureaucratic and it had taken me a while, struggling with my Spanish phrase book, to understand the system. Brian's only, and not entirely helpful, query as I tried to work things out was, 'When are we leaving?'

Once on the bus our names are checked off a list by the steward. Even without the heat of the sun and Brian's lackadaisical attitude my head is soon swimming. When finally we are on the move, Brian sits up and looks around the bus.

'There are plenty of spare seats, John. Why don't you take one in the shade where you can cool down?'

I feel anger rising but then appreciate his tone, gently teasing but also conciliatory. I take the seat across the aisle where I can see the road ahead. We are soon eating up the miles of the Pan American Highway. The name itself conjures up for me endless opportunity and adventure. At times we travel along valley sides at a thousand metres then swoop down to follow the rocky coast-line. It looks beautiful in the sunshine. I listen to the Neil Young tape that Anna gave me and find myself daydreaming, just enjoying the sense of rolling on. Looking ahead the road seems infinite, dead straight; all is flat as far as the eye can see. The road dips a foot to reveal miles more of two-lane blacktop. You can really sense you are covering the ground on flat earth like this. Calm now, I feel centred here in the desert – not really reflecting, not thinking ahead, just being of the moment.

Brian reads and dozes. I cannot help smiling. I am very happy to be with him – he has a big spirit. We are so comfortable most of the time; true, he seems unaware of those around him sometimes, but this comes from independence, not arrogance. Young's lyric 'Long may you run' plays in my ears. Yes, I think, you old bastard, long may you run – white beard shining in the sun.

This journey is scheduled to take more than four hours. After two it seems as if we have been on the road for a day, and time is dragging. Every now and then we stop and someone gets off. Sometimes there is a little side track, sometimes nothing. I watch the faces as we pull away. They remain impassive, merely blinking away the swirling dust. I feel lonely for them as they head off for heaven knows what remote spot.

I read what the guidebook has to say about Iquique, our destination.

'Oh, no!'

'What is it?' asks Bri.

'It says here that our next stop has huge fishmeal plants. After 1980 Chile was the world's largest producer of fishmeal, and sixty per cent goes through Iquique!'

'Isn't that just lovely? At this rate I'm going to be smoking as much as you.'

'Hold on though,' I say, reading on, 'the town's name comes from the Aymara word *ique-ique*, meaning "place of rest and tranquillity".'

'Let's hope it is. But I guess that'll depend on which way the wind is blowing.'

As the road scrolls down to the sea, a vast sand dune rises up. Until now there has been none of the rolling Saharan terrain that I associated with deserts, only flats and rocks and barren escarpments. Yet this huge, solitary hump just outside the town is not reassuring. Its rounded shape is gentler on the eye than rugged outcrops but the scale is intimidating. Small whirlwinds, visible by their shadows, race across the dune as it squats at the gates of this important city. One has the feeling that nature is just playing games, waiting for the moment to reassert its authority.

〰︎〰︎

The bus to Iquique travelled for some three hundred kilometres along the coastline edge of the northern desert. It had all the appearance of being one huge sand and gravel quarry. The view through the bus window could not intrigue the eye. Its emptiness and repetitiveness was broken here and there only by small crosses on the roadside, marking the place where someone had departed this life.

On the hillsides around Arica I noticed how the army had constructed its own symbol of anchor and crossed guns in white-painted boulders. It seemed the military was continuing the history of the geoglyphs that had begun with the Inca empire. It was an interesting comparison. Certainly the ancient Inca civilization was authoritarian and brutal. But back then kings were regarded as sons of the Sun. They were deities without human equal. The brutality of that empire was largely marked by wars of conquest or confined to religious ritual. For a moment I thought of the image of an Inca high priest standing on the temple steps, his arm raised high in the air and in his hand a knife. On a stone altar beside him lay the drugged body of his living, human sacrifice. Into that beating heart the priest would plunge his stone knife and pull out the pulsating bloody organ to be held aloft to the worshippers below him.

In comparison the role of the military junta in Chile was one of the most insidious examples of state repression in contemporary history. As I was thinking, my eyes again caught a glimpse of one of those simple roadside crosses. How many thousands of the disappeared have not even this simple memorial? I wondered how contemporary Chileans dealt with their recent bloody history. For the regime that had so dominated Chile's immediate past had also plunged a stone-cold knife into the heart of the Chilean people and ripped it out, pulsing and bleeding, only to be forgotten. I looked about me at the faces of the passengers on the bus and wondered what hidden secrets or what hidden grief pulsed in their hearts. History was not so distant as to be easily ignored.

But if the landscape outside the bus was sombre, and if it was perhaps conditioning such responses, then the atmosphere of the bus itself was determined not to let it be so. From an old battered transistor radio on the driver's dashboard, romantic ballads were being blasted out by some South American Sinatra or alternatively the airwaves were crackling with some frenetic salsa. I looked at the driver, who was not only oblivious to my contemplations but also seemed at times oblivious to the road. His head was rolling and nodding in time to the music and from a cigarette burning slowly in his mouth, a long column of ash dripped precariously. Like the roadside shrine we had discovered high in the hills, his window was adorned with miniature fluffy animals, teddy bears and rubber Disney toys. Everywhere there seemed to be ribbons, bows and bells. A dangling crucifix smashed into the windscreen with every roll and pitch of the bus. There was Santa Claus and Mary Magdalene and flower posies and miniature flags. It cheered me up, I don't know why – perhaps because, unlike the shrine on the mountain, this collage was somehow life affirming.

Chapter Three

~~

Iquique was bustling and vibrant and more colourful than Arica had been. But just like Arica there was the awful and inevitable smell of fish processing. The heat and the smell hit us the moment we descended from the bus. I was wearing a sweaty T-shirt, an old pair of shorts and an even more ancient pair of bedraggled sandals. John was immaculate in cotton slacks and a crisp clean shirt. I had an odd assortment of baggage all tied willy-nilly with elastic ropes to a small chrome trolley affair. John had one large bag containing all his clothes and another smaller bag smartly tossed over his shoulder carrying his documents, passport, pen, computer, compass, penknife, string, guidebooks, smokes and God knows what else.

We were an odd couple standing like two lost sheep in another town perched between desert and sea. Without hardly looking for it John pulled a street map from his satchel. If John was irrepressibly curious he was also an inveterate organizer. I watched him study the map and move his head slightly as he mumbled, 'Right, yes. Yes, OK. Yes,' while all the time his finger was drawing an imaginary line in the air. 'OK, let's go,' he commanded and struck off down a side street. 'Intrepid traveller, my arse,' I said scurrying behind him. We found the hotel, quickly registered and went up to our room. After dumping his bags, John headed out again, saying, 'I'll see you in the bar in a bit, I'm going to take a look around.' I nodded in agreement. The welcome blast of the air conditioner kept the town's heat and the smell of fish at bay. I slept easily; there was no need here to worry about gasping for air.

≡‖≡

Brian has been suffering from a minor stomach bug and is resting until evening. As dusk starts to fall I stroll out from our hotel into Plaza Prat. Globe street lamps and green lights strung out from the top of a clocktower light the square as families saunter about under the trees, the air filled with the lilt of children at play. I enjoy the peaceful atmosphere and realize that part of the pleasure comes from being alone for a while and meandering at will.

I stop and look up at the brightly lit Teatro Municipal. Its broad façade dominates the square and reflects the prosperity of the port in Victorian times when nitrates and minerals were shipped abroad from the mines inland. The Teatro is adorned with four statues of women depicting the seasons – though from what I've read about Iquique they should only honestly depict one: summer, summer, summer and, well, summer. As the sun sets, the mountains beyond this white edifice turn an ever deeper pink. As I near the hotel once more I spot turkey vultures wheeling and settling in a high palm across the road from our room. Perhaps they have spotted the ailing Brian.

∿∿

Later I made my way to the hotel bar. '*Una cervesa, por favor, señor.*' The bar was empty and the barman seemed glad of my company. Within a minute he set me up a tall frosted glass of beer and with it a small saucer of olives as big as walnuts. I sluiced it down and ordered another.

The waiter pulled the beer and smilingly asked where I was from. His curiosity was tempered by reserve. I told him that I was from Ireland and waited for a moment. It was obvious he was not used to foreign guests. There was a small misunderstanding when he thought that I was from Holland. I corrected him by repeating the word *Irlanda*, and when I received a quizzical look I spoke the words *Irlanda* and *Irlandés*, trilling my r's like a parrot. The encounter must have looked like a scene from *Fawlty Towers*. Finally, to get my point across I joked that I was the great-great-great-nephew of Bernardo O'Higgins, the liberator of Chile. The barman smiled nervously and said, 'Oh, yes,' as he watched me devour yet more olives. By now I was on my second dish.

I gathered from his furtive glances that my remark had unsettled him. I sipped my beer slowly and tried to look a little less demented than I imagined he thought me to be. I was becoming anxious that my throwaway joke had backfired. He passed me a couple of times rearranging bottles and glasses. Each time he took a long, lingering look at me. My discomfort grew. When I noticed him whisper to one or two locals who had come in, nodding towards me as he spoke, I was convinced my travels in Chile were about to end with a great deal of physical ignominy. I was wishing McCarthy would arrive to even up the odds. I had finished my second dish of olives and the beer was at its last half inch. I couldn't get up and run now, and if I coolly called for another drink it might force the barman to act out what I thought he was thinking and unceremoniously tip this demented, olive-eating insulter of the Great Liberator on to the street.

As I watched him from the corner of my eye, he emerged from behind the bar counter and ushered me towards the window. 'Come, come,' he said. I walked towards where he was standing, trying to look unperturbed. The hotel fronted on to a square and the waiter was pointing towards it. 'See, there you are. Here is your great-grand-uncle standing in the square in Iquique,' he said beaming widely. I looked out and saw he was pointing to the statue in the middle of the square. Sure enough there stood the great liberator, my great-great-grand-uncle, Bernardo.

For several minutes we chatted about why I had come to Chile. The barman seemed to think it even more funny than my joke about Bernardo. While he talked I devoured another plate of the massive olives, still catching glimpses of bemusement on my new friend's face.

John came dazzling through the door in one of those waistcoats that you sometimes see seasoned travellers, coarse fishermen and camera crews on location wearing, awash with pockets and very professional.

'Must say you're looking very dapper this evening, John.'

He ordered a beer and in the same breath said, 'Sorry, I can't say the same about your good self, old man.'

John knew of my fascination with Bernardo O'Higgins. During our captivity in Lebanon, I had talked about him repeatedly. When you spend time imprisoned in tiny rooms, and an even longer time imprisoned inside your own mind, people come to visit you. Bernardo was one of my visitors. In such circumstances you make them stay, imaginary or not.

I had since learned much about him. Bernardo was born in Chillán on 20 August 1778, the only son of a strict hard-working father, Ambrose O'Higgins, an Irish-born soldier and trader in the service of Spain. Ambrose was a Cecil Rhodes of his time. In Chile he saw a truly new world thriving with life and vast potential. He began making a reality of his dreams. He improved roads, built harbours and cities. He provided education and introduced new farming methods. Encountering the resistance of the colonial aristocracy who would not admit an Irish peasant into their social circle, he effortlessly countered their xenophobic ostracism by the simple expedient of returning to Spain to purchase a title, thus becoming Don Ambrose O'Higgins.

Late in life he had a son, Bernardo. The mother was a seventeen-year-old, Spanish, middle-class girl. Overcome with a mixture of Catholic guilt and perhaps confused with fatherhood and a wife young enough to be his granddaughter, Don Ambrose refused to share his home with his son though he visited him occasionally and maintained him. He was known to the young Bernardo only as his benefactor. No doubt some of the stories of Ireland and of his benefactor's dreams drifted into the young man's consciousness. But Bernardo grew up alone, desperately questioning his paternity but receiving no answers.

Though history has recorded Bernardo O'Higgins as the hero who finally defeated and expelled the Spanish from Chile, I was fascinated more by the man than where history had placed him. History for me is a human occurrence. The imperialist litanies that I was taught at school, the catalogue of dates and incidents and names, replete with births and deaths of long-departed kings and queens, meant nothing to me. They were merely something I was forced to learn by rote and have long since gratefully forgotten.

'Does the statue look like anything you imagined?' John asked.

'No, but then I'm not sure what I imagined him to look like. I suppose I expected a younger man with gaunt features and drawn eyes.'

'So what do you think?' John persevered.

'He looks too handsome, too mature, avuncular even, but I suppose all that paternalism is part of the package when you are the founding father.'

John ordered another two beers and said, 'If I was you, I wouldn't complain about paternalism.'

I smiled – John was the only other soul I had told about my wife Audrey being pregnant.

After a meal, I sat at the window and watched the ugly beige of the desert hills turn into a soft pink and pull together the flat pastels of violet, blue and black and bleached blue. The new high-rise buildings painted blue, yellow and a washed-out emerald green seemed to soak up the desert night. All around the square young lovers were promenading; mothers and fathers with their young children in little pedal pushchairs were walking them round and round the tiny space. I thought of my own child waiting to be born and smiled contentedly at John's earlier comments.

That night I slept fitfully, shunting back and forwards between bed and toilet, cursing my over-indulgence in those huge oily olives. The travelling of the last few days was beginning to catch up with me. I also was growing anxious about our journey into the deeper reaches of the desert. I lay back on my bed and listened to the noise of the square outside. Though I was desperately weary my restless mind had created a dreamy sense of displacement in me. On the bedside table I had left a copy of Pablo Neruda's poetic opus, the *Canto General*. I feverishly hunted through the book to find a favourite poem, hoping that it might lull me to sleep.

SPRING IN THE CITY

The sidewalk has been worn till it is only
a network of dirty holes
in which the tears of the rain gathered;
then came the sun, an invader
over the wasted ground
of the endlessly riddled city
from which all the horses fled.
At last, some lemons fell
and a red vestige of oranges
connected it with trees and feathers,
whispered falsely of orchards
which did not last long
but showed that somewhere
the shameless, silvered spring
was undressing among the orange blossoms.

Was I from that place? From the cold
texture of adjoining walls?
Did my spirit have to do with beer?
They asked me that when I went out,
when I entered myself again, when I went to bed,
they were asking me that, the walls,
the paint, the flies, the carpets
trodden so many times
by other inhabitants
who could be confused with me.
They had my nose and my shoes,
the same dead, sorrowing clothes,
the same pale, neat nails,
and a heart as open as a sideboard
in which accumulated bundles,
loves, journeys, and sand.
That's to say, everything in its happening
goes and stays inexorably.

Listening to the noises percolating through my open window, I
seemed to know the streets of which Neruda was writing. I had

been down them a hundred thousand times. These streets are metaphorical as well as literal. Like a wonderful Impressionist painting, they are closely observed and richly sensuous. Yet they pose questions. And they are the eternal questions about identity, place, meaning and purpose. Like a fine work of art, Neruda's poems are simple and direct, yet they hold you, and you reread them again and again. I have always believed all of life is a journey and felt myself to be a perpetual exile. With Neruda I felt I could travel into many landscapes: the metaphysical, the existential, and the simply exquisite landscape of Chile and South America.

But it was not simply the finely wrought craftsmanship of Neruda's poetry that made me choose him as my spirit guide. I felt a closeness to him that in some inexplicable way had preceded the gift of his poetry to me. There were many aspects of his childhood and adolescence that seemed to echo my own. I turned them over in my mind, trying to bring the man closer to me. Behind all his political protestation and historical iconography, there lives a great hunger.

He was baptized Neftali Ricardo Reyes Basoalto, but adopted a pseudonym at the age of sixteen to hide his poetic inclinations from his father. Neruda was his mother's first and only child. She was a teacher in a local school and suffered from tuberculosis. She died a month after giving birth to her son.

His father, Don José del Carmen Reyes Morales, was a foreman on the railroad. He was blond and blue eyed, a stern, hard-working man used to giving orders and having them obeyed. Two years after his wife's death Neruda's father remarried and the family moved south to the small frontier town of Temuco.

Neruda's stepmother, Dona Trinidad Candia Marverde, became the centre of the young Neruda's life. She provided the love and gentleness that was so missing from his relationship with his father. Later Neruda described her as his 'more-mother' and some-times the 'guardian angel of my childhood'. When he was six years old, Neruda was sent to the local school for boys. It was a large, rambling mansion with sparsely furnished rooms and a gloomy basement. By the time he was ten he was already composing poems. Because many of his schoolmates mocked him for his love of poetry, Neruda kept to himself after school, either staying at home or taking long walks in the woods. He read anything and everything he could get his hands on. He later wrote about these precious moments of solitude: 'I go upstairs to my room. I read Salgari. The rain pours down like a waterfall. In less than no time, night and the rain cover the whole world. I am alone writing poems in my maths notebook.'

I too was a child poet who spent many hours alone or going for long walks and had spent many nights alone in my room at home in Belfast, composing poems. I too felt different from my child-hood peers and for many years never spoke of my nocturnal scribblings. And now, here I was so many years later, sitting up in my bed at five o'clock in the morning feverishly writing metaphors and similes to capture my first few days in this intoxi-cating land.

Somehow the choice of Neruda as a spirit guide was not one chosen out of reason, but was an instinctive one, something given to me.

I reread the opening lines of the second stanza of the poem:

> Was I from that place? From the cold
> texture of adjoining walls?
> Did my spirit have to do with beer?
> They asked me that when I went out,
> when I entered myself again, when I went to bed,

I sensed that I too would be asking these questions in whatever city or whatever place my travels between extremes would land me.

The sun was coming up outside the window, declaring first light. I had not noticed the noise abate in the square beneath. I had forgotten sleep, for, like that first light, I was only slowly becoming aware of the fascination O'Higgins and Neruda held for me and the pull that had brought me to their native land.

It was inevitable, I suppose, that I should begin hunting through the Canto, to find Neruda's first mention of Bernardo. I went to the window unconscious of John sleeping solidly and snug in his bed, but knowing there was no one in the square to see me.

Looking across at the statue of Bernardo, I read Neruda's words of acknowledgement and celebration.

BERNARDO O'HIGGINS RIQUELME (1810)

O'Higgins, to celebrate you
in the twilight we must light up the room.
In the South's autumn twilight
with an infinite tremor of poplars.

You're Chile, between patriarch and cowboy,
a poncho from the provinces, a child
who doesn't know his name yet,
iron-willed and shy in school,
a sad little country boy.
In Santiago you're ill at ease, they
stare at your baggy black clothes,
and when they placed the ribbon across
your rustic statue's breast, the flag
of the country you gave us, it smelled
of wild mustard in the early morning.

Youth, Professor Winter
accustomed you to the rain,
you received your degrees from
the university of the Streets of London
and an impoverished wanderer,
wildfire of our freedom,
gave you a prudent eagle's counsel
and embarked you in History.

'What's your name?' laughed
the 'gentlemen' from Santiago:
child of love, on a winter's night,
your forsaken condition
shaped you with rough mortar
with the seriousness of a home or
of wood, definitive, worked in the South.

Time changes all, all but your face.
O'Higgins, you're an invariable clock
with a single hour on your candid sphere:
Chile's hour, the last minute
left on the red timetable
of combatant dignity.

So you're one and the same amid the rosewood
furniture and the daughters of Santiago,
as surrounded in Rancagua by gunpowder and death.

You're the same solid portrait
of him who has no father but fatherland,
land with orange blossoms
conquered by your artillery.

Over breakfast John commented on my drawn appearance. I explained that the night and the noise had made sleeping difficult. And that in any case I had kept awake all night in the company of Pablo Neruda and Bernardo O'Higgins. John remarked, 'This Bernardo has had a hold on you for some time.' In return I told him about my early morning thoughts that I would love to write the real story of Bernardo, not the historians' version. I was gabbing, I suppose, full of ghost-filled sleep.

We moved on to the itinerary for the next few days over the remains of our breakfast. The real purpose of our stopover in Iquique was to travel out into the desert pampas and visit the ghost mines of Santa Laura and Humberstone. When John mentioned them they sounded to me like characters in a gothic romance. He had already ascertained from the hotel staff that the quickest and easiest way to get to them was by taxi. We decided to look over the town of Iquique before business started.

≡ ||| ≡

At what seems like the crack of dawn I wake to the growl of large masonry drills. Our hotel is undergoing refurbishment. I reach for my earplugs and for once give thanks for Brian's snoring, which makes them such a necessary precaution, as I drift back into the cocoon of sleep.

Later, we saunter around the town. Iquique is a busy, friendly place with many wooden, balconied buildings, once the homes of the nitrate magnates, which overlook the wide avenues in the town centre.

'I like this town.'

'Yes, "a place of rest and tranquillity" it is.'

'I'm glad we're not moving on until tomorrow.'

'Yeah. Travelling like this, you never develop much of a routine. It's wearing after a while.'

Most of the time we have spent together in the past has been dominated by a mind-numbingly dull routine: wake up from fitful sleep, guards bring breakfast, take us to bathroom, read, if we have books and light, or talk, guards bring lunch, chat or doze, guards bring sandwich, hope for sleep. Occasional terrifying bouts of activity and moving gaols. In those days there was no time, no chance to prepare for anything, we just had to try to hang on amid the physical and emotional roller-coaster of miserable transfer. Our moves, bound and gagged, allowed no exchange of views, just the reassurance of the warm body close by. Here no such strictures exist. We can make our own plans.

The main street of colonial clapboard houses was interesting enough if one had an architect's eye. The dryness of the climate here had maintained them, but I was disappointed to find that none of these houses was open to the public. They were still occupied and part of the living environment of the town. Happily the museum was open, even though we seemed to be the only tourists. It was a small affair, adequately laid out, every nook and cranny stuffed with the rusted architecture of Chile's industrial age. Bits and pieces of engineering machinery and what seemed acres of hand tools filled the place. It had the feel of a tomb about it, but there was more than sufficient evidence in this small corner of Chile of how Europe had plundered the mineral wealth of this country like a ravenous wolf. European capitalism was the new conquistador. It had sweated the life blood out of the Chilean people and had left nothing in recompense but these rusty relics.

Everywhere the walls were lined with old sepia photographs of the mine owners and entrepreneurs. They stared out from the walls. Dylan Thomas's words were never more cogent or real than they were here with those staring, pious, 'dickie bird watching pictures of the dead'. This was the Victorian aristocracy of iron, with their tight starched collars and equally starched suits that looked two sizes too small. They displayed long lavish beards turned brittle with the dry climate and also huge curled moustaches. To my mind, still fevered from the previous night's imaginings, they had the look of the conqueror or overlord about them. And here I could imagine the rust like the dried blood of the labourers who had dug huge fortunes out of the earth. In those staring faces, I thought I could see the shadow of Neruda's father.

It was curious to me that the mines in this northern area of Chile had produced millions upon millions of tons of nitrate, mainly saltpetre. This same saltpetre is the principal constituent in the making of gunpowder and had undoubtedly supplied the armies for the slaughter of the First World War. Contrastingly, one of the mineral barons, Pedro Gamboni, became a multi-millionaire by producing iodine from the saltpetre. Iodine is a crude antiseptic and must have been used in thousands of field hospitals throughout the theatre of that same world war. And when the nitrates were not feeding the war machine, they were being bought in huge tonnage to support the nitrate fertilizer industry which was rapidly expanding in North America and Canada. Either way the nitrate barons won. They could produce the essential element which fed humanity, which contributed to human slaughter and which at the same time made the medicine that might heal the maimed.

Conversely I thought how paternalistic the portraits of those nitrate barons were. With their flowing grey beards and plump faces they had the look of a kindly Santa Claus, but it was far from the truth. The harsh exploitation of the labour force in the mines, the farms and in industry had been the persistent characteristic of Chilean society since the sixteenth century. From the first years of conquest well into the 1980s Chilean society reflected a dichotomy between attempts to create better living conditions and the realities of an economic and political order which rested upon the foundations of conquest, subjugation and coercion of the labour force. The museum was pallid evidence of all that.

I was momentarily thrown by the double-take these portraits had occasioned in me. One minute they were kindly and even lovable, like a favoured grandparent; the next they were the bloated, arrogant faces of the exploiter, the parasites who fed on gullibility and innocence.

I was also beginning to sense, however tentatively, Pablo Neruda's passionate commitment to the mestizo and the indigenous peoples of Chile and also his fervent support for classical Communism. There was one thing I felt saved him from the rage of the propagandist, and that was his sensuous love of the land he grew up in. At every point of his poetry he talks of 'his' people as the real treasure of Chile.

≡Ⅲ≡

The natural history section of the Regional Museum includes a freak shark embryo with two heads while an anthropology exhibit shows the curious pointed skulls of the Chinchorro people. They bound them from birth to change the shape – as part of their group identity and because it was deemed attractive. There is an extensive display of old photographs and relics from the great days of the nitrate mines. One of the leading figures of that time was James 'Santiago' Humberstone who ran a vast nitrate plant just outside Iquique. Here is the man's three-piece suit. Made of black, heavy wool it makes me feel clammy even in the cool confines of the museum.

There is no sign of such hot garb when we wander down to look at the packed beaches. There is a stench of fish but happily it is tempered, as is the heat, by a land breeze.

On the outskirts of town, modern, brightly coloured tower blocks rise up against the coastal hills that reach almost two thousand feet.

'Those flats with all that green, blue and red look like the mineral deposits we saw in the valleys round Lauca,' I say.

'Maybe,' muses Brian. 'To me they speak of man's need to bring his own colours to this dull landscape.'

There is nothing dull about the Centro Español where we dine that evening. It is an amazing Moorish edifice with great wall paintings depicting scenes from Cervantes. Looking at the ungainly, comic figures of Don Quixote and Sancho Panza riding their beasts puts us in mind of the trek we will be joining in a few weeks' time. Sitting in such an ornate restaurant, surrounded by elegant diners, it is hard to come to terms with all the wilderness we have travelled through. There is a sense of disorientation at moments like this when we are essentially in comfortable Europe yet really just a mile from the desert. In a short while we will be going high into the mountains on horseback. At times our schedule seems to dominate everything. This is certainly true for me: I am constantly running through our itinerary, rechecking whether we need to get tickets in advance and wondering whether we are missing some important aspect of Chile.

〰〰

The Moorish building was a bar-cum-restaurant. It was full of richly carved woods and huge brown leather sofas which you could disappear into. It also had the usual Arab feature of tall ceilings. All around the bar, along the stairs and in the restaurant were fabulous representations of that intricate symmetry of which the Arab mind is such a master. And hanging on the wall above where we sat were two massive and finely executed pictures of Don Quixote and Sancho Panza!

When one is travelling non-stop for long periods you don't really taste food when you sit down to eat it, you're usually too tired or hungry. But whatever I had been eating up in the Bolivian foothills and now in this desert landscape was beginning to take its toll.

'You're doing a lot of running to the toilet!' John said.

I nodded and commented that the name of Iquique was baby-talk for my condition.

'Tough shit,' said John. 'We really need to sort out what we're doing over the next few days.'

As John talked about our plans, I studied the quiet animation in his face and thought of his comic dismissal of my rumbling bowels. I thought of our time together in Beirut when I had been seriously ill and John had been anxious I might die within a few days. His ministrations to me then had been unrelenting and deeply moving. On one occasion, I remember him placing his hands on my stomach and praying earnestly for my recovery. I smiled to myself. No matter how he shrugged off my illness now, I would never forget that moment.

≡▥≡

I feel quite thrown when we receive a phone call just as we are turning in. Friends of acquaintances of Brian's have just come back to their flat in Iquique from Santiago. We are leaving tomorrow so the only time to meet is now. We take a taxi to their building.

Frank and Noni have a grand flat looking over the sea. It is one of only two occupied in a vast block owned by the company Frank works for, Anglo American. He is in charge of setting up the biggest mining project in the world, inland and high in the Andes. Frank has worked as a mining engineer in Africa and all over South America. He has been an expat for thirty years or so yet still seems very in touch with his Irish roots. A big man with neatly groomed grey hair and spectacles, he speaks in a deep, rumbling voice that often turns to a chuckle. He fights his corner well in the face of our cynicism about the multinational's concern for the environment.

'Countries like Chile could not develop their mineral potential without venture capitalism,' he insists and goes on, 'The days when the multinationals just dug out the goods and cleared off leaving a scarred landscape are gone. A big part of my job in preparing the mine site is to ensure that at every stage we do as little damage as possible and that we will eventually leave it as close to virgin as is humanly possible.'

We hope he is right. Certainly he believes what he says. Noni is a teacher, an outgoing and hilarious woman who makes us very welcome indeed. It is five in the morning when we eventually head back to the hotel. As we leave their building and look up to the two isolated sets of lights from the occupied apartments I cannot help feeling that Frank and Noni, though obviously happy, are themselves isolated. Theirs is a strange life.

One aspect of their terrific hospitality is the offer of the use of their flat in Santiago. For some reason I have reservations that I find hard to articulate. Perhaps it is the sense of obligation. Brian thinks this is mad.

'I don't want to be paying for a hotel when I don't have to,' he says as we get ready for bed.

'But we've already budgeted for the hotel in Santiago,' I argue, still not clear why I am bothered about it.

Bri shakes his head in weary bemusement. 'Look, in the apartment we'll be able to come and go as we please – nobody'll be wanting to get in and do the room. We'll be able to relax, cook meals for ourselves when we want, and eat what we want. As for the saving we make on the hotel, we can rebudget that into some other contingencies.'

I am noticing, more clearly than before, differences in the way we look at things. This clarity is not surprising now that we are out in the real world. In captivity they would not have been so important. There were far fewer, hardly any, real plans to make. Fantasies are endlessly negotiable: two people can sit side by side studying the same imaginary view and that mutual vision can still accommodate any number of either individual's particular desires.

I have been feeling responsible for our arrangements which, perhaps, is not fair on Brian. We have not argued but there are moments when he seems tense. Maybe he too is finding it hard to adapt to this new journey together.

He hates the constraint of plans. He likes to take things as they come and, when the mood suits, run with them. On the other hand he is far more anxious about getting to bus stations or airports in good time than me.

Despite the fact that we were out until the early hours Brian is up first thing. 'I'm away round to Frank and Noni's for that key,' he chirps happily, 'then I'll get some boxes for our stuff. By then maybe you'll be up out of your pit.'

Happy to let him get organized, I slump back on my pillow still feeling exhausted. Mildly irritated by his good spirits it occurs to me that all the cat-napping he does may give him the reserves for such early morning activity. He has a remarkable ability to leave his bed.

We are going to use the boxes to send some redundant clothes and books home. It is a relief to be lightening our loads somewhat. Either we brought too much gear or we should have larger bags. I had hoped my medium-sized rucksack would suffice, but already it needs both of us to sit on it to shut it. There is no room for anything acquired on the trip. A few T-shirts and a couple of finished books can be dispatched home. I have been spending a lot of time trying to work out how best to distribute my belongings. Ideally everything fits into one not too large bag. I even bought a cheap waistcoat that has many pockets into which I can fit all manner of stuff. It feels good to have wallets, passports, etc. close about me. I also have a shoulder bag which takes these things if the going gets too hot. I have a huge supply of films, notebooks and batteries for my Psion organizer, with which I am writing my notes and diary. I want to be the perfect traveller, seasoned, rugged yet with a certain *élan*. As it is I feel slightly daft. How can one be adequately equipped in a country where you move through every conceivable type of terrain and climate?

As we were intending to journey from the extreme north down to Puerto Williams in Tierra del Fuego, the most southerly inhabited place on the continent, we had brought clothes suitable for such climatic extremes as we would encounter. But it was becoming obvious that we had planned unwisely. Our journey south would involve many bus and train rides, sea trips and of course the terrifying adventure across the Andes on horseback. The thought of humping these bags around every point on the compass was not encouraging.

I scoured the streets of Iquique in search of some cardboard boxes. I was taking my role as Sancho Panza to heart. There I was, in the pink light of early morning, rifling through the litter left outside the shops and offices.

When I returned to our hotel, John was in an agitated state. He floundered about the room packing and unpacking, indecisively declaring, 'I'll keep this and send that home, or no, maybe I'll keep that.' I watched as he feverishly packed and unpacked the same clothes and laughed when the maid arrived with the freshly laundered shirts he had left with her the previous evening.

The clean shirts added to John's dilemma, and I could no longer control my laughter when John suddenly discovered that his smart 'traveller's trousers' were missing. 'Where are my trousers, where are my trousers?' he cried dementedly. I left him with his wardrobe and went to sort out my own.

≡|||≡

My continued hopes for linguistic enlightenment receive another rebuttal at the post office. I want to ask the woman behind the counter if she speaks English. As she looks at me baffled by my few words of Spanish, I realize that instead of saying 'Do you speak English?' I have said 'I speak English.' Brian takes over with a more direct approach.

'English?' he barks.

The lady waggles her head uncertainly. She does have a few words which is most fortunate as the posting process is quite a palaver. We have to go outside to buy brown paper and sticky tape. Brian had managed to find a couple of reasonably sized cardboard boxes, but they are in danger of splitting with the amount of stuff we have crammed into them.

'Perhaps we'd better go back to the hotel to wrap this lot up,' I suggest.

Brian shakes his head. 'No, let's do it here.'

'Where? There aren't any tables free.'

'There'll do,' he says, striding to an empty bit of floor and sitting down cross-legged. Initially we try taping up a box each, but the paper keeps unravelling just as one is about to apply the sticky tape. What's more, as we have to move out of the way of other startled customers, we end up in wild contortions as if we are playing some new version of Twister. After a few minutes we find ourselves looking at each other's red faces under our hats across a messy heap of exploding boxes, string and brown wrapping paper.

'One box at a time, I reckon.'

'Good idea,' agrees Bri.

Eventually the wrapping is done and we struggle to our feet to rejoin the queue at the lady's desk. She gives us a form and points to indicate that we now need to go out of the building to another department.

'What now?' asks Brian.

'Customs, I think,' I reply, trying to listen to the woman and read the form. We locate the customs department in an alley beside the post office. Here there are no English-speakers and my frantic flicking back and forth through phrase book and dictionary, trying to communicate, word by sporadic word, makes little headway. Brian steps forward again and his loud mantra of 'Irlanda! T-shirts!' gets us the necessary stamp on the form. We return once more to the lady at the front desk and our parcels are dispatched.

Maybe it is because I am still tired from our late night but walking back to the hotel I feel self-conscious and silly in my travelling gear, hat and waistcoat. People shout at us from a passing car. It may well have been good humoured but, feeling vulnerable, I assume they are taking the mick out of the gringos. Brian just mutters 'Bugger off' as the car speeds past.

〰

Santa Laura is a name full of wistfulness and romance. It made me think of a magnificent ship rolling across an ocean, not a crumbling disused mine in the desert. Approaching the mine, its silhouette against the expansive blue sky and greying desert looked more like the image its name had evoked than I could have believed. Only it wasn't a ship but rather an old gypsy caravan riding across the sands.

Our taxi from Iquique parked about half a mile from the site. As we neared its ghostly edifices, our boots biting hard into desert crust, the lumbering hulk of Santa Laura looked like a huge mechanical dinosaur that the winds had unearthed and given a sandy coating of dusty fur. For some reason, I thought of my school science lessons of magnets and iron filings.

Santa Laura is the only thing that breaks the continuity of desert and sky. Without the perspective of its gaunt galleries it would be impossible to distinguish between earth and air. The place had an aura which it declared as its own.

Fascinated, we trudged through this blasted cathedral of iron and lumber until the presence of it overwhelmed me. I felt I could almost hear the roar of its steam lungs belching out across the emptiness. I could smell the air acrid with nitrate. Everywhere was the ghostly din of hammers, gouges, shovels and pumps. The noise of iron under pressure was amplified deafeningly in the desert waste. Beneath it I imagined the voices of men cursing and sweating in the relentless heat.

I submerged myself in this opera of agony and heard the ghosts of Neruda's campesinos and mestizos, a chorus of the dead.

First comes José Cruz Achachalla. José was a starving child when he walked across the great sierras from Bolivia wrapped in coca leaves to protect him from the elements. The vultures that followed him seemed kinder than the white masters who had beaten his mother daily. The miners took him in and he was apprenticed in the mine's dark galleries. Fingernail by fingernail he gathered the hidden tin, knowing neither where nor why the silvery ingots were dispatched.

But José had only traded hunger for hunger and poverty for poverty. For forty years he beetled in the bowels of the earth. When he joined with his comrades for another peso on his salary, he tasted the red wind of police truncheons on his back.

Now José is out of work with nowhere to go. No one knows him in the village he left so long ago. He is as old as the stones and cannot cross the mountains again. He lives by the roadside now, a cripple begging crusts. José has reached the end of the line. His voice screams across the still desert, 'Let them bury me in tin, the tin alone knows me.'

Next comes Cristobol Miranda, who tells his own story. 'I am the shoveller of nitrate snow. We are the heroes of an acid-etched dawn, subject to the fates of death, receiving only for our reward the torrential nitrate. Into our breast the acid enters bloating hearts and rotting lungs. My eyes are burned, I see only shadows, my soul's in the shovel that rises loading and unloading, blood and snow, while around me, only the desert stops.'

In tattered clothes Eufrosino Ramiriz leads blind Cristobol to sit in his dark corner. He declares, 'We took the hot copper sheets with our hands and fed them to the power shovel. Because of this men lost feet and hold out stumps for hands. But I was given the gate when my crippled hands could not lift the scalding sheets. Listen to my heart, the copper crushes it. I can hardly walk. I look for work I cannot find. I am bent still carrying invisible sheets of copper that are killing me.'

From out of the shadows a broken giant of a man lumbers forward. For a moment he looks upon the ghosts of Cristobol and Eufrosino. Then with a voice crumbling like broken stones in his mouth, he says:

'From afar you will see nothing but sand banks, then you will see structures, cables, railings with their trucks and miles of rubble.' Then he gasps deeply for a breath. 'Fatigue and suffering are not visible. They are moving underground, crushing beings. When I entered I could lift the shaft with my shoulders, but when I left I was yellow, hunchbacked and withered. Antimony consumed my innards. I walked like a starving ghost. They buried me out there unmarked, no one can tell you where because the sand and wind batter and devour crosses. And there they left me where the nitrate still eats me, even in death.'

I found a small graveyard adjacent to the overseer's house. The fossilized trunks of a few trees still stand in front of it. I could also discern the long-neglected remains of a small garden. I wondered what that bleak garden must have meant to those who laboured here. Did they revere it like a holy place? Did this feeble garden make the overseer more powerful than his lash and the batons of his police? But even as I was thinking and pondering the desolate beauty of this garden I heard a soft woman's voice behind me.

'I am Margarita Naranjo. I am dead. I spent my entire life here, my parents before me and my brothers and sisters too. We gave our life-blood to the American company. One night they came for no reason and took away our men to the concentration camp. When they dragged my husband away and beat him into the truck, I felt I could no longer breathe. There is much betrayal and much injustice here. From that day I knew I could not eat until he was returned to me. When my friends remonstrated with the over-seer, he roared with laughter at their pleading. I keep sleeping and dying and clenching my teeth that no soup or water can enter me.' Suddenly the unearthly woman's soft voice turned wondrous, and questioningly she said, 'He never returned, he never returned, and little by little I died away and they buried me. I remember the old women weeping and singing a song I had sung so often. I look for my husband Antonio, he wasn't there, they didn't allow him to come. I'm here dead, there's nothing but solitude about me. But I shall sing my wind song until Antonio comes for me.'

The eerie voices of Santa Laura had exhausted and unnerved me. They echoed out of every nook and cranny, and I needed to be away from them.

As we walked back to our taxi parked on the desert roadside, we passed a small group of Americans. The men were explaining the working process of the mine to their wives. Their expertise told me they were engineers. They had the enthusiasm of little boys with a new train set. Their wives simply nodded complacently, like bored turkeys. I doubted they could hear the voices I had heard.

The road to Humberstone from Santa Laura runs through the dry salt pampas. The monotonous emptiness of the place concen-trated my mind. I was thinking of those old photos of the nitrate barons and the explorers in the museum, trying to reconcile their fatherly images with the ghostly voices in Santa Laura. But the history of the nitrate industry is a complex and bloody one involv-ing international disputes and open warfare between Peru, Bolivia and Chile. Ultimately these 'Fertilizer Wars' led to boundary changes which are still the subject of controversy today.

When Chile had claimed large expanses of Peruvian and Bolivian territory by force rather than reason, invoking at least one element of the national motto, the expansion of Chile's nitrate reserves brought its own problems. A national committee integrating the élite triumvirate of landowner, merchants and mine owners set about the rapid industrial exploitation of these reserves. Their proposed intention was to 'achieve the stable base of economic and political equilibrium' through industrial development. The fact that only three of the surnames of this extremely powerful national body were of Spanish origin says much. The decisions reached here were being made by men whose own surnames declared them either English or German or French. Their allegiance was not a national one. The industries they sought to develop were wholly owned or financed by foreign investment.

The question of how to integrate the wealth of the desert was a vexed one. Private foreign investors wanted no truck with a nationalized industry. They had no interest in the labour question. Profit alone was paramount. With such fortunes at stake it was easy to understand the development of political nepotism and financial chicanery in the national parliament. As the labour force realized its own exploitation it determined to make its voice heard above all this political double-talk. With the added element that the world nitrate market was a volatile one, the inevitable result was civil war. Only in this instance it was not a civil war, but rather a war of internal economic interest fuelled by foreign investment.

In such a cauldron, who would hear the voices of those at the mine-face who spat blood from poisoned lungs, or the amputee from those same hell-holes who starved on the road that the mine owners had carved out of the desert, and along which they exported the large mineral wealth in truckloads of nitrate snow? Elsewhere in Chile and in Europe someone was making untold fortunes but here the only reward was hunger, homelessness and death.

With such thoughts on our minds, we left our taxi and made our way to the small office at the entrance to Humberstone.

≡|||≡

It takes a while for me to grasp that the man on the gate is telling us we cannot go in. At first I assume it is because we have no tickets and point to the kiosk.

'*Boleto* [tickets]?'

'*No, cerrado!*' he replies.

'I don't believe it. He says it's closed.'

'What?' comes Brian's bristling reply. 'Show him your letter!'

Before leaving London the Chilean embassy had been kind enough to give me a letter of introduction, explaining that we were working on a book and that 'To whom it may concern' should be as helpful as possible. The gate man peruses the letter very carefully, hands it back smiling and shrugging. 'Cerrado.'

He points to a notice. Laboriously I translate it word by word.

'I think we have to go and get permission from some government office in Iquique.'

'Frigg that,' says Brian.

'Quite. How fucking ridiculous! We come all the way out here and then they tell us we've got to go all the way back. Stupid bloody guidebooks,' I moan, waving one under Brian's nose. ' "Two dollars fifty entrance charge, take food and water as you will want to stay a while. Guided tours on some days." I'm writing to these idiots when we get back.'

'OK, OK. What are we going to do? Go back?'

'It's a real shame. It does sound special – a ghost town.'

Even as I voice my complaints, a large Mercedes pulls up and two couples emerge.

'I'll go and see if they can help.'

They can. Not only do Señor Carlos Calderon and his friend Alejandro Armstrong speak good English but Carlos turns out to be a congressman for the district around Valparaíso. He exudes the confidence of one used to getting things done. Even with tight shorts emphasizing his pot belly and revealing varicose-veined legs he is every inch the experienced politician. He talks to the man on the gate and then to a policeman who has been sitting in his patrol car a hundred yards away.

'You mentioned a letter of introduction. May I see it?' He studies the letter and then explains, 'I am going to the local police station to speak to the area commander so that we may visit Oficina Humberstone. If you and your friend wait here we will come back soon. I will take your letter, OK?'

Our new friends rejoin the two women waiting by the Mercedes and drive off, following the police car.

'Excellent!' I say to Brian, 'I reckon he'll get us in if anyone can.'

'Looks better, that's for sure,' Bri says and then points to a little café across the road. 'It's thirsty work out here. Let's get a drink.'

It is a hot and desolate spot. Music blares from a radio and the slightly jaded, over-made-up lady who runs the place is cooking up some powerful-smelling concoction, redolent of curry. Behind the café is a wasteland of car wrecks and mechanical junk. We sip Cokes and look back to the distant hulk of Santa Laura through the flapping canvas of a tattered windbreak.

〜〜〜

As we sat waiting the absurdity of our situation struck me. Here we were sitting at a white plastic table in the middle of the desert supping cold drinks. Above us the canopy that was meant to shade us from the sun was torn in tatters by the wind. A few yards from us our taxi driver walked backwards and forwards scratching his head or sitting in the open doorway of his car, reading the paper. We were Vladimir and Estragon waiting for Godot, waiting for a miracle, waiting for something, anything. While I was waiting, pondering what was so important about going to visit a ghost mining town, the miracle happened.

≡Ⅲ≡

Some thirty minutes later the Mercedes and its police escort returns. We walk over and Carlos tells us that he spoke to the local governor from the police station and has permission for his party and us to go round the plant. He then leads the formal introductions, first his wife and then his sister, who is married to Alejandro. 'Carlos and I are brothers-in-law,' confirms Alejandro who has the dashing good looks of a Fifties film star. Both ladies are handsome and elegant but have little English.

We all saunter in as the gate man happily raises the barrier. The policeman accompanies us as a courtesy escort, though his mirrored sunglasses give him an ominous appearance despite his smiles. I tell Carlos that we had no idea one needed special permission to enter the plant – that our guidebooks talked of it as a going tourist concern. He nods. 'This was true, and the government has made Oficina Humberstone a national monument. But just before this happened the plant had changed hands – it is owned privately. The owner wants to sell the timber, good, valuable Oregon pine, for other construction projects and so there is a long legal dispute as to what happens next.'

Humberstone proves to be worth the frustrations of getting in. It is a remarkable place. Built as a result of the nitrate boom of the 1860s it was originally called Oficina La Palma but was renamed after its long-time manager, Santiago Humberstone, when he retired in 1925. A busy man was Santiago. As well as administering the *oficina* and perfecting methods for extracting nitrates from the caliche of the desert, he was also involved in building the railways to carry the nitrates to the coast.

Out of nowhere a guide appears. A tiny, deeply sunburned woman, Juanita appears impish as she grins from behind large sunglasses. The two couples clearly find her conversation delightful and Carlos and Alejandro, often encouraged by their wives, pass on information to us as we walk around. The complex is vast, a town really. Five thousand workers and their families lived and worked here, with separate quarters for single men and married folk – and a guard to ensure that no women entered the singles enclave. Juanita showed us the market where workers could buy goods from the company using the company's own money.

'The workers didn't have much choice then. Did the company take advantage of them?' I ask Alejandro.

After conferring with Juanita he tells me, 'In many mines with this system, yes. But I understand that this *oficina* was more kind, there was good treatment for the workers.'

As if to support this view we enter a room with a large zinc-topped bar – an ice cream parlour! Juanita leads us outside and across a square to see the church and then, via a library, to the hospital. Here she points out a legend on the wall, handwritten by a man who states he was born there and is now a professor at Dallas University in Texas. It must be very strange to return from one of the world's most modern cities and find your birthplace a ghost town.

Humberstone closed down in 1961 but in the nitrate industry's heyday, between the 1860s and the First World War, the export taxes were so lucrative that the government in Santiago was able to fund vast public programmes with them. This meant that the general population was kept happy, and political and economic reform avoided. Yet it was in this region that trade unionism took root in the face of harsh regimes at the nitrate *oficinas* and at the copper and other mines. There were a number of workers' revolts and the very thing they produced was turned against them when their protests were savagely suppressed in a hail of bullets.

At Humberstone, though, there was more gentle drama. Juanita leads us into a massive theatre. Brian and I join our friends in the front row seats as our effusive little guide tells us that in the boom times there was so much money available that top rank troupes were brought in to entertain the workers and that Iquique once hosted the great Caruso. She tells another story that has the two couples doubled up. Señora Calderon turns to her husband urging him to translate.

'Once she was showing a man around the *oficina*. She did not like him, says he was very grand. He seems to have thought that Señorita Juanita, a little woman in the desert, was not showing enough respect. They were in this theatre when he said in a loud voice, "I am an artist from Santiago." She stood on that stage and looked down on him and said, "Well, I am the Sophia Loren of Humberstone." That kept him quiet!'

Brian and I applaud.

The theatre was not the only leisure facility available to the Humberstone workforce. There was a dance hall where even now, in the last week of November, there is an annual party for those who worked or grew up there. There was also a huge swimming pool. This was built out of steel plates, probably from ships' hulls, because, unlike cement, steel would not be eroded by the nitrate in the soil. Water for the pool and for all human consumption had to be brought or piped in from the hills as the local wells produced only brackish stuff heavily salted with the nitrate.

'Strange, isn't it,' says Brian as we look down into the empty pool, 'that this lifeless earth should produce the raw materials for fertilizer. Camps like this, that had no life-sustaining water, prepared stuff that helped other land flourish.'

'Still, there was one advantage as far as I can see. The nitrate kept rats and spiders away. I'd have liked some of that for all those mice and cockroaches in Beirut.'

Our last stop is at the one occupied building on the site. Juanita tells us that a lady lives there, a kind of janitor it seems, and that last year she killed a burglar with an iron bar. As she tells us this we are startled by a fierce chattering above our heads. A little monkey jumps from side to side of the tin roof on a length of chain, its eyes wide and its teeth bared in a snarl. We back away from its eerie anger.

At the gate we say goodbye to Carlos, Alejandro and their wives who invite us to visit them in Santiago if we have time. We find our taxi driver and head back to Iquique, reflecting on our good fortune.

Chapter Four

≡Ⅲ≡

The bus to Calama stops for twenty minutes at Rio Loa which is nothing but a customs point by the sea, in the middle of nowhere. The heat beats down as every bag is checked, for we are leaving the First Region, Tarapaca, and entering the Second, Antofagasta. There are twelve regions and we aim to pass through them all. We have covered three hundred kilometres; a mere four thousand to go. Everyone is pleasant enough, the customs officers asking where we are from, but I still feel that churning in the stomach I get at customs, borders and checkpoints. Given I have done and plan to do nothing wrong there is no real reason for this tension. Partly it's the sense of there being no way back: the subconscious remembrance of sitting, sometimes for hours, bound and gagged, often with a gun at one's head, waiting for the guards to decide it was safe to move on. The remoteness of this spot – the blank, dusty plain around us – adds to the feeling of vulnerability.

After cracking along at a good clip we slow as the road starts winding inland. This is a relief from the rocking and rolling as the bus swung high up among the clifftops. The curtains had been drawn against the sun but every now and then, as we shimmied through another abysmal chicane, I would catch a dizzying glimpse of a sheer drop below my window. I resented anyone sleeping, ignorant of our impending doom.

Brian in the 'utter wilderness' above Arica.

John and Eduardo, close to the edge.

Brian on the streets of another hillside ghost town.

Karlen and Brian.
'Not asleep – just resting my eyes.'

TOP: Vicuña and llama in the mist in Lauca National Park.

BOTTOM: 'A landscape to relate to', between El Tatio and Baños de Puritama.

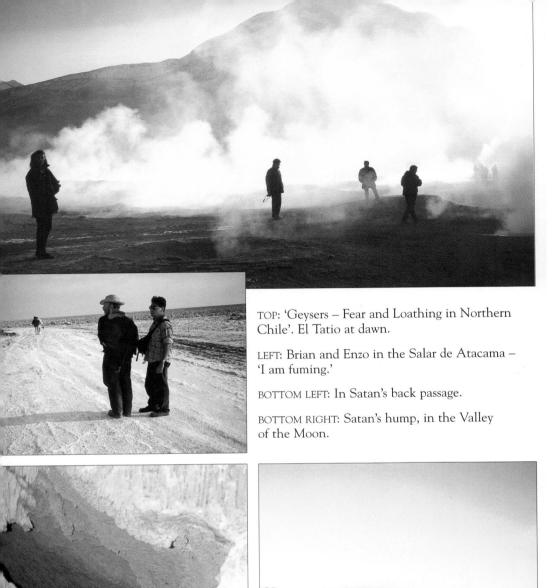

TOP: 'Geysers – Fear and Loathing in Northern Chile'. El Tatio at dawn.

LEFT: Brian and Enzo in the Salar de Atacama – 'I am fuming.'

BOTTOM LEFT: In Satan's back passage.

BOTTOM RIGHT: Satan's hump, in the Valley of the Moon.

Moonscape at dusk.

Santa Laura –
'Back where he belongs.'

A restored façade at La Moneda,
Presidential Palace, Santiago.

An encounter with the spirit guide, Pablo Neruda, at
La Chascona, Santiago.

A quiet moment with Tio Pablo.

Neruda's home at Isla Negra, with Tom and Jorge.

'Death to the Torturers', Valparaíso.

TOP: Clean air, green water, Los Azules. Day One in the High Andes.

RIGHT: 'This trek should be a breeze...'

BOTTOM: Travelling light. Mauricio loading a mule.

Butch and Sundance in the Big Country.

As afternoon moves to evening the careless sleepers stir and curtains are opened again. We come out of Tocopilla up a boulder-strewn, sheer-sided and tortuously winding valley to witness a glorious sunset: its heart on the horizon the colour of burning copper, cooling to the softest of blues higher in the sky and, framing all this, white feathery clouds. It keeps catching you unawares, the light and terrain mingling suddenly to make your heart leap.

Although the landscape is often harsh it looks actually malign only where man has disturbed the surface; his leavings from the mines or diggings look squalid. In the winding valley I saw the abandoned workings of the *piquineros* (small, independent mining gangs). They looked like little black mouths that had spewed out rock, dust and the wooden chutes and rocker contraptions that reminded me of photographs of the California gold rush. Imagining the life of such prospectors at the turn of the century makes me shudder. To be in such a remote spot, with just a few mementoes of a home and family far away, must have been tough enough but to burrow deep beneath the parched surface would have required great courage or desperation.

We drive through Maria Elena, one of only two working nitrate *oficinas* left. It looks very much like Humberstone, rows and rows of one-storey wooden chalets, all with the same colour blue on the fences. Like Humberstone it has a theatre, market, library, shops and hospital and started out as a private company town but now it is a proper municipality and the plant is owned by the state company. We stop at a railway line to let heavy trains roll slowly past, their open cars filled with rocks. The *oficina* is dominated by a giant chimney and other huge constructions. Once the bus has struggled over the tracks I look back at Maria Elena. Uniform and bleak, it appears just as I had imagined a South American mining town. As we leave it behind in the dust from our tyres and the fading sunset, the washed-out chalets and the few street lamps present a dilapidated vision of suspended animation.

We continue along the uneven road which improves, but only briefly, at the junction with the Pan American Highway. Once across that we head deeper inland and the road is once more an unpaved track. It is a strange feeling leaving that great road behind, as if one is heading away from civilization and back in time. Just outside Chuquicamata we slow right down as the track turns to sand. Fine clouds of dust fill the bus and dry our throats.

We had a one-night stop at the town of Calama which was the nearest place to Chuquicamata, the biggest open-cast mine on the planet. Someone had described it to us as like looking across and into the Grand Canyon. I could not understand why John wanted to visit this place. I was trying to find a reason for persuading myself to go but could find none. It might be interesting to compare this working mine with Humberstone and Santa Laura but that seemed an insufficient motive for staring into a gigantic hole in the ground. Chile was, after all, such a visually intoxicating country. It is a feast to the eye and to the senses but the idea of Chuquicamata seemed the opposite of all that.

We went to bed early after supper. On the way to my room I found a huge picture of Chuquicamata hanging on one of the hotel walls. It was a nightscape of deep blackness relieved by thousands of lights, giving the impression of a vast city. I studied it for several moments trying to imagine myself there.

I read Pablo's poetry long into the night. Whether it was my weariness, Neruda's exotic imagery, or even a tinge of guilt for not accompanying John, I slept fitfully. It was obvious that the ghosts of Humberstone and Santa Laura had followed us here to Calama and into my sleep. I dreamed of Chuquicamata.

The mine glittered like a ghostly *Marie Celeste*. I was in the bowels of its massive aperture, which closed around me like a gigantic bird enveloping me in its suffocating, dusty plumage. The implacable walls towered everywhere about me and were veined with a green patina of copper seams. I walked the terraces that had been walked by generations of miners before me. I seemed to be trapped in a maze of excavated galleries in an infinity of stone. Everywhere around me I saw insubstantial forms of men claw and pick at the earth. There was a strange aquamarine sheen to their bodies as they laboured furiously like turquoise ants. They were mindless things. The copper god hidden in the earth had laid its sulphurous breath on them and was pulling them into itself.

The labourers were oblivious of me and I alone seemed free of
the frightening lure of the idol. I looked up to the uppermost ridge
of the mine's cliff-like walls. The perimeter lights were indistinguishable from the stars in heaven.

But morning came and I awoke unmindful of where I had been.
On my way to breakfast I passed the picture I had seen the
previous evening, and briefly images of my dreaming sleep echoed
back to me. I bumped into John as he was leaving for the mine,
and returned to my room to pack for our onward journey.
Neruda's poetry lay open on the bed where it had fallen as I drifted
into sleep.

> It was a grimy multitude,
> hunger and shreds, solitude,
> that excavated the gallery.
> That night I didn't see
> the countless wounds file by
> along the mine's cruel rim.
>
> But I was part of those torments.

≡Ⅲ≡

It is early in the morning as I sit outside the office for the
Chuquicamata copper mine along with a few other tourists,
Chileans, Germans and French. Brian decided against coming and
is back at the hotel reading Neruda, or more likely kipping, I suspect. I am jealous, having slept badly last night despite being very
tired. After driving for ages virtually on the flat, it is easy to forget how high we still are here – 2,700 metres – and I could not get
off to sleep since every time I lay down I had to take deep breaths.
When I did get off to sleep I woke every hour or so and had many
strange dreams including one in which my watch was broken. The
dream had been so clear that this morning I checked my watch
against Bri's. They were wildly out.

'God,' I had exclaimed, 'that's amazing! I dreamed my
watch was bust and it is. No, wait a minute, mine says seven
o'clock which sounds right, yours says one o'clock. The

dream was almost there – it's your watch that's bust!'

'No, it isn't!'

'Look!' I said.

'Yeah, I know. Mine is still on Dublin time. I like to know what time it is back home, know what Audrey will be doing, keeps her close. You know?'

Curiously enough, as I wandered round this town before coming to the mine I noticed that all the clocks on the major buildings had stopped. Odd.

I was driven here from Calama by Carlo. A nice, chubby man in his late fifties, he tells me he was born and bred here but is now a US citizen.

'So have you come home for good now?'

'No. I am here every September to April and drive the taxi. Then I go back to Connecticut and drive a truck.' He has one of those high-pitched, lisping voices that would be bang on for a Hollywood Central Casting 'Mehican bandeetoh'.

'Do you have family in the States?' I ask as we near the mine.

'Been married fife times! But now I alone, last wife she die.'

'Oh, I am sorry.'

'No problem. Thass life, inneet? I meet you here after you do mine.'

We tourists file into a room where we are issued with hard hats and sit down to watch a video, in Spanish then English, about the mine. It is all very technical stuff. Suffice it to say they dig up a hell of a lot of rock, process a hell of a lot of copper, and make a hell of a lot of money. The mine is a colossal hole; the largest open-cast mine in the world. It has been going since the early years of the twentieth century and has another thirty years' reserves. It is over five kilometres wide already and 750 metres deep. It will be 1,100 metres deep at the end which means, I think, that it will be deeper than the height of anything in the UK except Ben Nevis. Given the altitude they're starting from, even when they reach the bottom the Chuqui miners will still be higher than anywhere in Britain.

Despite the scale the mine is, surprisingly, not exciting but depressing. The refining area is like a city; a nightmare vision of huge sheds, conveyor belts, rock-crushing pyramids, pipes and chimneys spewing smoke and flame. The dull green slag heaps ooze wreaths of black smoke as great trucks crawl across them like cockroaches. It looks what it is, a perversion of nature. I am as glad as anyone that we have plenty of copper but, environmental concerns aside, watching the workers, covered head to foot in overalls, hard hats and breathing apparatus, I have the feeling that human beings have created something here beyond their control. This is the ultimate consequence of the industrial revolution.

On the way back to Calama, Carlo tells me he left in 1970.

'Oh,' I say, 'before the troubles?'

'Yes, my family suffer very much in those time.'

'They were socialists?'

'Eh? No! Is before Pinochet they suffer. The Chaos!'

'I heard that times were very difficult. But wasn't the dictatorship the wrong way to go?'

'Sure, many bad thinns happen – here and other places. But is all secret. Mose people juss wan food. My family have money, but no food. When you ungry you donn care who give you bread. Yes?'

His pragmatism is more convincing than Karlen's dogged acceptance of Pinochet. The situation was obviously dire. It still seems odd though that all the oppression and torture gives rise to so little comment. We carry on in silence until we reach Calama when he whizzes me round the town, pointing out the busy bars where the waitresses, wearing shorts and tight tops, stand at the doorways. This is a novel sight in Chile; mostly people seem to behave and dress with great decorum. But this is a big mining town so perhaps one should expect things to be a little wilder here.

When John returned we had a light lunch and he complained about his trip to the mine. He had paid a few dollars for a tour which simply amounted to being loaded on to a truck and driven around the periphery. All he could see were yellow trucks moving about the mine floor like they were Dinky toys. It had obviously been a real anti-climax. I told him about my dream.

'Thanks a bunch. Maybe I should have stayed here and given

you and Pablo Neruda the few dollars instead,' he said.

It was time to move on and leave Chuquicamata's gaping hole behind. We waited for several hours in Calama's dust-choked streets. The booking office for the bus doubled as a grocery store-cum-café. It was hardly an office as such but more a corner shop that sold everything including tickets. So we had to queue for our travel passes along with the locals queuing for everything from babies' dummies to back-breaking bags of flour. Grateful to be rid of our baggage we stashed it behind the counter and went walking.

≡Ⅲ≡

Despite the element of wildness there remains an overriding sense of safety and honesty and we do not worry about leaving our bags at the rather chaotic bus company office while we kill time waiting for the next departure for San Pedro. We stroll around a large market where you can buy almost anything from live poultry to music tapes. There are many, many clothes stalls whose stock is pretty old-fashioned. We look at hats.

'I'd like something more substantial than this straw thing for the mountains,' says Brian, trying on various types. He scowls at the tiny mirror the stallholder puts in front of him as he dons a wide-brimmed stetson. 'Nah, I don't think so, what d'you reckon?'

'Ludicrous!'

We saunter on through the arcades until I spot a stall selling the knee-length, stiff leather chaps some of the cowboys or *huasos* wear.

'Now they would be really good for horse trekking,' I say. 'They are a bit pricey though.'

I hold up a pair, the black leather glistening, and know I want them. It's partly because I love having the right gear but also because I can see myself looking the part wearing them up on a horse. Brian is watching me and knows I am about to buy.

'Where are you going to put them?'

'On my legs, you fool!'

'Not on the trek! Where are you going to put them now? Don't you think you've got enough clobber already? We've just sent a load of stuff home. Do you really want to cart those things all over the Atacama Desert and beyond?'

He's right, of course; it would not be sensible. Damn him for his practicality.

~~~

We were on time for the bus, but obviously the bus was not on time for us. We walked in a radius circling the depot, fearful that we would miss our connection. Each time we returned the numbers of people waiting had grown. Our anxiety made our perambulations shorter. It wasn't the number of travellers so much as their baggage that worried us. Whole families were here with generations of luggage packed in massive blue and white bags that looked like squat mattresses.

Calama was obviously a transit town. It was important because of Chuquicamata and drew many people because of the work and the availability of goods. But to me Calama was not a place to live. It was only a place to work. Curiously, as we walked about the town, I noticed that, apart from the market and a few mediocre grocery shops, only the hairdressing emporiums were open. I suppose wealth brings with it affectation, or whatever it is that dissociates people from their natural landscape. Everywhere we walked were billboard hoardings advertising well-known trade names which were synonymous with North America.

Back at the bus depot, European backpackers were obvious among the raucous family groups of Chilean travellers. I had for-gotten how skinny a land Chile was, and that these 'real' travellers could have been en route from Argentina or from anywhere else in Chile or South America.

As I watched the underbelly of the dilapidated bus being stuffed with baggage and belongings, I wondered if it would ever be able to move. The locals had no time for us incomers and noisily jockeyed to ensure their voluminous bags were stored before any of ours. It wasn't the fact that Don John had packed away some of his apparel in my bag that worried me, it was where it might be stored and how long it would take to unpack this whale of a bus to find it when we reached our destination. One look at the faces of our fellow travellers told me that they were going far beyond where we would leave them. Don John nonchalantly did not bother his backside about my worries.

After some anxious moments jostling with the locals, I finally got our bags carefully stowed away near the front of the over-stuffed luggage compartment. I was insistent that they remain close to the door. When the driver who was half-heartedly over-seeing the loading tried to shove them to the rear, I hastily dragged them back to the front. He seemed unimpressed and left me to my idiosyncrasy.

After all the luggage had been packed and the doors locked, I boarded the bus and flopped into my seat. Some of the locals were looking at me questioningly. I knew that my concerns were irrational and that I hardly understood them myself, never mind explaining them to others.

Our buckled bus roared out of Calama in a burst of black smoke. It didn't bode well for our onward journey, but the many faces ranged about me seemed unperturbed. For endless miles we were inundated with the driver's battered radio blasting out tijuana brass band sambas, chattering Indians and crying children, while our very own San Pedro Chitty-Chitty-Bang-Bang moved on and on through the Atacaman landscape.

The monotony of what passed outside my window made me yearn for the confusion of voices and faces at our destination. No matter where I looked, I could see no sign of life. The word 'desert' derives from the Latin *desere* meaning to abandon or forsake, and 'wilderness' may have given rise to the verb 'wilder' meaning 'to cause to be perplexed'. The names of some of the world's deserts reflect these terms. I thought of the Skeleton Coast, the Empty Quarter and the Devil's Playground. For the several hours of our journey, it seemed that the meaning of those names was written on the scorched earth before people had even found these words or their significance for themselves.

In my reverie, suddenly I began to understand my worries about our bags locked in the underbelly of the bus. I was sweating, and not simply from the heat. Rather it was from a memory of those terrifying journeys we made through the Lebanon, squashed in the undercarriage of a lorry, taped up like mummies, baking in our own sweat and smothering in the stench of diesel fumes. But the memory washed over me as quickly as it had arrived. I looked out on to the burning landscape.

The Atacama has only one counterpart in the whole of the earth's geography, the Namib in Africa. They are the world's only coastal deserts. For millennia, waves from the world's largest oceans have hammered the coasts of Africa and South America making them among the most untamed and desolate places on earth.

Paradoxically for a desert, the atmosphere of the Atacama is directly influenced by the sea. The presence of the icy Humboldt current flowing from the Antarctic and following the west coast of South America creates a layer of moist air directly above the surface of the desert while a blanket of air heated by the sun hovers above it. This phenomenon is an inversion of the accepted laws of physics which state that air temperature decreases as elevation increases. But the Atacama is a contrary place in more ways than one because of this peculiar quirk of physical laws. It is a desert constantly immersed in thick fog blown in off the sea by prevailing winds caused by the rotation of the earth. Thus for many hours and for distances of up to fifty miles inland the desert is locked in the grip of fog-shrouded aridity. It is the kind of place where you could shave your beard off without any lather on your skin.

And this inversion of the physical laws is not restricted solely to the interplay between land and sea but also between the air, the mountains and the land behind them. The Atacama resides in what scientists call a reversed rain shadow. Simply translated, this means that the extreme altitude of the Andes prevents moisture from crossing over to slake the parched wastes beyond.

What could anyone expect from a place that turns natural law on its head and is persistently and remorselessly antipathetic to human needs?

The bus ride to San Pedro de Atacama was long and tedious. I found the monotony of the recurrent landscape increasingly irritating. John, on the other hand, was oblivious to my state. He was furiously fingering his miniature laptop. What could he be writing about? What inspiration was framed in the window he was forever looking out of? I sat back to probe the source of my irritation. The emptiness of the landscape was certainly un-stimulating but that did not satisfactorily explain my own feelings. Perhaps they had their origin in disappointment or even some-thing stronger, like disillusion.

I was expecting to be moved by the mystery of it all. Where was this magical desert that had illuminated the mind of the mystics? The literature of every language writes of the desert as a place of inner enlightenment and spiritual awakening. The American Wallace Stegner once wrote, 'Deserts are not the country of big returns but are the country of spiritual healing, contemplation, meditation, solitude, quiet, awe, and peace of mind and body.' I don't know from where Stegner received his information, but at this moment I was feeling the complete opposite. I was not look-ing for religious affirmation, I was looking for inspiration, the inspiration that moved the pens of men like Antoine de Saint-Exupéry with his quasi-mystical night flights over the deserts of Africa. Where were T. E. Lawrence's *Seven Pillars of Wisdom*? I would have leaped through the roof of this baking bus just to see the shadow of one of them. Where was it all? Where was it? And what had so intrigued McCarthy that his fingers kept caressing the keyboard like it was some sacred tabulator? I saw nothing, and felt only the heat multiplying as it drummed on the window. For another hour I suffered while John's fingers gently tapped away, until I could bear it no longer.

'What do you find so fascinating anyway?' It was more an ex-plosion of my own frustration than a question.

John looked at me for a moment and then without speaking, he winked slyly and tapped his nose with an all-knowing gesture.

'Bollocks,' I hissed as he returned to his keyboard and I lay back sweltering and uncomfortable, my head as empty as the desert outside.

I tried to sleep but the air percolating into our bus made it impossible. In any case, John kept nudging me in the ribs.

'Brian, we left the *camanchaca* behind many many miles ago, but your foghorn is disturbing everyone else on this bus!'

I had given up on the desert and my expectations of it. Perhaps it had given up on me too. Even sleep, it seemed, had abandoned me. Only irritation and disillusionment remained.

Thinking Neruda might give me some comfort, I leafed hap-hazardly through my copies of *Isla Negra* and the *Canto General* to see what I might find there. One of his poems, entitled 'Atacama', was too rich for me. It was swirling in such sensual and oblique imagery that I could not reconcile it with the landscape through which we were passing. It only added to the torment of my heat-baked brain.

In another of his homages to the desert, he seems to fall on his knees in abject worship. His description of it is tinged with a bittersweet, overblown romanticism:

> A thousand years of silence in a wine glass
> Of calcareous blue, of distance and moon
> shape the night's naked geography.

Neruda declares he loves this wilderness but it is more than love, it is adoration and he states it repeatedly, mantra-like: 'I love you, pure land, like so many contrary things I've loved', and again, 'I love you, pure sister of the ocean'. His chants of adoration build up like the response to the Mass, until he concludes:

> This was the world's virile bosom
> And I loved the system of your unswerving form
> the extensive precision of your emptiness.

It was enough. Here was John tumbling out acres of words beside me, while the desert around us crushed me with its nothingness. Every desert mystic from the invention of the written word was a frigging liar, and now even my confederate and invisible companion presented me with visions as sumptuous as a tropical night. How could this be the 'world's virile bosom'? Nothing could be nurtured here. Nothing would want to be nurtured here, for that matter.

The oasis village of San Pedro de Atacama sits approximately eight thousand feet above sea level and lies at the northern edge of Chile's largest salt flat, the Salar de Atacama which we were to visit in the next few days – though after the trip through the desert on the bus, I couldn't for the life of me understand why!

When we arrived at the village terminus I fell out of the bus like a drowning man gasping for air. As always, John was ready with a street map of this isolated desert village in his hand and quickly discovered the way to our hotel. I retrieved our bags from the undercarriage of the bus and hastily strapped mine to my little chrome trolley. But it was a ridiculous contrivance for this place. There were no footpaths and for the most part the roads were rutted dirt tracks. Dragging my luggage over such terrain was like dragging a dead sow behind me. I said nothing as I sweated and grunted in the footsteps of Don John, desert explorer *extra-ordinaire*.

Our hotel was a newly built complex of cabins. We washed and changed before heading back to the village. John, as always, was immaculate. I was sure he must have a travel iron concealed in his luggage. After all, if he could arrive in a tiny desert village in the arsehole of nowhere and miraculously produce a detailed street map, what else might he not have hidden away in that conjuror's bag of his?

The main street of the village was little more than a hundred yards long. What had once been a terrace of single-storey, crude wood-and-adobe homes with a single window and door was being transformed into shops, bars, restaurants and more than a few travel offices. Obviously San Pedro was a jumping-off point for desert aficionados from every part of the world. I was surprised at the number of people. More than two-thirds of them looked European but as the native Chilean has so many mixed bloodlines in him one can never be sure. But one thing I could be sure of was that it would not be long before Don Quixote would transmute into Indiana Jones and I would be subjected to the most rigorous set of proposed treks into the desert. I was correct. Before I had even had time to discover a good bar, Indiana Quixote McCarthy had arranged several expeditions and hired a local English-speaking guide. With the confirmation of that last accomplishment I knew I was done for. There was no point arguing.

Several hours later in one of the tavernas, I was busy sampling the local delicacies while John explained our itinerary for the next few days. As each new venture unfolded, I ordered another bottle of wine, fearful that Indiana's enthusiasm would not allow us to complete the essential task of sampling all of Chile's production before we returned home. Home, that was a place that increased in desirability as John's expeditionary plans were revealed.

We discussed the journey so far. John declared that if he ever heard the word geoglyph again, he would strangle the person who used it. This reminded me of the woman and her two infants in a tiny shanty hut in the Azapa valley. Her home was built from scraps of corrugated iron, old cardboard and bits of broken wood. Inside were the barest of necessities, a table, two broken chairs and a construction of old fruit cases that served as a cabinet to hold her few possessions. Yet in the centre of the room blazing away incoherently was a huge TV, the kind that is watched by sport fanatics in bars back home. Her lifestyle was little removed from her Inca predecessors but her means of communication was a long way from the stone images on the hillside behind her.

We talked about those airless nights in the hills above and beyond Arica when we would wake suddenly gasping for breath. John admitted that the sensation had terrified him and I confessed the same. One confession prompted another. We admitted openly that the proposed horse trek over the top of the Andes frightened us more than we cared to think about. Neither of us was a horse-man and we were tentatively laying down the seeds of an excuse to cancel that particular expedition. Yet neither of us wanted to be the first to suggest it. Anyway all compass points had to be covered and there were few other options for that west–east leg. Although I was genuinely ill and John was solicitous, I felt I would have to be gasping my last breath, for real, to get out of this one.

John reminded me of the story I had told him while we were held in Lebanon. When I was about seventeen and trying to impress my girlfriend, I had taken her to a horse-riding establish-ment somewhere outside Belfast. The young woman running the stable had asked us if we knew how to ride. My girlfriend of that time admitted she didn't, while I, being full of macho confidence, said, 'Sure, no problem.' The young woman looked at me with a knowing eye. She asked one of the stable hands to prepare a horse for my girlfriend, then looking at me, she said ominously, 'Bring out Billy.' I soon understood her meaning when Billy was led roaring and snorting out of the stable. My own adolescent arrogance had condemned me to ride this dragon. Needless to say, I ended up making the most pathetic idiot of myself. We both laughed at the memory as Don Indiana McCarthy remarked that 'Cocky people with no brains inevitably come a cropper.' I promised I would remind him of his own words before each of his expeditions into the desert. In any case, I recalled how he had nearly drowned one of his own girlfriends on a canoeing holiday in France, doing exactly the same thing as I had. 'Ah, but that was different,' he said, pouring us another glass of wine. 'You see, I thought she could swim.'

While we were busy reminiscing like two regular old codgers, the bar around us filled up. It felt like some hippy festival, with everyone in bleached jeans and washed-out T-shirts. For a moment I thought I was part of the scene in my own T-shirt and shorts, but after a second glance I felt desperately old. Who was I trying to fool?

As we were drinking in the youthful atmosphere, as well as the wine, a few of the newly arrived customers joined us at our table. They were a ragbag of different nationalities who were all passing through San Pedro. We spoke with them the way incidental travellers do, about where they had come from and where they were going. Our new friends were impressed by our intended journey. One young man named Ronrico, a student from Santiago, had come to San Pedro simply to get away from his home town. He was tall and lean with long blond hair, more Aryan than South American.

He spoke to us at great length. He was an engineering student who bitterly rejected the profession he felt he was being pushed into. 'There is no culture in our country. The young people in university study only for the professions, engineering, the law, medicine. The arts are not encouraged.' He explained how, after the military coup of 1973, the regime had introduced sweeping university reform. This entailed reducing state funding, raising fees, and eliminating such subversive subjects as the arts, psychology, sociology and politics.

I complained to him that there was no such thing as a country without culture. If he believed that, he was simply accepting those reforms he was complaining so bitterly about. At this stage the wine was in my head and Neruda was whispering adamantly in my ear. 'What about Gabriela Mistral and Pablo Neruda, Chile's Nobel laureates? What about Vilotta Parra and men like Victor Jara?' I reeled off the names carelessly. I was anxious to ascertain if he knew that for many people in Europe, Chilean culture was synonymous with subversion and the struggle against authority. I knew I was becoming over-excited and John's castigating look confirmed it. Ronrico was unmoved by my passion and his answer was simple. 'There's no money in art and no one wants to teach it.'

It was pointless to pursue the question. Ronrico was young, intelligent, aware and dissatisfied. Out of such responses, cultural renaissance is inevitable.

On the way home I explained to John how I had felt deserted by Neruda on our trip to San Pedro. 'Deserted, that's us!' John exclaimed, laughing. I had to join in.

We both stopped simultaneously. The road was pitch black. John's small pencil torch was doing nothing to aid our homeward journey. Above us the sky was spangled with a hundred thousand million stars. I had never witnessed such a display before. I laced one arm around John's shoulder and, thrusting the other towards the heavens, quoted, ' "Look at the stars, Joxer, look at the stars." '

John looked skyward and said uncertainly, 'Sean O'Casey, *Playboy of the Western World*?'

'No, John boy, that was Synge.'

'Sing? Sing what?'

≡⫼≡

Walking back through the darkened streets, the occasional pool of light spills from a doorway to show a knot of people bidding each other good night. It is very peaceful and becomes yet more tranquil as we leave the main thoroughfares behind and walk between high adobe walls, our footsteps muffled by the sandy path. Our chat about new acquaintances and tomorrow's trip into the Atacama peters out as our eyes adjust to the absence of any man-made light. Yet it is not dark, we are not stumbling since our way is lit by stars. They are magical: so many, some so sharp, others lost in a bright cloud with their fellows, and all around them the deepest blues, and the profoundest black. It is almost as if you are in touch with the power generating up there, looking into such a distance, and the light, so bright and immediate, is really so very old.

〜〜

Before finally retiring for the night, I flicked through Neruda's poetic map of Chile. I wanted to find in the tracery of his verse some insight that would unlock the secret of the desert and give me an advantage over it. His poem dedicated to the Atacama offered little consolation. It was full of complex imagery which strained and obscured the energy of the poem. I read and reread until the verse seemed to collapse in a nightmare of obscurity.

Eventually I switched off the light and lay back in the darkness, thinking that old Neruda must have been suffering from high altitude hallucinations, or at least drinking as much wine as us when he penned those lines.

The next morning was bright and loud. The lack of any other noise seemed to intensify the thrilling song of the desert cicadas. They reminded me of an amplified dentist's drill.

I decided to dress and go for a walk. It couldn't have been much after the full flush of dawn and, walking the rutted road, I felt like the last person on the earth. Above and around me the desert light was expansive. Its fluorescence toned down an impending sense of melancholy that hung in the air. As I neared the sleeping village and passed the outlying homes, the warmth of the back streets and sense of human presence erased it completely. I was enjoying the stillness of the place and remembering how earlier, in the 1900s, this village was a major stop for cattle drives on their way from Argentina to the nitrate mines. If it wasn't cattle to feed the miners then the place might well have been filled with stockmen and droves of mules brought to do the 'donkey work' in those same mines. But today there were no braying mules or lowing cattle, just the cicadas, and an occasional accompaniment from a cockerel or a barking dog.

As I turned into one of the back alleys leading directly to the village square, I was confronted by the curious spectacle of two horses and a mule wandering aimlessly towards me. They were, I suspected, the descendants of those earlier mule trains. Their casual gait as they strolled nearer had the air of long and familiar possession about it. I stood and watched the scene until the almost black mule and one of the ponies passed me as if I wasn't there. The other pony, a yellowing grey colour under a film of dust, sauntered towards me and stopped a few feet away. The whole scene had the look of a clip from a Fellini film. In the silence of the deserted street it was ghostly and unreal.

I waited for a moment and then moved slowly towards the animal. It stood still until I was only a few feet away and then walked a couple of paces and stopped. It was teasing me. I looked to the other horse and mule, both of whom had their heads turned to watch. They stared, then moved on dismissively. The bone-coloured pony stood its ground but did not look at me. It was determined I should come to it. I walked up to it and patted its shoulder and neck. Its head was massive and looked far too heavy for its scrawny body. Its huge brown eye surveyed me with the scrutiny of an inquisitor.

I rounded its flanks, patting clouds of dust as I did so and came up on the other side of its head. It was an ugly beast but its eyes were deep and soft. It had Mona Lisa eyes, those curious, unmoving eyes that follow you everywhere. Apart from an occasional quiver of muscle at its shoulder and the dipping of its head like a slow pendulum, the animal was the epitome of incredible patience. It was an old mare, I noticed as I moved to stand in front of it. A length of its mane had been plaited in yellow and blue ribbon and hung down its forehead. It was filthy, which made me think what a perfect mount it would make for Don John.

I recalled our confessions from the night before. Looking at this hulk of horseflesh, I doubled my intention of abandoning the Andes expedition. I was terrified of heights and had not sat on a horse for more than a quarter of a century. I could probably have found a hundred other excuses but at the root of it I was scared and didn't know how to deal with it.

I moved to the horse's shoulder and, taking a fistful of mane in

113

my hand, half-heartedly attempted to hoist myself on to its back. I expected the creature to bolt and leave me sprawling in the dust but it stood as docile as stone. As a result, my already deflated ego was flattened even more. I gave up on my feeble attempt and patted its head again in a gesture of apology. Those great soft eyes seemed to be reading my thoughts. I drew a deeply penetrating reassurance from them. In their stillness they seemed to be pulling me into themselves and at the same time dragging me out of the fear that was paralysing me. For some moments we stood eyeball to eyeball but it was no contest of wills. Then it slowly moved off and I followed with my hand placed gently on its flank.

Maybe it was the silence and the strange desert light but somehow the village seemed larger and appeared to open itself out to me. My eye seemed to penetrate into every obscure recess, discovering in each dark corner little cameos of life. Clothes flapping on a line. Shoes discarded at a doorway, or children's playthings scrambled on a porch.

Everywhere around us the wind-washed clapboard and eroded adobe took on the worn texture of a patchwork quilt. We must have made a queer sight, like a dumb animal leading a blind man through a street. But, however curious, it was an illuminating communion between man and beast. This old mare was showing me more than the village. It was showing me how to see, and I was walking as if in a trance. My eyes were glutted.

Suddenly it stopped, rolled its eyes for a moment and trotted off, turning a corner and disappearing as magically as it had appeared.

I was alone again but comforted. The old quilt of the village wrapped itself around me. I wandered into the square and passed the adobe house where Pedro de Valdivia in 1540 had rested with his coterie of conquistadors and Peruvian Indians. Opposite was the Iglesia San Pedro, a seventeenth-century church built from adobe and cactus wood, and held together with large welts of leather that may well have been made from the hides of cattle and mules too old or too ill to make the desert crossing with the entourage.

The village was beginning to awaken and I decided to return to see if John had risen. Along the main street the pink adobe walls looked like a woman's make-up compact. As I walked homeward, dark Indian faces began appearing in doorways like curious turtles.

Around the breakfast bars and tourist offices, the young travellers were settling in. For all their gaudy T-shirts emblazoned with the multifarious patented names and products of American consumerism, I thought that San Pedro had not changed so much. Valdivia's conquering army and then the stockmen with their herds had simply been replaced with this new transient population. It was inevitable, I supposed. The three or four days when those stockmen rested over with their animals were called 'La Tablada'. I was still unsure what our own 'Tablada' would produce. We still had McCarthy's hairy expeditions in front of us, but I was consoled by the earlier companionship of the old mare. Whatever happened on our forays into the Atacama, we had always the relative comfort of San Pedro to return to.

When I reached the hotel, John was up and chirpy as the cicadas that had entertained me earlier. He was bursting for breakfast and when I told him I had already been for a walk, he asked if I had met anyone. 'A couple of old nags and a mule,' I said.

Chapter Five

≡|||≡

San Pedro, with its regular streets of adobe houses, is just what one would imagine a South American town to be. The interiors of the houses look fairly basic through their open doors. Some have gardens shaded by fine plants and trees where senior citizens chat and doze, dogs loafing at their feet. Ancient and battered pick-up trucks cruise slowly past stirring up lazy clouds of dust. Now it is the weekend, the square is busy with crowds of folk walking around, children playing in the dust while the men and women take part in a kind of boules, called Rayuella, in which they throw heavy metal pucks from twenty feet at a yard-square tray of mud with a wire across it. The winner is the one who gets the puck nearest the wire. A couple of soldiers strolling around remind us we are near both the Bolivian and Argentinian borders.

People cheerfully return our greetings as we wander the back streets in the heat, every now and then catching a refreshing glimpse of a snow-capped volcano. We have been thinking it would be a good idea to spend some time on horseback as our planned week-long trek is drawing closer and we are both having moments of anxiety; our experience of riding is virtually zero so even a couple of hours in the saddle would, we hope, be encouraging. It turns out that all the stables are closed or their horses all hired out. If we can we will try again tomorrow.

Later we head out of San Pedro in a minibus crammed with other passengers. We are on our way to the salt flats of the Salar de Atacama. Our guide, Enzo, points out a pillar of dust shimmying across the fields; a little tornado or twister.

'We call it a *diablo*, a devil!'

Enzo is about my height, slightly tubby and, judging by his clothes, very keen on the colours blue and purple. He has a large bumbag with water bottles and also a plastic bag for food and tapes. He speaks very lightly in terrific English that he learned from books. He also speaks German and French and is learning Japanese and Italian.

'Have you visited all these countries?' Brian asks.

'No, not yet. I want to set up my own tour company, run trips all over South America. Then, when I've made my fortune I'll go everywhere!'

As we drive on Enzo talks about the Atacameño Indians and how their language, Cunza, has all but disappeared.

'There are very few pure Indians left here and those who are pure, or nearly, see everyone else as outsiders. They don't trust the other locals so they can't build any political strength to fight for their culture and homes. It's the same all over, no one gets together to make things happen.'

'Do you think people are sort of scared of making a noise – a hangover from Pinochet?'

'No, it's not that, there's no fear, just too many selfish groups. This area is turning to desert more and more as the mines take the water from the Andes. One day it will all be dead.'

He points to a plantation of trees.

'Those are *tamarugo*, native trees, very tough. There was a project to replant a whole forest. This is all there is. First Allende stopped investment and then Pinochet abandoned it too.'

'But with the area's mining doing so much for the national economy, can't you demand more investment and support?' asks Brian.

'The north takes up a third of the country, but has only about eight per cent of the population. No one in Santiago listens. The northerners tend to be more reserved than the outgoing southerners. Anyway it's still the same problem. The Indians don't trust anyone. The descendants of the Spanish don't like the descendants of the other immigrants and the Catholics hate the Protestants and vice versa.'

'But I thought people were proud of their country,' I say. 'I mean, ultimately you're all Chilean.'

'Oh sure, we tell you gringos that,' Enzo replies, laughing.

The minibus stops at the little town of Toconao and Enzo gets the key to the old Roman Catholic church. As we walk around inside Brian asks, 'We've seen a lot of churches for other denominations – Baptists, Mormons. I thought Chile was very Catholic?'

'Many are, but the people of Indian descent still resent the old church as being part of the conquistadors' work. Also it's a way for them to get education. The Baptists, the Mormons, the Adventists all provide free schools, clothes and sometimes medical facilities.'

We enter the Salar de Atacama at the very heart of the world's driest zone and it is raining. With windscreen wipers going the driver slows down to avoid the huge puddles. No one seems that put out. Yet rain is meant to be so rare here. Or is it one of those things that, while uncommon, is not unheard of? I visited the West Indies once and it poured with rain. Everyone kept saying, 'What bad luck – it's never like this,' before I realized that it often was, particularly at that time of year, and that they wanted me to feel unlucky rather than cheated.

Unlike my Caribbean experience, the rain and water now vanish in seconds. Soon we leave the van to walk to the middle of the flats, where there is a nature reserve. An almost totally evaporated saline lake, the Salar is a vast white plain, one of the world's largest salt flats and surrounded by three mountain ranges: the Andes, the Cordillera de Sal and the Cordillera de Domeyko. A surreal terrain of salt-encrusted earth and solid salt rock extends dead level as far as the eye can see before the world leaps up to the mountains and to the perfect volcanic cones.

Away across the flat we catch the occasional flash of pink as a flamingo wheels up and returns to the ground. It seems odd that such a delicate-looking creature should nest and thrive in such an alien landscape. However, there are shallow saline pools which provide tiny fish and crustacea that the flamingos and other, smaller birds feed on. Squatting down beside one of these pools I see the minute creatures wriggling. Their appearance is not appetizing and the stench from the water is foul. This landscape is somehow imaginary, too freakish and barren to warrant so much space. Save for the few creatures the only things that grow here are salt crystals which rear up grotesquely a foot or more in places.

Near me Enzo is arguing with a woman about Chile's economy. They are speaking in English though I learned earlier that she comes originally from the town of Antofagasta. Anyway she reckons that Chile is doing fine and does not want to hear Enzo's more gloomy view that while the economy sounds good according to the reports of the IMF and the World Bank, the national debt is still vast.

'A third of the people are living in poverty. Health care and schools are going downhill,' he argues.

'No, no. You are wrong . . .'

They are both getting heated and switch to Spanish. I turn back to the view.

Great clouds are louring over the Andes – a strange and brooding sight against the white glare of the flats at our feet. We are waiting for the sunset, though apart from trying to get some shots of flying flamingos (which I know will be hopeless), there does not seem to be much point: we have seen all there is to see. This is not a place for relaxed contemplation, yet Brian has been sitting on his own for a while a little way off. I go over to him.

'What do you reckon?'

'I'm fuming!'

The vehemence of Brian's reactions still takes me unawares sometimes and I can find myself rather scared of his emotion. This is not merely a phenomenon of my friendship with Bri but is, or has been, the way I often respond to strong reactions in others. It is a hindrance sometimes that in the face of another's anger, instead of my own hackles rising, I become eager to placate. Perhaps this is due to being English, keeping one's emotions in constant check, but I think it also arises from a fear of things getting out of control. Nowadays I am less anxious, largely because of witnessing Bri's explosions over the years and realizing that they do not bring the world to an end. So after a moment of being startled I listen with keen interest as well as some amusement as he fumes on: 'I'm raging about those guys, T. E. Lawrence and Saint-Exupéry and what-do-you-call-him Thesiger. All that stuff about religious experiences in the desert. My arse!'

I cannot help laughing at his furious face and he scowls at me.

'No, I'm not disagreeing with you,' I say, becoming more sober. 'At first I thought, wow! But now I'm just bored and I keep thinking of the long drive back in that packed bus.'

He gives this a cursory nod but his sense of loathing is still running hot.

'This place is an affront. It is useless. What is anyone doing coming to look at a place that is so dead?'

〜〜

The desert had not thus far impressed me. It had got under my skin and I was feeling discontented as if I had somehow missed something. With this in mind I had little expectation of the Salar. Well, what could one expect of a saline lake that has almost completely evaporated? Our arrival there confirmed me in my disappointment.

The place was grim beyond belief. As I walked around it trying to get a sense of its caustic emptiness, words fell from me in despair. This environment was ugly and hostile, a lamentable land mass that would give no respite to my loathing of it. For the life of me, I couldn't understand why we, or anyone else, would wish to see it. This was a vista of total corruption.

The salt earth under my foot was poisonous and I complained bitterly to John for bringing us here. I can't remember everything I said. It was probably unrepeatable, but the overwhelming scenes of stagnation and lifelessness were too much for me. 'Nothing could live here, if anything ever wanted to,' I said. 'There's not even a rock or a hump or a hill you could shit or piss behind!' This was my final rejection of it and to emphasize my feelings I jumped up and down, trying to break into its impenetrable and horrid surface. Nothing gave, it was dead and utterly petrified. I noticed

John looking askance at me. His expression said everything. The desert had finally got to me.

We were soon on our way back to San Pedro. I sat silently hating the place as we bumped over it. The sea of rock-salt stone that stretched for miles before us looked like nothing more than scabrous droppings from the testicles of Satan. The place was drawing language out of me like pus. I closed my eyes and wished myself to be instantaneously away from it.

Somewhere on our journey we passed a strange sight. Before us lay what seemed like acre upon acre of piled bags of cement. Here and there dotted among these were stacks of concrete block. Our guide explained that an American company had come to set up a factory to process the vast quantities of lithium and borax which could be drawn out of the Salar. They had abandoned the project before they even began building, had simply upped camp and left everything lying there. I didn't need to ask why. I understood it in my bones.

Beside me John and our guide were unaware of my seething, silent response. I listened half-heartedly to their conversation. The guide was explaining how the landscape keeps moving and changing. But I couldn't or wouldn't believe it. This place was eternal and execrable. I closed my ears, I didn't want to know that there was more of it.

A few miles further on he pointed out a small flock of flamingos 'feeding' off the Salar. I was incredulous. How could anything live, never mind feed here?

'What are they feeding on?' I demanded, almost barking at him.

Seemingly oblivious to my tone, he explained that only flamingos exist here because they have a miraculous filter in their beak which enables them to clean and swallow the micro-organisms from the tiny salt pools. They then regurgitate the blood-soaked food and feed it to their young. This confirmation that there was some kind of life here, no matter how minuscule, should have soothed me. I thought about it for many miles. The image of the blood-soaked food seemed appropriate to the Salar for it was leaching all sense of life out of me, leaving me to stumble around with nothing but the language of revulsion as my response.

After another hour or so, as we were approaching San Pedro I watched the evening light come up. It was as if it had been brushed with those pink flamingos' feathers. The sky was filled with a soft fusion of blues and pinks and greys, but it looked to me like a massive bruise.

≡⦚⦚≡

As the sun goes down behind the hills a deep, blood red, I imagine some bloated beast returning to its lair after gorging on the flats all day, leaving the flamingos as sentinels at its bitter table.

Everyone is tired on the drive back and it is a relief when it gets dark enough that you can look around and not worry about catching someone's eye.

Back in San Pedro we pad about on a small shopping expedition, buying some water and picnic makings for tomorrow. The shops have little to offer, just a few necessities and fruit, reminding me of the general store on the Isle of Eigg with its frontier feel. We have been here only a little over a day yet the place is very familiar.

⟨∿∿⟩

Having showered and changed for our supper, we strolled lazily through the narrow streets peering into the tiny bars. Most of them were as yet empty and I had had enough of empty spaces. To kill time John suggested visiting the museum. It was as if we were in some capital city instead of a village in a huge expanse of desert. We walked past the church and main square to the far end of the village. The museum had been built by a Belgian Jesuit and was reputedly one of the finest in South America. I must admit walking around it was surprising. Here the archaeologist, the anthropologist and the historian would all find something fascinating to study. But for me it was the mummies.

There were several of them, each so perfectly preserved by the dry air that they looked like sleeping people rather than corpses thousands of years old. With their flesh, fingernails, glazed eyes, and hair neatly plaited and tied with colourful ribbons, they had a real presence. As I studied them I began to feel uncomfortable, as if I was a voyeur. Among the jewellery and the hand-woven textiles there was a selection of instruments used for the preparation of psychedelic plants and mushrooms. This caused me to ask questions. I could easily understand why anyone living in the sterile landscape I had suffered earlier would take mind-expanding drugs. I could understand how the wondrous deities of the Inca civilizations had evolved and sustained themselves in such an environment. But the mushroom was a fungal organism dependent on moisture, of which there was so little here. Was it the run-off from the distant vista of snow-capped volcanoes that sustained them? I suppose I was too weary of the desert to probe its quirky secrets.

Before leaving I took a photo of the mummified remains of a young woman and immediately wished I hadn't.

Outside the village was beginning to come to life. Many of the travellers had returned from their expeditions and were milling about. Everywhere was humming with a mixture of accents and languages. Although it was evening it was still light and the light had the clarity of early morning. I was hungry and anxious to get away from the dead into the living village.

'Come on, John, I could eat the leg of the lamb of God!' I called out as he emerged from the museum.

We had been advised, because we would be at high altitude the next morning, not to drink much and to eat only a light meal. Having put up with the endlessly dreary salt flats, I wanted to spoil myself and thought a feast of roast chicken, some beans and fresh bread washed down with a jug or two of red wine was the least I deserved, but John insisted on an early night as we needed to leave at 4 a.m. What's the rush? I thought. The desert had been here for thousands of years and wasn't going to disappear overnight.

As we walked back to our hotel along the thronged main street, our ears were suddenly deafened by the blast of several car horns. Behind us a wedding procession of cars was inching its way through the crowd. An ancient, dilapidated Renault 4 with its roof hacksawed off carried the bride and groom. The newly married couple were wearing the traditional black suit and white gown. The bride's dress was heavy with lace and brocade and her face covered in a flimsy veil. Her outfit must have been an heirloom from her grandmother or her great-grandmother.

The groom's suit was 1950s vintage, and here and there patches of dust mixed with the patches of confetti. Like a drunken dragon following them came a stream of Dodge and Chevrolet half-trucks, some of which were probably of the same era as the groom's suit. Each of these vehicles was crammed with families all dressed in their Sunday best. As the procession passed, the shopkeepers and householders came out into the street and began laughing, clapping and whistling. Then everyone, stranger and neighbour alike, danced and ran after the cars. Obviously there was no such thing as 'invited guests only'. The whole village was a guest and everyone was welcome. John and I looked at each other momentarily then, without a word, turned and walked into the nearest cantina where we ceremoniously toasted the bride and groom and then we toasted them again. The whole event was in such contrast to the day that had preceded it that we forgot about the early-to-bed ruling.

It was 1 a.m. when I finally turned out my bedside light. In three hours we would be back on the road, bumping through the blackness into the mountains. I was not looking forward to it. Sleep was impossible. All night the wedding festivities and the band seemed to grow louder. I cursed them but was happy for this confirmation of life. The desert was, after all, fecund and fertile. There would be love-making in the night. I was glad of it and excused the revellers their noisy pleasure.

≡▮▮≡

At El Tatio geysers, the sun is still not up and it is freezing except where the ground steams. This is a strange and eerie place full of gurgling sounds and the smell of rotten eggs. The drive up took more than four hours. The van was packed and I was grateful once more for my earplugs that gave me some distance from the other bodies trying to sleep around me and deadened the grinding sounds as the vehicle rattled over ruts in the track. There was quite a sense of pilgrimage though as ahead up the mountain one could see the lights of other vehicles and at times, looking back down the hairpins, yet more glimmerings. I was anxious about the altitude and started puffing slightly but in the end it was just the cramped seating that got to me.

The muscular pain was, however, massaged by the way the sky changed during the ninety-kilometre drive. At the moment of first light the mountainsides were lit up pure white, like a negative appearing in the darkroom. Then a star pattern emerged just above the line of the ridge. Later the outline sharpened and the mountaintops were silhouetted against the blueing sky. At dawn, I realized I was remembering Edward Fitzgerald's lines from *The Rubáiyát of Omar Khayyám* which my mother had loved to quote and I could hear her voice now:

> Awake! for Morning in the Bowl of Night
> Has flung the Stone that puts the Stars to Flight:
> And Lo! the Hunter of the East has caught
> The Sultan's Turret in a Noose of Light.

≡⫴≡

There is an entry in my notebook which reads 'Geysers – Fear and Loathing in North Chile'. I don't remember when I physically wrote those notes but I remember that my encounter with those geysers was at odds with everything I had read about them. One guidebook declares, 'The colours on the ground and the metal blue of the sky at the dawn, framed by the rising steam columns, make a simply breathtaking sight.' Another claims, 'The visible impact of the steaming Fumaroles at sunrise in the azure clarity of the altiplano is unforgettable, and the individual structures when the boiling water evaporates and leaves behind dissolved minerals are strikingly beautiful.' After these descriptions I was anticipating something stunning and hugely impressive. Such was my expectation that I forgot my hangover and my lack of sleep.

We reached our destination at about 6.30. Dawn had arrived but not with any azure clarity. The place was cold and overcast. The predominant colour was a murky endemic grey. Until now I could not have imagined anything worse than the Salar. This may have been the highest geyser field in the world, but for me it was the devil's very own throne room, surrounded by the ice-covered surface of a desiccated earth.

I had disregarded the advice to bring warm clothing and anyway I had posted home my heaviest sweater from Iquique. I shivered in the cool morning air and cursed McCarthy's curiosity for bringing us to another oblivion. Several people had arrived before us and were wandering about aimlessly. They seemed to appear and disappear in and out of plumes of smoke. Everywhere around them funnels of steam hissed up like yellowing, bubbling contagion and seemed to turn the people into ghostly silhouettes of lost souls. The air was thin at this height and I took a short deep breath and retched. The air was filled with the sulphurous odour of ammonia. I couldn't simply stand here, shivering and choking. As we walked forward into this putrid air, it seemed the earth beneath us was boiling and spewing forth huge calloused warts. We were standing in a massive basin-like structure. On the low hills above us gigantic boulders hung precariously like congealed blood clots. I felt I was standing in Hell's own cauldron and watched the earth spitting forth, as from Satan's lips, nothing but abomination and nausea. Whatever the guidebooks had said, I found no comfort here. The atmosphere of the place was filled with the incense of contempt.

Near the centre our guide pointed out the rusting relic of what had been a fresh water plant. There had been two attempts to tap the energy for geothermal power and the fresh water plant was for the workers who came to earn a living here. But what was left of it looked like nothing more than a massive scaffold. I was convinced that nothing could purify this ulcerous water. Everything was toxic and repellent. It was as if the earth was groaning a bilious insult at us. I watched as the other visitors were drawn to the rim of the boiling geysers. Our guide warned us of the dangers of such activity. He told us the story of a Frenchman who had stood too near a geyser's mouth. The surface had crumbled under his feet and he had fallen into the liquid. Though his friends had been able to pull him out, he died before a helicopter could reach him. I could imagine the salts and minerals of the superheated water eating into the raw burns in his flesh. The man had boiled to death in a cauldron of chemicals.

≡Ⅲ≡

El Tatio is the highest geyser field in the world and there are said to be more than a hundred geysers here. Some are just bubbling pools in small surface fissures, others are little volcano-like cones which send up more impressive plumes of steam. As the sun begins warming the land, a light breeze develops and the figures of other visitors are revealed then concealed again by the spreading clouds. Every now and then Brian appears, shoulders hunched against the cold, looking less than happy. His dark clothes and greying beard and hair give him a wild, mountain-man look in the shifting miasmas of steam. Suddenly he is wearing a hood which I haven't seen before.

'Found it,' he says, smiling slightly. 'Good honest pruck!'

He stays close to the steam to get the best of the warmth. I can tell he is not enjoying himself.

'Not really your kind of place,' I suggest.

'Well, you know! Up at the skrake of dawn, drive for hours in a crammed bus. For what? I'm freezing and there's nothing but steam everywhere. What are we all doing here? Maybe it's just because you're supposed to come. Sure, it's a strange experience, but so would be jumping in a freezing river!'

'It'll warm up with the sun. I guess I'd expected the geysers to be more dramatic – like Yellowstone Park or something – but I like it, I like making the effort to see a weird natural phenomenon. And the light on the way up here, it was worth it just for that.'

'Maybe. I'm going to warm up in the truck for a bit.'

We gather back at our truck as the driver gives out cheese sandwiches and tea while boiling eggs in a geyser pool. Stupidly I smoke a cigarette and feel giddy for a minute. As the sun rises higher, I experience another form of giddiness – at the splendour of the snow-covered hillsides above us shining in the brightening light. Beams of sunshine appear among the higher mountain crags to act as searchlights sweeping the plateau and turning the banks of steam white for a few seconds.

We go to look at a large pool that bubbles at a temperature of 80° Fahrenheit. Brian, clearly happier with the warmth from sun and food, nudges me. 'Going close to the edge, are you?' He is teasing me about my slip in Lauca.

With the sun high up we head downhill, now able to enjoy the spectacular scenery in daylight. The road sweeps across the altiplano, high tundra, which, at around twelve thousand feet, has a dusting of snow in places and in others is bare shingle. A little further down we see vicuñas grazing on short, wiry grass. We stop to take photographs. This huge space, overseen by the Putana Volcano and lesser mountains around the horizon, makes me laugh out loud: not amused laughter but simply an expression of joy. The promise of this stark but beautiful landscape and the crispness of the early morning light and the slight chill of the air give me a great burst of optimism.

'There's something you can relate to here, you know,' murmurs Brian beside me. As ever his face is furrowed in concentration, but his eyes move rapidly, taking in the beauty around us, the expression now of welcome rather than rejection.

I was glad when our driver started up our minibus and began slowly to drive off. In the cold morning air the exhaust fumes from the diesel engine rose up in smoky drifts to blend with the sulphurous mists at El Tatio. I cupped my hands at my mouth and blew into them to warm them. The exhalation of my breath steamed into the air like the fumes. As I looked out on the wilderness beyond my window, I was reminded of a story about another of these dried-up lakes. It was called Salar de Pugsa. Legend has it that a village is buried in the salt sediments, punished like the biblical Sodom for its wickedness. Looking out on the bitterness beyond me, I could easily imagine this to be true.

As I tried to make notes by picturing again the Salar and El Tatio landscapes, I suddenly remembered those powerful religious paintings in the tiny church at Parinacota, with their naive illustrations of Hell. When I merged together my visions and El Tatio I felt for a moment that I had been one of those terrified figures in the magnificent apocalyptic paintings.

It was pointless trying to pen notes on the lurching bus, though McCarthy did so contentedly. This time I wasn't jealous of his efficient machine. As the bus rolled on, I was somehow sure I would not forget these inimical desert places. I looked away from my notebook and watched the land pass outside. I wanted it to be Connemara. I wanted it to be home. I wasn't sure what these desert days had done to me. Perhaps the emptiness and the desolation had made me lonely.

Outside it was as if the sky of the previous evening had dropped to earth. Those flamingo-hued clouds had surrendered and rolled over the gentle hills, lighting up the green and yellow tufted grass and softening the harsh white of the distant snow and frost. These mountains might be beautiful to some and I could see how that would be so, but in me they induced only a sense of despair and melancholy.

I opened my copy of Neruda's *Love Sonnets* as a consolation and read and slept on our way to the Valley of the Moon. The jarring bus could not withhold sleep from me. I was exhausted in every way.

As we descended the air became softer and the land greener and greener. I woke and sat for several hours soaking up the seclusion. I had withdrawn into the sonnets. The expression of erotic feeling and human affection conveyed a warmth and intimacy that I absorbed like a sponge. The poet's effervescent lyricism was a much needed counter to the fierce scatology I was experiencing. In and out of his poignant lyrics I moved as I slept or stared at this vacant vista of his homeland.

I was sleeping and dreaming of pumas when the bus came to a stop. John nudged me gently and informed me we should take a walk. Outside it was bright and warm. But in the fresh air the sun did not have the same soothing effect as reading Neruda. Our guide had brought us to the top of a narrow gorge at the bottom of which there was a stream flowing with warm Andean mountain water. We could bathe if we wished. The idea was unbelievably attractive. He warned us that we would have to go down and climb up again on foot. We didn't hesitate.

I noticed that someone had painted some words in bright red paint on the boulders lining the path. They read, '*Dios Es Amor, Jesu Cristo Viene Por*', then the number '2' was inscribed and followed by '*A La Terra*'. Below this inscription in bigger letters the words '*Jesus Te Ama*' blazed out.

I was amazed that someone should come so far into the hills to paint this evangelical inscription. But why not? Christianity was a desert religion, after all.

When we reached the valley floor, I immediately understood the appropriateness of the graffiti. The whole course of the stream was lined with people and the area was ablaze with colour. Here and there families were eating and pouring drinks. In places where the stream had cut a deep basin into the river bed, men, women and children were bathing contentedly. Small tents and make-shift shelters were everywhere. The scene before me was biblical and could have been lifted out of an illustrated version of the loaves and fishes parable. Jesus and his disciples could have been sitting behind a rock, somewhere out of sight.

Don John, as always, could not resist the water's invitation. With unbelievable Quixotic foresight he had even brought a pair of swimming shorts into the desert. I laughed at his skinny white body with its brown forearms, topped by a well-weathered face. He stood out a mile from the desert people bathing beside him. But this was a place of welcome and respite and Patcha Mama and '*Jesus Te Ama*' knew no distinction.

≡Ⅲ≡

Off the high plateau we start the steep descent back to the Valley of the Moon and San Pedro, stopping to visit the Baños de Puritama. We have heard about the beauty of these thermal pools but the earth is brown again and as we park there is nothing to see except a few cacti. Yet after a brief walk we find ourselves at an oasis in a hidden gorge. Suddenly there are plants and grasses of rich green and a sense of peace and sanctuary. I cannot resist a bathe. The pool is about two feet deep with a gravel bottom and some plants among which tiny fish swim. The water is indeed hot and soothing. My skin is white as white in the water. Our fellow travellers are there too but somehow this is not a time to chat. We newcomers tend to sit and grin stupidly at the sheer pleasure of being in such an unusual place. Barely fifty feet away the harsh desert landscape reasserts itself but here we are safe in the balmy waters.

It is becoming clear to me that although we imagined great vistas, desert plains and mountains in captivity, the reality is far, far greater. What we are seeing could not be dreamed. One might conjure an oasis pool or distant salt flats flashing white in the sunlight but to put the two together and dream up the sensations of sitting in a volcanic spring while looking down to the bitter wastes of the Salar de Atacama, three thousand feet below you and more than twenty miles away, is beyond anyone's most fertile invention.

In the same way that the imagination has difficulty assembling the disparate parts of such scenery it also fails to prepare one for the range of emotional reactions it can provoke. Excitement, happiness, awe and even fear were likely enough but not that they should come all together and create a more profound feeling. From this soothing spot I am peering through a looking glass to that other world of the harsh salt lake and I feel at once secure and vulnerable – as if I am sailing along in safe waters while, on the horizon, a massive, black thunderhead looms continually.

While Don Quixote wallowed in the river, Sancho Panza lay back in the shade of one of those biblical stones and drank in the exuberance of the place with a grateful sense of wonder. I was glad I had brought Neruda's love sonnets. There could have been no more appropriate place on earth to read them. But our respite was short-lived. We had to be in the Valley of the Moon before sunset, so we trudged up the hill and set out for our final destination before returning to San Pedro.

The stopover in the idyllic canyon placed the bleakness of the remainder of our journey in high relief. Once more we were submerged in this forlorn emptiness. For another several hours I sat stunned and almost smothered by this expansive abyss. I turned to John who was again rapidly tapping on his machine. I scribbled in my notebook, 'This is the land of Ismael and of Cain.' I closed my eyes and dreamed my puma dream again.

En route to the Valley of the Moon Enzo detoured to show us an old salt mine. Some minutes before we came to a stop, he pointed out three huge salt pillars standing upright on the flat desert tundra. He called them the Tres Marias. There was nothing feminine about them. In fact there was nothing human at all. But I suppose in a place like the Atacama, the mind needs to believe in something more than this emptiness. I understood how this landscape would induce connections with the crucifixion. And equally I could imagine why someone would give the name Tres Marias to the landmark. Faith promises us something better than this boundless waste. The image conjured up by the name was one of maternal succour. I could well understand the necessity of it in such a wilderness.

The salt mine was nothing more than a few tumbledown stone huts and a hole in the ground, but as we returned to the bus a curious sight confronted us. There, as if he had appeared out of nowhere, was an old miner who apparently lived in a hut near the mine. He was ancient and his face was as dried up as the ground on which we stood. His shirt was sorely in need of a good wash and appeared several sizes too big. The sleeves seemed to have been torn off rather than tailored. His baggy trousers were tied below the knee with a string to make them fit. A piece of rope served as a belt and sandals completed his attire. He was selling gem salt. On a battered wooden box in front of him sat large chunks of exquisitely clear crystal. They shimmered with white fire in the light. I was too astounded by his sudden appearance to be much interested in his wares. I stood back a few feet from him and watched, entranced. He was passive and unmoved. He made no effort to cajole us into purchasing the fabulous crystals. He was completely dissociated from the world in which he sat, a Charon-like figure. I wandered off, thinking I had encountered the living image of Ismael and Cain whose land I felt this was. I didn't purchase any of his gem crystals, but I took his image away with me in my memory, like a ghostly hologram.

≡ ‖ ≡

We have seen some massive dunes which are much more attractive than arid plains. So perhaps the great desert writers were turned on by rolling dunes rather than the barren rocky, salty flats that have been the norm around here. Brian is calmer, though I thought he would blow a fuse when Enzo described another flat dull bit we had crossed earlier as the Plateau of Patience. Not Brian's forte with deserts so far.

Now we are in another salty area, but it is quite unlike the Salar. Salt has been mined here for human consumption from early Indian times until quite recently. There is absolutely no vegetation and even an old, derelict building is constructed out of salt blocks. As we look at this scene we ask Enzo about the large number of army and police personnel we have seen in the area.

'We are near the Bolivian border, so they watch for smugglers.'

'But there seem to be police checkpoints at the edge of some of the towns,' I observe. 'What do people think of the police, since Pinochet?'

'Since the coup and the horrors that followed, people haven't felt the same about cops or *pacos* as we call them. Uniforms used to be respected, then they were feared. Now, well, people reckon they wear them off duty to get favours – you know, free drinks and cab rides. The Carabineros' motto is *Siempre Amigo*, Always a Friend. It'll be a while before you can say that without laughing!'

'We've spoken to a few people about the Pinochet years and most don't seem that bothered or just don't want to talk about it,' Brian tells him.

'Yeah, I know,' says Enzo. 'For me it was a very bad time. Yes, Allende had really messed things up, but there was no need for what the military did. I was picked up once in Santiago, for nothing. Same thing happened to friends. It was bad. Everyone knows that but like I've said before, the country's so spread out and there are so many views it all just gets passed over somehow.'

〰〰

I awoke when the bus stopped. Imitating a station announcer John intoned in my ear, 'All passengers wishing to visit the Valley of the Moon, please alight here. Next stop, San Pedro.'

It was a short walk into the valley proper. The landscape was as huge and lunar as any place called the Valley of the Moon should be. Everywhere around us crater-like walls of sediment rose up vertically, eroded by millennia of winds that gave the valley an eerie atmosphere. It didn't repulse me in the way that other places had. I was drawn into it. There was something fantastical about it. It was sterile and barren and the whole valley seemed to be made up of endless sharp-crested hills. There was an extraordinary quality about it that I could not fathom. It seemed a place set apart from the Atacama. I thought I had run out of words and patience with expeditions to these hideous nowheres, but the Valley of the Moon was different. I was unsure what it was except that I sensed a kind of sorcery here, but one that was beneficent. The abuse I was ready to hurl at McCarthy for bringing me to another vale of malevolence dissolved in my mouth. But it wasn't long before I found it again.

Enzo brought us to a halt, before what I thought might have been a cave, or a weathered fissure in the gnarled valley walls that towered over us. He politely asked if we were afraid of confined spaces. It was an unintentional irony – there was little about confined spaces we didn't know and in any case I wanted to tell him I had been suffering from agoraphobia ever since we had arrived in the Atacama. Instead we quietly confirmed that neither of us was bothered and with that he led us into the mouth of the cave. As we walked into the passage he called back to us that the cave narrowed and that as we would have to crawl some distance, if we had some torches, we should use them. John was, as always, prepared for any eventuality and I became aware of the thin beam of light from his miniature pencil torch.

On and on we crawled and grunted, with Sancho Panza heaving great lungfuls of condemnation on our guide, McCarthy, this frigging cave in particular, the Atacama Desert in general, and God Almighty for inventing yaks which were the start of this fiasco.

For several hundred yards we crawled through the blackness and I gouged lumps of flesh out of myself on the broken cave walls. I could feel my hands starting to smart from the chemical salts that made up the surfaces over which we were scrambling. I knew there would be no water to wash the sting out of them and I cursed again, then called back to ask John if he had brought gloves.

'Of course,' he answered.

'Bastard.'

There was nothing for it but to grunt and bear it, occasionally punctuating the silence with an exclamation of the saviour's surname as I left another piece of skin on the rock. The place was devouring me inch by inch. To my relief, the guide called out, 'Almost there, soon fresh air.' A poet, a torturer and a traveller all rolled into one, I thought to myself, as he emerged from the cave's mouth and the daylight flooded down to me. Soon we were all out, and our guide told us that we would have to climb a little distance.

'Climb?' I said, looking at John with a face that told him I was ready to decapitate both him and the guide on the spot.

'Only a few feet,' said the guide, assuming my exclamation was harmless.

The climb was simple and within minutes we were looking across the Valley of the Moon. I was impressed. The cave had acted as a kind of ladder. We had been climbing as we had been crawling. We stood surveying the majestic lunar landscape unfolding in the distance. After a few minutes the guide commented on the time and the imminence of sunset. We had to move more quickly and he was off at once with us following sheeplike after him.

I was feeling exhausted but didn't want to admit it, though my huffing and puffing concealed nothing. Sir Edmund Hillary McCarthy seemed unruffled as he patted the dust off his shoulders. I decided to keep my mouth shut until this trial was over but when we finally arrived at the foot of a massive sand dune and were told we would not only have to climb to the top and then walk along its steeply ascending ridge, but also scale the plateau high above us where it met the 'sediment' cliff face, my response was, 'Holy fuck!'

I have two problems: one, I am terrified of heights; and two, at forty-six and after the exertions of the last few days, I was feeling seventy-six years old. I had no intention of bringing on a coronary collapse and being left here as the proverbial Man in the Moon Valley. I gabbled all this to John in a state of defiant panic. He knew I was serious and told me to wait and catch my breath. I looked along the ridge of the mammoth dune. Other climbers were ploughing their way towards the plateau. They were ant men from where I stood. I really didn't think I could make it. Humour was no longer sustaining me. What was staring me in the face was no joke. 'I'm going for a little walk while I think about this,' I said. John simply nodded in agreement. He knew I was very, very anxious. Our guide too sensed my apprehension and politely said nothing.

I walked only a few feet from my companions and looked again at the looming dune. This was Sisyphus's own hill of torment and I was standing in a sublunary Hades. I was Brian Keenan, not some sado-masochistic Greek hero obsessed with pushing great boulders endlessly up and down mountains. Without being fully conscious of it, I walked further away from the monster confronting me before turning to view it again.

I watched the progress of the climbers who had set out before we arrived. They were even more insect-like than before. I was about to return and tell John to go on without me when I looked again at the demon dune.

But it wasn't a demon. I was looking at that imaginary desert I had wished for. With its soft curve and upward flow, it had all the sensual exoticism of my mystical desert. In this hard, brutal, un-relenting land I had found a feminine soulscape. The dune was voluptuous and inviting. My eyes scanned the luxurious flow of the dune to the plateau. I wanted to be up there.

However, even as I walked back to John, my enthusiasm was rapidly waning. I had to commit myself before I lost my nerve. 'OK, let's go.' The others said nothing and we walked to the foot of the dune. To my total astonishment the guide announced that we must climb barefoot.

'Barefoot?' I exclaimed. 'Is this some kind of penance or some-thing? Who's up on that plateau, God Almighty?'

Don John disregarded my pathetic remarks and began undoing his laces, commenting, 'I suspect boots full of sand would make the climb more difficult and uncomfortable.'

I couldn't argue and began the barefoot slog heavenward think-ing what a supercool smart-arse McCarthy was.

We reached the ridge faster than I had expected, but the effort nearly killed me. I had no breath to curse, though my mind was reeling with expletives. I suspect God on the mountaintop forbade it and left me only sufficient energy to climb. We rested at the beginning of the ridge and looked down. Now the ants were below us. The guide glanced at his watch and said we must move on. I had expected this section to be easier but it wasn't. We seemed to sink deeper on this level than on the incline. I stopped every few paces to rest and breathe. It became more difficult with each stop. Throughout the long traverse John stood behind me saying not a word, stopping when I stopped and starting when I did. By following in my footsteps he was taking the evil eye off me. Others passed us on the trail and John could easily have gone ahead, but he chose to wait patiently. In every way he was a very 'parfit gentil knyght', as Chaucer would say.

As we neared the last leg, I could see the climb up on to the plateau was a short one. I rounded on Don John and, with my chest heaving asthmatically, complained, 'First you have me slithering up the devil's arsehole on my hands and knees, then slogging over this great hump on his ugly back! Do you have any plans for later?'

From the top of the plateau the undulations of the desert escarpments seemed endless and gave the impression that one was looking out over the cloud floor. The visual feast made the climb seem trivial. At this height and at this hour the sun and moon hung above us in perfect juxtaposition. In the deafening silence that came booming across hundreds of miles of desert we could see as clearly as if the horizon was only a few feet from us. You could believe you were in another world. In a way you were. I looked down on the valley beneath us. It seemed a long way away, yet I was not intimidated by it. The guide pointed out what he called the Inca Theatre, a natural amphitheatre cut into the earth. It was an incredible monument to nature's powerful artistry. For a long time I looked at it and the eternal land mass beyond. I imagined I was looking down on one vast celestial city. John and I sat in our separate quiet, relacing our boots, feeling like tiny microcosms caught up in a cosmic moment that we could only gape at, dumbfounded.

The sun was beginning to set and I was starting to hallucinate. The earth was glowing in the queer trance-inducing sunset. The landscape below me became a living thing, breathing different shapes and colours as the sun descended.

I had found myself an eyrie-like cranny in the wall of the plateau to shelter from the cool wind, and was feeling like a young eaglet trembling as the breeze fluffed its feathers. The panorama was changing with a slow intensity. For a brief moment I wanted to lean out and let the thermal carry me away, to soar and swoop in this endlessly intoxicating radiance. Instead I got up to walk and catch what I could of the magical cinematography of land and light.

My eyes scanned across again to the Inca Theatre. I thought of the vastness of that empire. I had wondered why anyone would want to conquer and claim such emptiness, but now I knew. The Inca worshipped the sun, and I was standing in the sleeping quarters of this magnificent deity. I now understood why the empire's messengers would run for days on end, stopping only at sunrise and sunset to praise their king who was the earthly representative of their golden god. Into the glowing evening I called out, '"Atahuallpa, Sapa, Inca, Inca, Capac. I am Atahuallpa Capac, Son of the Sun, Son of the Moon, Lord of the Four Quarters. Who does not kneel to me?"' They were the half-remembered words from Peter Shaffer's play about the conquest of Peru, *The Royal Hunt of the Sun*. I saw John look at me curiously as I mouthed out the words. I quickly explained their origin. I had forgotten them completely until now. But in the prescient evening they came flooding back. Inside me I heard the voice of the Sun God:

'Atahuallpa speaks! Atahuallpa needs. Atahuallpa commands. Bring gold. From the palaces. From the temples. From all buildings in the great palaces. From walls of pleasure and roofs of Omen. From floors of feasting and ceilings of death. Bring him the gold of Quito and Pachamacac! Bring him the gold of Colcanota! Bring him the gold of Caolae! Of Aymaraes and Arequipa! Bring him the gold of the Chimu! Put up a mountain of gold and free your Sun from his prison of clouds.'

And here it was in front of me, a land turned luminous as if there was some alchemy in my subconscious memory. As the last arc of the sun hung over the edge of our horizon, Atahuallpa,

Son of the Sun, spoke his last words:

'There is my father sun! You see now only by his wish; yet try to see into him and he will darken your eyes forever. With hot burning he pulls up the corn and we will feed. With cold burning he shrinks it and we starve. These are his burning and our life. Do not speak to me of your god. He is nowhere.'

It was disconcerting and intriguing to find myself remembering these lines so vividly. The little church hall in Belfast's Cromwell Road which had served as a rehearsal centre for the Youth Theatre was a long way in time and space from the plateau of the Valley of the Moon. Somehow my memory was as incandescent as the air around me. I wandered about the place again, wanting to get a final glimpse of the pulsing chiaroscuro before me. I was looking for one image which would imprint itself on my memory and that I would see every time I recalled my visit. I could not find it, yet it was everywhere in the auroral symphony that was playing silently around me.

Too soon it was time to go and we slowly descended the plateau wall on to the ridge. It was still a long way down but our eyes were elevated into the glowing sky. If I had cursed the penitential upward climb, I began the descent subdued and awestruck.

As I stood on the topmost edge of the ridge and looked down on the incline to the valley floor, I was overcome by an irresistible urge. I was going to jump off the edge of the ridge and keep jumping until I reached the bottom. I turned to John and smiled, my eyes wide with the lunacy in me. He looked back at me, his face passive and knowing. He never spoke a word. I looked back down the dune and tried to restrain myself. I told myself I was forty-six, not six. What would happen if I broke my ankle in this fit of insanity? What would people think of this demented half-wit hopscotching down these desert mountains?

Within a second, I had removed my boots and tossed them and the rest of my belongings at McCarthy. I launched myself off the ridge and bellowed a salutation to the night. 'BOING!' I roared and 'BOING!' again, as I landed and lifted off again. 'BOING, BOING, BOING!' I shouted with every leap while the laughter was choking me. Far above me on the ridge, I could see John and our guide echoing my laughter.

When I reached the bottom I was covered in red sand like the reddleman from Thomas Hardy's *Return of the Native*. I was sweating and breathless but incredibly happy, in the most uncomplicated and childlike way. I sat up from where I had fallen in my final leap and looked upward. I had been higher than the highest plateau I had stood on but I didn't know how to explain it to myself, let alone anyone else.

≡Ⅲ≡

From above, laughing at Brian's antics, I suddenly remember him telling me about Jack Kerouac's *Dharma Bums*. The narrator, Ray Smith, is out in the mountains with Japhy Ryder. 'I looked up and saw Japhy running down the mountain in huge twenty-foot leaps, running, leaping, landing with a great drive of his booted heels, bouncing five feet or so, running, then taking another long crazy yelling yodelaying sail down the sides of the world and in that flash I realized it's impossible to fall off mountains.' Unlike Ray Smith, I do not follow suit and take flight down the mountain, preferring a more leisurely descent, but I do share the profound peace of revelation and reassurance – we should be safe enough on those horses.

〰〰

On our journey back to San Pedro I confessed to John that if all his other expeditions had not impressed me, this one made up for them all. He smiled knowingly and said, 'Yes, I had the distinct impression you enjoyed that.' He paused. 'Especially the last bit.' The rest of the journey was a long drive through another section of no-man's-land. I looked out on to it as we passed through, but I saw nothing. My mind was still in the Valley of the Moon.

'So tell me about that mumbo-jumbo you were singing up on the plateau.'

I quoted back to John the lines of the play: ' "Atahuallpa, Sapa Inca, Inca Capac/Atahuallpa, Son of the Sun, Son of the Moon, Lord of the Four Quarters." '

'Enough, enough. Now that we know you can speak Inca, you might like to stay here as a guide, given that you like it so much. I can see it all now. Specialist tours of the Valley of the Moon by the only Inca-speaking Irishman in South America. Now let's see . . .'

I knew John was well away and I was about to be subjected to a mischievous teasing for the next few hours. I pre-empted the torture by cutting him off before he got started. 'OK, John, roll it up and put it away!'

Outside the barren wastes drifted past us. This time they did not produce the same smouldering in me but paradoxically the thrilling moments on the mountaintop drove home to me the powerful loneliness of the place we were passing through. It wasn't the isolation so much as the absence of anything to stimulate the mind. I tried to imagine myself existing in such an uninhabitable void. I couldn't, I wouldn't, my soul would perish here. The sooner we were out of this the better, I thought.

As we drove into San Pedro we were confronted by the bustle of people and the smells of coffee and roasting meat. The intensity of the day's several experiences struck home. Later that evening as I lay on my bed taking notes I remember thinking of one of the closing scenes from the play that I had recalled on those dizzying golden heights.

Francisco Pizarro was the commander of a group of conquistadors who had come to plunder Peru. But Pizarro was a man in search of something greater than gold. Age and the grave haunted him and all sense of joy was eroded from his life. Time was his prison. At the edge of despair he cried out for release. 'There's a jailer, there must be. At the last, last of lasts, he will let us out. He will, he will.' Utterly inconsolable, he comes to believe that his prisoner Atahuallpa, living god-king of the Inca, is that immortal jailer. In a moving scene Pizarro is converted by Atahuallpa. The Sun King takes a handful of ichu grass and a stone. The conquistador general confesses into the grass for an hour. Then the Inca god-king throws away the grass, strikes Pizarro on the back with his stone and making a sign of purification receives him into the Inca world.

The recollection made me pause from my note-taking. I was trying to find the words to describe the supernatural atmosphere of the Valley of the Moon. I took my pen and wrote cryptically, 'I have spoken into ichu grass and felt the blow of Inca stone upon my back.' I paused before finally climbing into bed. Near the reading lamp sat Neruda's poetry, my alternative guidebook. The experience of the desert had brought me closer to understanding the poet's sometimes hallucinatory surrealism and sensuous imagery. That night I didn't need to read anything.

I went to sleep with desert pumas panting through my dreams. My sleep was troubled, but not by nightmares. We were leaving the desert for good tomorrow. But the desert had not yet finished with me. The night was cold and my head was still compartmentalizing everything we had experienced. Sleep was pointless, so I threw on a pair of trousers and a shirt and went outside to the porch, wrapping myself in a blanket. The sky was incredible, as if a million starbursts had been frozen at their moment of explosion. It was impossible to distinguish any reference points there. Under this pre-dawn canopy I could easily believe there were as many stars in that sky as there were grains of sand in the desert. For several hours I sat losing myself in those unknown galaxies.

As the night skyscape melted into sunrise I penned a quick note to fax home first thing before we departed:

Hello Sweetheart,

We have just come back from 10 hrs in the high hills on the Bolivian border, then through the relentless emptiness of the Atacama desert. I am wheezing and puffing like a colic donkey in the thin air.

I miss you very much and last night wrote this poem, under the influence of my friend Pablo.

Silent and staring I hunt the red emptiness
My feet are burned. The baked stones have
broken my claws to the quick
I am prey of this infernal sun
Great hunger consumes me

I am thirsty for your spring water laughter
I want to drink the liquid blue of your eyes

But bone-cold darkness gnaws at me, and
I await your creature call in my ravenous heart
I am the puma of the night
Sniffing starlight

We finally leave the desert tomorrow for La Serena. I will ring from there.

What do you think of 'Joachim' for Junior?

Love and special hugs,

Brian

San Pedro de Atacama

≡ ||| ≡

We packed before turning in last night. Although dog tired I could not sleep for choking and gasping. Now I have some idea of what Terry Waite went through with his asthma. Sometimes he was up most of the night struggling for breath. The medicine he was given worked some of the time, but inevitably there were days when the attacks were too bad or, even worse, when the guards did not have what he needed. I am frightened enough here in freedom: heaven knows how much worse the panic was in those cells.

We struggle off in the filling light, Brian stopping every hundred feet or so to realign his wheely-bag device. Taking a last look at the volcano rising white we walk up the now familiar stony, sandy track escorted by a black dog wearing a rakish maroon scarf. It is very peaceful so early, most doors still closed tight but there are one or two people about. We look back down the long, straight and dusty street – there are two boys, two dogs and thin sunlight. When we reach the square, the bus is already quite full. There is a woman carrying a large child of perhaps six or seven in a papoose. She wears a full, brightly coloured skirt and her husband sports a wide-brimmed hat. A young couple board: he is skinny with long black hair framing a high-cheekboned face, ugly really; she is beautiful, with short hair, pretty face and physique and a sweet, trilling voice and laugh. They are clearly much in love. At the front of the bus a young German woman drones on and on in an impossibly dull voice.

It feels good to be moving south; it will be a relief to have more green in the scenery. A ridge of mountains ahead offers a new horizon as today we will go far.

Chapter Six

∿

La Serena

Name is suggestive of peace and relaxation after our desert trials: place to charge batteries.

Arrived Hotel Francisco de Aguirre to curious looks from reception staff. Waited patiently while they discussed some problem with the reservations. Manager was called and examined his booking lists. First he looked at us, then at his staff, then at our passports, then back to us and once more at his staff. Spontaneously they all burst out laughing. John and I looked at each other in confusion. Soon all was revealed: 'Please excuse us, señors, we have given you the bridal suite!'

≡Ⅲ≡

The Club Social in La Serena is a strange gaff. You come up a couple of flights of stairs to a large room with an extremely high ceiling. There is a profound air of antiquity in the main restaurant, from the quaint and rickety furniture to the old couple eating silently a few tables away. The waiter too is past his prime but is enthusiastic and, with patience and the phrase book, helps us to work out the menu.

While waiting for our meal we become intrigued with the goings on in a room adjacent to the restaurant. Some youngish men bustled up and disappeared in there. The waiter took in drinks, squeezing sideways through the door and making every effort to keep it as closed as possible. There has been shouting.

'A drama group?' I wonder.

'Maybe, certainly sounds a bit excitable for Rotarians, but why the secrecy? Ah! A card school!'

Our ponderings are interrupted by the arrival of the food which, oddly, seems to come from the *baños damas*, the ladies. Anyway it is good, as is the wine. When the immediate needs of hunger and thirst are assuaged, our attention returns to the gathering next door. The waiter has been slinking in and out with more and more booze and the shouting is getting louder.

'A bit rowdy for cards, isn't it – maybe politicos?'

'That's it,' says Brian conspiratorially. 'They're Nazis! The Boys from Brazil on a busman's holiday to the coast.'

La Serena, one of the oldest cities in the country, is full of colonial and mock-colonial mansions. There is quite a touristy air here but it is pleasant just wandering around or stopping at La Recova market for a beer while looking over the stalls in the square as jazzy Latin music blares out from a record store. It is a colourful place selling all manner of handicrafts, clothes and food; men mingle with the crowd offering olives and other morsels to taste before buying. A man with a beribboned llama touts for photographs.

I spot some trousers in a department store sale. They have leg pockets and, still obsessed with being the perfect travelling man, I must buy them. It is less than simple. Once you have made your choice you then have to queue with a ticket, pay the money and pick up the goods – in a sealed bag – from another desk. I am surprised I do not have to show my passport.

A group of gypsy women beg aggressively in the square, the Plaza de Armas. Their faces and clothes seem to have come from another age and strike me as being Asian rather than American. Their insistence undermines the peaceful atmosphere created by trees, flowers, bandstand and sculpture. The town seems to be a centre for the arts. There are a number of galleries and exhibitions and placards advertising the imminent annual literary festival. So maybe culture is not entirely dead in Chile.

∿∿

La Serena

Bookstalls everywhere, but cannot find a translation of Gabriela Mistral's work anywhere. We will be visiting her birthplace in a week or so – must check with master planner McCarthy!

Town coming down with churches. Every religious order has one here. Found death mask of Gabriela Mistral in church of San Francisco. She was some kind of lay sister in the order of St Francis: looks very stern – a mother superior in waiting!

Don Quixote bought new trousers today (millions of pockets) . . . and I suspect some silver paint for his lance! What was the fiasco in post office in Iquique all about? Looking forward to our Kerouac-esque run down the mythical Pan American Highway.

≡⦀≡

I feel a need to have things organized. Once the basic decisions, where we are going and how, are made and the basic details, tickets, etc. are sorted out then I relax and lose much of the tension. All this is fine on a simple trip but here, where weeks of logistics stretch out ahead, I realize that as I try to take in the immediate experience I am also reading up on the next place, thinking about the journey there and onward again.

I sense that Brian is getting pretty fed up with me having my nose endlessly in a guidebook and forever trying to decide what we should go and see next. At lunch today I suggested the town's archaeological museum. He was not really interested.

'Oh John, we've seen a few already, this will be more of the same. You can't go looking too hard for interesting stuff, sometimes you just have to wait till it comes to you.'

We are agreed that a trip to one of the area's famed astronomical observatories is a good idea. My guidebook says you need to phone a couple of days beforehand but when I ask the friendly lady at reception in our hotel to help get us into La Tololo observatory she offers little hope, telling me that bookings have to be made three months in advance. Apart from getting livid with the guidebook – and it is fairly unrewarding ranting at a small and now battered volume – there seems little we can do. I present the lady with our letter from the Chilean Embassy in London and she promises to make every effort on our behalf.

Top of our agenda is hiring a car – we plan to meander down to Santiago under our own steam. I drag himself off into town with some names and addresses culled from the *South American Handbook*. This is an excellent publication, so much so that every traveller we meet has one. However it seems that the La Serena section has not been revised for a while. A restaurant in the neighbouring port of Coquimbo proved illusory and now the first car hire company has moved. An old fellow eagerly gives me elaborate directions to the new address and I reckon I have a general idea of what he is saying. Brian is getting restless, I know, but he does not complain. Near where I think we are heading, Brian spots a Turista office sign and goes in.

With a few phrases of Spanish and English, the young woman behind the desk understands what we are about and starts phoning round for us. I had just wanted an address. Anyway she finally recommends that we go to the Gala hire company. Just before we depart, I realize that the travel company was on the first floor. Our kind lady was working in an estate agent's.

Eventually we get a vehicle sorted out. It is a largish pick-up truck. Brian has arranged this so, feeling negative, I have my doubts – there is no boot so where will we keep our bags safely? Secretly I think it might be fun.

Despite the best efforts of our friend at reception, the observatory says we cannot visit. A major disappointment.

There is a big do on at the hotel tonight. Many guests are being entertained in a marquee on the terrace. The cabaret man plays 'Yes Sir, That's My Baby'. At which point I decide it is time for bed.

∿∿

La Serena

Both feeling frustrated. Truth is, we're not getting what we're looking for – whatever that is! It's hardly inspiring and makes for poor communication. Neither of us has the answer to the other's frustration!

Am spending too much time with my nose in Neruda. John buried in guidebooks. Have a strong impression John does not like Neruda, so can't talk about that either. Three days here too long.

Rang Audrey. Everything OK with pregnancy. I am feeling homesick and guilty and I don't know why!

≡⫿⫿≡

We get the truck and Brian starts driving it alarmingly to Vicuña. I am not the best passenger and cannot stop myself from shouting, 'For God's sake, Bri, don't do it!' as he races past another dawdling car.

Normally he doesn't go over 50 m.p.h., yet here he is thrashing a strange vehicle on uneven roads. To take my mind off imminent crashes I look out at the countryside. The Elqui valley is magnificent: very lush in parts, just dusty in others. Above there are scrub- and cactus-covered hillsides. I try to make a few notes about the views but find it is impossible. Brian hunches over the wheel, right on the tail of a long truck. Suddenly he guns the engine and we overtake and I involuntarily brace myself with legs and arms but manage to keep quiet, grit my teeth and decide that note-taking with white knuckles will not be very productive.

At Vicuña we visit the Gabriela Mistral museum. Although she won the Nobel Prize for Literature in 1945, no one seems to have translated her work.

∿∿

Vicuña

After long drive, badly disappointed. Mistral museum small, and informative if you speak Spanish. Black and white photos;

Gabriela looks very masculine with broad shoulders (she seems to have smoked as much as McCarthy) and wears severe suits. There is more man than woman here! Father deserted her as a child, close relationship with mother. Her restored room would make a wonderful painting. I am depressed I cannot take photos and that even here there are no translations.

Vicuña is a sad little town. I can imagine her writing here even if I can't read it!

≡Ⅲ≡

Inland is all barren hills and cactus but the coastline is dotted with teeming resorts. Most of the local population escapes to the beach, it seems. We are in a little town called Tongoy. It reminds me of Whitby – seaside and working port. There must be more than a hundred bright yellow, twenty-foot-long fishing boats. In the late afternoon light, a couple of fishermen stand as they row to their moorings.

As the sun goes down over the bay there is much noise; the laughter and squeals of happy family holidays. This place has a warm atmosphere: odd then that I should feel a chill about me. Paradise triste or something. But it has been good, driving and feeling that we are making our own way. Grudgingly I have to acknowledge that Brian's vehicle is ideal.

∿∿

Tongoy

Long long drive. Stupendous coastline and packed beaches. Caught a debilitating cold. Gets worse by the hour. Everyone looks at me as I cough, rasping out of the pit of my chest.

Monotony of constant travel is getting to us. It wearies you in a way that you are not really conscious of. Good dinner: fish market restaurant full of life. I am barking like a seal and not the best of company.

≡Ⅲ≡

Exploring below our little hotel I discover feverish activity in the deepening gloom of dusk as the fish market closes. Deep in the shadows one stallholder hacks and chops at chunks of fish – and finger, I shouldn't wonder. Fish are stacked away in coolboxes as kids nip among trestle tables under awnings. Just along the quay a painted saintly statue looks rather forlornly out to sea while a few people sit fishing. As I follow the saint's gaze out across the blue-black bay I notice a small buoy a hundred yards away. Then it turns to reveal the great gobbling beak of a pelican.

We walk down the dusty track to a beach where there are many fish restaurants and a shoal of waiters gather round and try to reel us in. The restaurants are largely indistinguishable so we just take pot luck.

I have had a bit of a cold for a couple of days and Brian is very tired too so we sit pretty much in silence, though it is companionable. It is a bustling place; across a rough cement path from us huge fish hang ready for the men working away cutting them up. The food is good and we are entertained by a guy with an accordion who wanders through the tables yodelling songs. It seems awfully out of tune to us but some of the family groups appear to love him. Brian looks across at me. There is an impish gleam in his eye.

'Do you think that if I tell him about the bridal suite in La Serena, he might play a tune for us?'

᠕᠕

Tongoy

Another night in Tongoy, I don't know why. There is really no reason to stay on. Some wonderful old wooden houses apparently built by ships' carpenters a century ago.

My snoring is keeping John awake. Says he would prefer the accordion player in the room. Do my best but can't stop – what can I do, cut my nose off? Even Neruda is boring me now.

≡Ⅲ≡

In the morning we head south again. The day is bright and sunny and we are both feeling much restored after a good rest. Brian, though, is still coughing badly. But his driving is more as I know it from back home. We progress in a calm and sedate manner, only bumping off the edge of the tarmac occasionally – when something to the left or right particularly draws his attention.

A winding dust road leads us to the Fray Jorge National Park. The hillsides are covered with cacti, some with brilliant red flowers. A couple of the few houses use the plants as fences – living barbed wire. Under an electricity pylon a young goatherd shelters from the fiercer power of the sun while tending his flock. The road becomes bumpy and we judder as if using one of those electronic cellulite-reducing belts that were in vogue a few years ago. Just before we reach the park, we see the heavy clouds that hang permanently over the coastal range here as if beyond them lies the promise of a strange Shangri-La after the long and dusty ride.

The rocky road steepens as we near the treeline, wheels skidding and spinning. The temperature drops and the vegetation becomes a little denser. Although there are many plants and small stunted trees, the overall effect is of grey, not green. Clouds stream in from the sea – visible at times a way off and far below.

There isn't much colour up here: one tiny purple flower and a plant with bright red blooms, the *quintral*. The colours are especially vivid against the grey of dead tree stumps and the sky. At one point as we walk through a small wood on a raised wooden pathway I am reminded of walking through pine woods in the Swiss Alps on family holidays.

It is strange driving back to the red dust of the desert lands later, the cool and damp of the park becoming a pleasant memory like the last cold beer. We stop to buy a couple of cactus fruit, prickly pears, from two little boys in the road. They do not seem sure about taking the money I proffer, but their big sister comes up and puts them right about the procedure with daft gringos. Two foxes appear brazenly on the track, presumably hanging out for leftovers. They look mangy and bedraggled.

‿∧∧‿

Road to Los Vilos

Held up today by two bandits with bushy tails!

Don Quixote paid king's ransom for a few prickly pears that grow wild in the scrubland. Pan Amer. H'way – roadside stalls selling cheese, bread and what looks like the corpses of dead lizards.

John is darting in and out of traffic like a demented roadrunner in a Disney cartoon – Me – Beep, beep – Whoosh!!!

Beaches like refugee camps. Roadside villages choked with dust. Can't raise enthusiasm for that Kerouac-esque experience.

Mad mule bolted blindly on the highway from the scrubland. Careered along a stretch of h'way oblivious of the oncoming traffic. Mule killer McCarthy roared on heedlessly!!

≡⫴≡

Entering the town of Ovalle we pass the usual shanties lining the hillsides. There are many tourist campsites on the beaches but here, inland, is an encampment of larger, gypsy tents, with a little child wandering naked among them.

The Club Commercial is about the only place open on a Sunday. There are a few families eating in the big hall where, as usual, a television is on – this time showing tennis which no one watches. We eat *lomo a lo pobre* (meat of the poor) – which, given it consists of a whacking great steak with onions, chips and fried eggs, seems a definite misnomer.

At times we wander off on sideroads, drifting through small towns, stopping to eat or have a look, then we take another chunk out of the distance left to Santiago by cruising down the Pan American Highway. I like driving the pick-up, zooming along at a good clip and taking in the sights. Getting used to the ways of Chilean traffic – the ancient little tractors and horse carts and the huge modern trucks – gives one a sense of fitting into the local scene.

The landscape varies as much as ever: areas of green and then more desert, plenty of scrub and cacti. At times the many still forms of these plants ranged over wide hillsides make me think of people waiting, expectant of some revelation.

The roads heading inland are lined with orchards, vineyards, wheat and corn fields. The snow-capped Andes and their brown lower slopes dominate the distant view while in the foreground one gets an odd vista when looking up the tunnel-like avenues between the vines. It is as if there is a green underworld of soft pastel light and then, 'above ground', sharper lines and harsh earth.

Every now and then, as we lap up the miles on the Pan American, we come across little centres of roadside marketing. Sometimes people come out from little stalls holding cheese and fruit aloft to the passing vehicles. A few miles further on and people appear from tiny wooden sentry boxes waving goat carcasses before going back inside as the last in a stream of cars passes. Further south still and the roadsides flutter with men and women in white coats and hats waving madly at the traffic, selling what look like sweet snacks. Sometimes in the middle of nowhere there is a lone shack with a guy selling watermelons.

On the hard shoulder people move in ancient carts, on motorcycles, on horseback and then there are men in smart suits and sunglasses on foot who look completely out of place.

We are more talkative and actually looking at maps and guidebooks together. I find myself lightening up and cracking a few weak jokes which Brian acknowledges with a tolerant chuckle. Although we have not talked at any length about our mutual irritations we are both aware of them. As in earlier times we have thought about them, mulled them over and I suspect that, like me, Bri has acknowledged some of my concerns while re-evaluating his. We have, in our own ways, reached a compromise. Without having to spell it out we both sense that a bridge has been crossed and the air is clear again. Mostly he dozes when I am driving – he still has a bad cough but says he is in much better shape and always does his share at the wheel. A couple of days ago I would have been secretly raging at his erratic driving but now I feel far safer with him. Whether this is because now I am happy asking him to slow down or simply because we have not hit anything, despite my elaborate wincing and wailing, I am not sure.

〰〰

Los Vilos

Chile's gold coast. Miles of white beaches. Old cars with roofs stacked with camping gear bundled up in old blankets and candy-striped sheets. Renault 4s, VW Beetles, and a ragbag of American automobiles as old as myself make up our coastal convoy.

Greenery popping up everywhere. Horses around every corner. My cough getting worse. Maybe psychosomatic.

Horseride over Andes – serious influenza – cancel Andean expedition – much relief – illness cured!

Vilu is Mapuche Indian for snake but I cannot see why Los Vilos is named after it. Many hotels named after famous seafaring characters. I recognize some names from Melville's *Moby Dick*!

☰∥☰

Los Vilos is a compact little resort full of run-down-looking café restaurants. The *feria artesanal* (craft market) has the same old tat – hats, wristbands (*pulserias*), rock and film god posters, crystals and jewellery – that we have seen everywhere. Actually most of the naff stuff probably could be found anywhere in the tourist world: Blackpool or Benidorm, Florence or Phuket.

We have a small room in a string of cabanas in the intriguingly named Hosteria Lord Willow. With its homely wooden walls and noise of happy families, it seems an ideal cheap holiday environment. There is an amazing view out across the bay where there are a few fishing boats and, far out, some rocky islets. It is lovely but very windy. Nevertheless, caught up in the seaside ambience I decide I must have my first dip in the Pacific. Brian photographs me, laughing at my timid entrance to the great ocean. It is freezing and my swim extremely brief.

∿

Viña del Mar

Road to Viña lush with market gardens, fruit fields, vineyards and flowers. Every imaginable colour is coming out of the earth. Horses again remind me I am anxious about climbing over the Andes on one of them. 8½ kilos of avocados for 1½ dollars. Don John would probably have paid 500!

Viña – capital of noise! Watched paper collector pull an enormous bundle of cardboard thro' the choked streets. His burden was balanced precariously on a tiny trolley of skateboard wheels that a horse would have had trouble pulling. Discovered mosquitoes in our hotel – sure sign we have left the desert's dry heat. I HATE THEM. Made our lives a misery in Lebanon and their droning buzz flashes me back there. I cannot bear them in my room and spend some time hunting them with bloodthirsty zeal.

≡⫴≡

Viña del Mar is really not our type of place – Oxford Circus meets Blackpool but twice as busy and ten times as hot. After some frustration parking the truck, we have a sandwich – in a balcony bar above a street blaring with people, music, car alarms, amusement arcades and honking traffic. We head early to bed in the run-down Hotel Español.

∿

Viña del Mar

Left Viña as fast as Mad Max McCarthy could negotiate the chaotic traffic. Up into the hills filled with the scent of pine and eucalyptus, wanted to eat the leaves to cure my cough. Santiago next stop.

Long, tedious, sometimes hairy trip. We are both overtired and nervy. Jack Kerouac died of extreme fatigue on the road. Must get music for the mountains and doctor for me.

≡|||≡

We have a good run down from Viña to Santiago. Brian is fulsome in his praise of my handling of the capital's crazed traffic – there are fighting armadas of buses – and likewise I am delighted with his foresight in Iquique as we finally relax in Frank and Noni's apartment.

Part Two

Santiago

•

Andes

•

Chiloé

Chapter Seven

After being on the road for a while, Frank and Noni's flat is a blessed relief. It feels luxurious to be able to loaf about in our own stationary space. There is a bedroom, bathroom, open-plan kitchen and living area. We are in a smart residential district about twenty minutes from the centre, the streets meticulously clean with wide verges and many trees. There are only one or two low buildings; the majority, like ours, are high-rise apartment blocks. We are high up so there is little traffic noise and we enjoy a cooling breeze. Our first action is inaction. We dump the bags and Brian dozes on the sofa in the living room while I flake out on one of the beds. Three hours later we awake refreshed, although it is very hot even up here.

It is hotter still in the Metro going downtown, yet most travellers, both men and women, are in suits. A small queue develops behind us as we try to work out what ticket we need. I offer a few phrases centred around the word *boleto* and the station name we are aiming for but the man in the kiosk keeps repeating something that I cannot follow. We stand aside to let the other passengers through and then try again.

'I think we can get a book of tickets,' says Brian, scrutinizing a notice in the kiosk window.

'Ah, good. What does it say?'

'*Boleto, carnet*,' he says and returns to the now deserted window. '*Dos carnet, por favor, señor!*' he requests and the man immediately hands them over in exchange for Brian's pesos.

We now approach the barrier to the platforms. Brian sticks his ticket in the slot on the post and waits for it to come out again. It doesn't.

'Now what?' he asks. 'That carnet isn't going to last long at this rate.'

'Is there another slot? Maybe it comes out on the other side.'

We both lean around the turnstile to test this theory. Nothing. I am beginning to feel very hot. It is warm down here but the press of commuters is also raising my body heat.

'Let's see what the others do.'

We garner some strange looks as we take up positions facing each other so that the passengers have to pass between us. One woman is clearly edgy when our heads follow, perhaps a little too closely, as she inserts her ticket. She hurries through to the other side as Brian exclaims, 'How simple! You don't get the ticket back, the fares must be standard wherever you go.'

We watch another couple of travellers just to make sure and then get ourselves through. We work out the platform we need and descend to it. I try to avoid those who seemed irritated with us above. The Metro is very clean but the colour scheme, of tiny white and brown tiles surrounded by walls painted orange and green, is drab. The advertisements are boring and once we have counted the number of stops we have to go, we realize that the Santiago de Chile Metro is as dull as most underground railways.

Although Brian still has not shaken off his bad cough, we are in pretty good shape and excellent spirits and for a few days we do not have to worry about where we will be staying. 'Thank God you got the key from Noni,' I say as we wait for the train. 'It'll be good going back later, having a shower and cooking a simple supper.'

'Aye! I want to get some decent rest before we head up into the mountains. At least we can have a bit of a routine for a while, after all that driving and humping bags around.'

We had heard that there was a major problem with pollution in Santiago. The mountains ringing the city prevent the wind blowing the smog away and we see clouds of noxious black smoke pumping out of the racing buses. It might be just my imagination but I feel a little breathless as we saunter around the centre. Brian snorts when I tell him this: 'Typical bloody Brit, nose stuck up wanting more air than youse need! It's all those cigarettes you're supposed to have given up!'

It may be due to the pollution but I begin to feel as I used to when I suffered badly from hay fever in my teens. Phrase book at the ready I go in search of medication. I get nowhere slowly attempting to explain *fiebre del hano* to a pharmacy assistant. I settle for Panadol.

Standing in the Plaza de La Constitución in front of La Moneda, the presidential palace, I feel rather numb. The military coup against President Allende in September 1973 had seen this squat colonial building bombed by the nation's air force. After giving a last speech over the radio, Allende had, as far as we know, shot himself. His body was put in an unmarked grave and not reburied properly until 1990. In that final address, made as the bombs rained down on La Moneda, Allende said, 'I believe in Chile and her destiny. Other men will survive this bitter and grey moment . . . sooner than you think avenues shall again be opened down which free man shall march towards a better society . . . These are my last words. I am convinced that my sacrifice shall not be in vain. I am convinced that at least it shall serve as a moral judgement on the felony, cowardice and treason that lay waste our land.'

Democracy has returned to Chile and the avenues to a better society are open again but we have discovered a very mixed response to the notion that Allende's death has served as any kind of moral judgement.

It is strange to be looking at a building that one has seen many times in news footage and photographs; planes swooping low and smoke erupting from the windows in the dying moments of democracy. The palace was restored by Pinochet in 1981 and looks impressive, even though it is dominated by higher buildings on all sides. After the coup, many thousands of leftists were killed or disappeared and I had expected to feel some powerful reaction to this place. Yet in the hot afternoon sun with people wandering about in gay summer clothes I feel a muffled sense of anti-climax.

It is as if even the buildings have understood the national ambivalence about the 'military period'; there is no monument or plaque to record what happened here. In the mid-Seventies, bad but, to some minds, necessary things occurred but now it is time to move on; better not to look closely at those years; safer to plaster over a few cracks in the nation's psyche and accept a refurbished façade for the common good. One day those who suffered at the hands of the dictatorship may be properly acknowledged and those who conducted the terror may be brought to justice. Perhaps there is something in the nation's collective subconscious that warns that emotions too long held in check might produce too violent and disturbing a reaction if the boil is lanced too soon. Going closer to the main entrance, we see the honour guard in pristine uniforms, their knee-length leather boots gleaming as they strut about. They are all young men and were probably not even born at the time of the coup, yet still they convey a sense of menace.

Back at the flat we prepare some food. Brian is slicing tomatoes.

'Ah there you are. The tomato farm is mine!'

'What?' I turn to see him peeling a small sticker off a tomato.

Grinning proudly he replaces it on his forehead. It says 'Rocky'. 'That's me, Rocky, and don't you forget it!' He does a few jabs and feints, huffing and puffing, as he used to do to vent his frustrations in Lebanon.

'Take that, you bastard!' he would mutter as he let rip with another haymaker. He always looked the part to me. With a low centre of gravity he is hard to knock off balance and has powerful shoulders, not to mention a determination to overcome, or rather a refusal to be overcome. Sometimes he forgot where he was as he did a passing imitation of Sly Stallone or Robert De Niro shadow-boxing around the small room. On one occasion, ignoring the Marquis of Queensberry, he had followed a blitzkrieg of hefty punches with a savage kick. His taunt of 'Take that, you waster' was cut off abruptly. Sadly he had used his right foot which was still chained to the floor. He tottered off balance and slumped against the wall as he caught his breath and the initial agony ran through and out of his body. 'Wise it, Brian, for God's sake!' he said to himself.

I waited a moment, concerned that he might have done some real damage but also amused by his antics. 'Are you all right?'

He turned to me, tears of pain still around his eyes but he was laughing. 'Don't!'

'Don't what, Bri?' I said, getting up.

'Just don't you, don't start, all right!'

'Start? Me?' I said, pretending to hobble, waving a fist down an imaginary road: 'Come back here, you cowards, and I'll sort you out – you just got me off balance! Just a fluke!'

After supper we lounge with coffees in front of the television. There is a big item on the news that seems to be about torture, showing a victim talking followed by officials and file footage of demonstrations and military camps. I will try to get an English language paper tomorrow and see if the story is covered there. The issue is clearly not dead; instead it is seen as worthy of prime time coverage. Perhaps with some of the contacts we have been given, we will get a better line on the general view of the Pinochet years.

After the news the weather graphics tell us that it will be hotter tomorrow with temperatures into the nineties. An early evening breeze has died so we have a fan going. A Clint Eastwood western dubbed in Spanish comes on, interrupted by commercials. Some of the stores have English names like Johnson's and Ripley's which sound odd in the middle of a fast flow of Spanish.

Many times in Beirut we sat in wilting heat, sometimes with a fan going, sometimes watching the television when suddenly an Arabic voiceover would say in English, 'Jolibon Biscuits, they're really Jolly Good.' Lighting a cigarette then, I would automatically cup my hand around it so that the fan could not steal any of the precious smoke.

Now I automatically number it as the third smoke of the day and recommit myself to giving up. The focus has moved from making the packet last to making it the last packet. Cigarettes were a useful prop then, now they are not needed. Now we can turn off the television and look at our books and make plans, not the plans of pipe dreams but those of definite action for tomorrow. Instead of just imagining the gear I might want, I can go through my bags, checking off torches, knives, hats and boots with the confidence that we are going on a trek.

Next morning, as Brian fries up eggs and bacon, we talk through our concerns about altitude sickness, his cough, and the potential stomach upsets to which I am vulnerable when travelling. These are normal worries and yet for a moment I do feel anxious. I have learned that prolonged traumatic experiences, where one is often in a state of heightened tension, may leave a hangover effect where one can confuse excitement with fear. For a time after coming back from Lebanon I experienced this, but now I quickly see that while my concerns may call for caution, they need not inspire distress. As we eat breakfast we run through another gear check.

'D'you reckon we'd be better off getting some cheap bags for the pack ponies?' I wonder.

'I was thinking the same – I don't want this bag going over a precipice on a crazy horse! Do you remember where that market was yesterday where we saw some?'

'I do. We could go there after we've picked up Tom.'

Tom Owen Edmunds, a friend and photographer, is joining us for a couple of weeks and will be coming on the big trek.

'Do you mind doing the airport run on your own? This cough is bad and I need to rest – I didn't sleep last night.'

'Is that so, Rocky? You'll definitely need a doc in that case. Snoring while awake is potentially fatal, I've heard.'

'Yeah, yeah, yeah . . . anyway Tom'll most likely want to come back here and dump his bags before doing any shopping.'

I enjoy the solo trip by Metro then bus to the airport. I like to get my bearings and feel part of the scene to a degree. I suppose this could be a way of avoiding vulnerability, by being in control and able to carry out decisions as soon as they are made. It is part of feeling at home with oneself, I would imagine, even when one is in a new environment. Certainly I enjoy greater confidence and some pride in rapidly establishing a sense of place. It is also good having our base at the flat since we do not need to make any detailed rendezvous plans.

Tom's flight from London is posted as *Arribado* almost as soon as I reach the airport, which means it is early. Soon Tom comes beaming through customs, light glinting on his spectacles as he looks expectantly around.

I have been looking forward to Tom joining us. His wife Katie Hickman and he spent a lot of time travelling around the country when her father was Britain's ambassador to Chile in the mid-Eighties, so he knows the country well and he speaks Spanish. Tom is a great photographer and what's more he is great company. I worked with him when making a television series, *Island Race*. He did the photos for the book and at various times as we made our way around the British coast he would appear, stay a couple of days and then disappear again. Tom is a wide-open person, full of mirth, positive and unselfconscious. With his Eton accent and diction and his slicked-back hair, he could be the archetype of the bright young things of the pre-war years. He is in his thirties, though with his big grin and eager expression he often appears younger. Tom has travelled a great deal more than me and I value his judgement. There is always a pleasant mix of banter and serious chat with Tom and while working on *Island Race* we became comfortable at acknowledging vulnerabilities to each other. He and Brian have met only briefly and I wonder how they will get on. As they both have a great sense of humour I am sure it will be fine.

∿∿

I was relieved to have the small apartment to myself. I really hate the heat and the smog of the city streets, and my cough was getting worse with every breath. In any case I wanted to catch up on some notes and do some reading. McCarthy was forever planning our physical route and I needed to fix my own. Neruda and O'Higgins were still ghostly outriders on our journey to the earth's end.

I was still hungover from the desert. It had created an un-resolved state of contradiction in me. Indeed at one point, probably at the height of my loathing, I momentarily thought of tossing Neruda and his poetry into the Atacama, but those last few hours spent in the Valley of the Moon had changed my mind. Loathing had been overcome by illumination. I wanted to re-establish my relationship with Neruda. Since the beginning of our travels I had felt I was getting closer to this man. The parallels between our childhoods seemed stronger now. The *Canto General*, one of the highest poetic achievements of the century, was written in the middle of the author's life and at an age similar to my own. With profound insight reminiscent of Whitman, Neruda creates a tapestry of his personal and creative life as well as of the history of South America and Chile in particular. I wanted to feel my own responses in the elaborate embroidery of his work.

If the Valley of the Moon had been something of a turning point for me, then I looked to that turning point in Neruda's poetry, the majestic *Heights of Macchu Picchu*. It is a record of the poet's ascent and conversion and also much more. I like to think that my tortuous climb along ridges up to the plateau had something in common with Neruda's arduous ascent to the ancient Inca fortress.

I had read the poem several times during our many stopovers from San Pedro and couldn't really get to grips with it. Now, in the quiet of our small apartment perched high above the clamour and heat of the streets and with my mind able to reflect on my own desert ascent, I took it up again.

I looked around our apartment. It really wasn't much bigger than some of the cells we had been held in. So here we were back in tiny rooms, making epic journeys. I thought of the hugeness of that dreadful desert and how strange it was that now I was out of it, part of me wandered back there. Part 6 of Neruda's poem roared out at me as if I was again on that desert plateau:

> And so I scaled the ladder of the earth
> amid the atrocious maze of lost jungles
> up to you, Macchu Picchu.
> High citadel of terraced stones,
> at long last the dwelling of him whom the earth
> did not conceal in its slumbering vestments.
> In you, as in two parallel lines,
> the cradle of lightning and man
> was rocked in a wind of thorns.
>
> Mother of stone, sea spray of the condors
>
> Towering reef of the human dawn . . .

a thousand years of air, months, weeks of air,
of blue wind, of iron cordillera,
like gentle hurricanes of footsteps
polishing the solitary precinct of stone.

Few times in my life have I experienced that mysterious, overwhelming release that a place can impose on the imagination.
However, Neruda was a man primed for such a response. He was
at the height of his career as a diplomat, internationally acclaimed
as a poet and loved by the Chilean masses. He was educated,
wealthy and deeply in love with his wife and companion of many
years. Earlier in the same poem he writes:

How many times in the wintry streets of a city or in
a bus or a boat at dusk, or in the deepest
loneliness, a night of revelry beneath the sound
of shadows and bells, in the very grotto of human
pleasure
I've tried to stop and seek the eternal
unfathomable lode
that I touched before on stone or in the lightning
unleashed by a kiss

I had been experiencing my own such frustration during our
travels, desperately looking for something, yet not knowing what
it was or how to find it. But, I confided to myself, 'all things come
to those who find the patience to let things happen'. My desert
experience confirmed it.

Towards the end of his magnificent poem Neruda declares, 'give
me the struggle, the iron, the volcanoes'. Many years later in his
Memoirs he confirms the importance of Macchu Picchu. He
writes, 'on those heights, among those glorious, scattered ruins, I
had found the principles of faith I needed to continue with my
poetry'. In my own high place, amid the scattered ruins of the
Valley of the Moon, I had felt very close to Neruda's affirmation,
if not his resolve. But little did I know that very soon, in another
high place, I too would be given 'the struggle, the iron, the
volcanoes'.

≡|||≡

'Brian poppet, give me a little more poetry. To me just a little bit, dear, that's right, hand just touching the grapes. Perfect. Good. Hahahaha!'

How Tom's photographs ever come out when there is so much laughter I do not know. One would think the camera shake would render everything a blur. I remembered feeling very relaxed being filmed by Tom, none of that awful self-consciousness at being targeted by a lens, but I had forgotten how much the relaxation comes from his endless banter; he teases his subjects incessantly. Brian seems to be loving it.

We are at Neruda's Santiago home, La Chascona, a wonderful house up a back street on the San Cristóbal hill behind the zoo. Neruda collected things from all over the world and installed them here and at his other houses. I am jealous of the place and keep thinking, this is my dream home. Various rooms – study, library, dining room and bar – are spread out over the hillside so that one wanders up flower- and vine-shaded paths to the next amazing chamber. Neruda died of cancer just after Pinochet's coup had ousted the Communist government he had served. The troops destroyed much of this house, leaving it a shambles; a deliberate desecration of what might have become a temple to free speech and the freedom of the spirit. The house has been restored by the Neruda Foundation but there is a display of photographs showing what the military did and these two elements of La Chascona make it a powerful witness, not only to what went wrong in Chile, but also to the ultimate value and strength of cultural freedom.

Oddly but appropriately two of the guides here are Irish: Orla from Belfast and Vanessa from Dublin. The poet's sense of fun has survived the bad years and we are filled with a spirit of cheeky joviality as we wander around. We are told that Neruda, a man known for great generosity, also had a terrible habit of admiring things in other people's houses and not letting the hosts rest until they agreed to give the object to him. Brian admires this healthy attitude to 'honest pruck'.

'I nicked an *uva* from Pablo Neruda,' he quips, stuffing his face with a fistful of grapes liberated from the poet's patio vine.

I was delighted with Orla and Vanessa, and quietly convinced myself that Pablo had arranged it just for me.

I loved the exuberance of the place. A sense of liberation and love of life penetrated every room. His home was like his poetry, full of hints of fantasy, allegory and hedonism. Neruda's presence was everywhere writ large on the house. He had built it, seemingly haphazardly without any architect's plans or permission from authority. In a sense, the house had the same structure as a poem on first reading – awkward and confused. Yet wandering through it was like wandering through his poems. Suddenly everything fell into place. A romantic avant-garde poet could not have lived anywhere else.

As much as I was reeling from the delight in being here, another part of me was deeply humbled. It was as if I had entered into a sacred tabernacle. I wanted to touch everything and sit on his seat, but I was afraid. It was as if his house was full of holy relics that had the power to curse and to bless. Briefly I wished everyone would go away. I wanted to spend the night alone in the house and sit with the old man himself. But unfortunately there are some things in life which one can only wish for.

La Chascona is built next door to a zoo. I could well understand why. Neruda's love of the natural world permeates every line he writes. I could imagine him sitting here listening to the roar of animals and the song of birds. I could imagine the transport it gave him. But the idea of caged animals could not inspire me. I had known that condition for too long. So why would the poet find inspiration in such a state? Perhaps he found in it a metaphor for his own imprisoned nation. But it was more than that. Neruda used elaborate metaphors drawn from the world of nature to break the 'sense' of his poetry from the confines of language itself. The thought reminded me that I would not find the whole Neruda in this fantastic dwelling. Neruda was in the mind, the emotion of the people and in the extremes of the landscape itself. I left La Chascona refreshed and hungry for more. I might not have met him but I knew he was there.

≡Ⅲ≡

We head downtown, Tom and Brian anxious for food, me anxious for holdalls and *botas*, to protect the calves and ankles from becoming sore while riding. The holdalls are quickly bought but the *botas* prove more difficult. We find an information point at the entrance to a large shopping mall and Tom is directed to find out about them. He says quite a lot in Spanish but does not seem to be getting through so he begins a curious high-kicking dance, pointing at his lower leg and gamely reiterating, '*Botas*, *botas!*'

Brian and I become almost hysterical though, sadly, Tom's moment of theatre does not help. We decide food might fuel a more productive search.

Attempting to order our lunch in an upstairs balcony restaurant overlooking the market area, we begin to appreciate that Tom's Spanish is rather more enthusiastic than useful. He talks with great animation to the waitress as Brian and I wait expectantly to hear what is on the bill of fare for the day. Tom rounds off the conversation with a flourish of his arms and a graceful '*Gracias*' and the woman goes to tend to another customer.

'So what's best do you think?' I ask him.

'Well, I'm sure it's all delicious!'

'Yes,' says Bri, 'but are we talking fish, steak or what?'

'Well, I did get a bit lost. My Spanish is a little rusty,' he admits as we all start laughing.

However, with the aid of the dictionary Tom soon works out what is what and orders our meal with his customary gusto.

After lunch we manage to locate a shop selling *botas* but agree that they are too expensive. By way of compensation for this lost opportunity to acquire more gear I decide to buy a spare pair of sunglasses.

'What do you think of these, Tom?' I ask, donning a pair of mean-looking wraparound shades.

'Were you thinking of effecting a complete change of image?' he wonders with more than a hint of mockery, holding up a traditional tortoiseshell pair like those I already have.

'You don't think they're me then?'

'No!'
I decide to stay tortoiseshell.

That evening we meet up with some of Tom and Katie's friends – Jorge and Eunie Lopez. He is a film producer, she a landscape designer. They suggest going to an Italian or French restaurant, explaining that Chilean food tends to be pretty plain. We have found this to a degree but have hoped that Santiago might offer something better. Perhaps Chilean cuisine is as vague a concept as Chilean national identity. Jorge and Eunie remember a possible venue in the old Bellavista district and we all pile into their station wagon to drive across town.

Tom and our hosts catch up on news of families and mutual friends, then we talk about our plans and what Bri and I have discovered so far in Chile. We talk of our confusion over attitudes to the 'military period'.

'How come there is such acceptance of what Pinochet did?' we ask.

'Well, you have to understand the Chaos that we had by '73,' says Jorge.

'Chaos, that's what you call it?'

'Yes, it was "the Chaos". The country was getting more and more out of control. People had come to think that whatever you wanted to do, the government should help. But there was no money, and the economy was in crisis.'

'And the US, Kissinger and the big companies weren't helping that,' says Brian.

'No, sure, they were doing their best to screw Allende. When Allende took over, he nationalized the copper industry and the communication networks, so some very big US companies lost a lot – and he wouldn't pay them compensation. Kissinger was shit scared of a democratic Communist state – it was his worst nightmare, especially on the same continent.'

Chile's extreme left was doing all it could, advocating the use of force if necessary, to push towards a Marxist state, while the Communist Party itself backed off from going so far and shared the right's desire for Allende to rein in the left. This he seemed unable or unwilling to do.

As we drive along, Jorge slows the car and says, 'That's a military barracks. This is a rich neighbourhood. In the Chaos, the housewives would come and jeer at the soldiers and call them chicken. People were getting hungry and angry, especially the middle classes; they looked to the military to do something.'

At the outset the junta received the support of the powerful oligarchy that had always dominated Chilean life, as well as a sizeable part of the middle class. Moderate political forces, including many Christian Democrat Party supporters, believed that the military takeover was just a necessary stage en route to restoring the status quo as it had been before 1970. Very soon, though, it became clear that the military, Pinochet in particular, had political objectives of their own: the destruction of any leftist thought and activity. Rather than being the liberators from the nightmare of the Chaos, they became what Jacobo Timerman calls in his book *Chile: Death in the South* 'an army of occupation'.

By now we have arrived at the restaurant and set about ordering food and drinks. Here in the capital, with two lifelong residents, it seems we are in the one and only place where we can be sure of gaining a true flavour of Chile. As predicted, the meal is quite plain but very good and there is a band, two musicians and two dancers, performing traditional stuff from the various regions of the country. For a brief and embarrassing moment, we join in the Quecca, a courtship dance where the woman acts out being a flustered hen bird. I am relieved when we can return to the table. I had wanted to taste the real Chile but had not expected that this would include being escorted to and from the table by indigenous equivalents of Butlins Redcoats.

At one point I notice a policeman in his khaki, military-style uniform standing by the bar, being photographed, all smiles, with some revellers. It is funny how an outsider can be so preoccupied about the history of the place he is visiting that he finds its present unexpected. My thoughts about the killing and disappearance of thousands of people and how it seems so easily to have been forgotten or forgiven, mean that I am surprised by the scene I witness at the bar.

As we leave the restaurant Jorge tells us that the newspapers and television are still full of debate on the question of bringing to justice those who had abused human rights. 'But there is still a long way to go,' he says.

'I saw in the English language newspaper, *News Review*, that President Frei has signed a Press Freedom declaration,' I say. 'Will that make a difference?'

'Maybe, yes. It still has to get through Congress. It is always the same thing: "Why go over the past and stir up trouble? Just get on with running the country and the economy." '

When we get back to Jorge's car a street person, an old man, 'helps' us out of the parking space to earn a few coins. A tall scarecrow figure with sharp, aquiline features, dressed in tatters, he wears a pristine military hat festooned with braid; the dictator manqué of the back streets.

The next day Jorge takes us to Valparaíso, stopping off at Isla Negra so we can see one of Neruda's other homes. It is very similar in feel to La Chascona, except that it is by the sea. Somehow, despite one or two lovely rooms, I feel less sympathetic to Neruda here than I did at the Santiago house. Here the curious collections and nautical themes, ships' figureheads and ships in bottles, seem to suggest that the need to possess came to obscure any genuine joy in these artefacts. My ambivalence may have something to do with our guide, a rather strange American woman who seems to know little beyond parrot-fashion guidebook stuff and has an obvious desire for a tip. I find her unreal and the mercenary attitude sits ill with the great Communist poet's generous reputation.

Jorge seems a little unhappy and I remember him saying last night that he came here and stood with the crowds outside for Neruda's funeral.

'Does thinking of those days upset you?' I ask.

'Yes, but that is not what worries me now. Many times I have asked the Neruda Foundation to let me film the place for one of my documentary series on Chile. Always they say no unless we pay a lot of money. Foreign TV producers have more money so they pay. It means that Chilean people cannot see the museums on their own television. I think the Foundation is badly run.'

The views of the sea are magnificent and it is amusing that

Neruda had a little boat on a terrace beside the house where he took cocktails on board but, being terrified of the ocean, never set sail on it. I suppose it is fine in its way, yet the image of him sitting there half-cut in his captain's hat, holding court with his circle of friends, suggests a drunken potentate who acts on his whims, careless of others. Perhaps he was acting from a sense of pure fun, or was happy to mock himself.

Brian was over the moon when he read, among the poet's other confessions, that he was a 'fabulous snorer'.

If La Chascona had hints of fantasy, allegory and hedonism about it, then Isla Negra epitomized these qualities absolutely. The house was positioned on a hill overlooking the sea. Gazing out from the main room towards the end of the garden, where Neruda had erected a ship's mast, it was easy to imagine one was standing at the helm steering this house out to sea.

His collections were everywhere and of every description. Ships in bottles, butterflies, rocks, shells, spiders and God knows what else. The whole house seems to have been devoted to these curiosities. But the surrealism of his verse really emerges when one enters a room wholly given over to a giant papier-mâché horse and several barbers' poles and other shop signs which Neruda had remembered from his childhood and later made a point of acquiring for himself. The house had the sense of a playroom about it. Even the reverse side of one of the toilet doors had several photos of coy semi-clad ladies on display, 'to entertain his male guests', the guide explained.

The living room had the same surreal air about it. Everywhere the walls were mounted with antique ships' figureheads. They looked like they were floating around the room. I loved the abandon of this house and felt that someone who had written so openly about his emotional responses and laid bare his psyche was entitled to create such a living space. Each room looked like a three-dimensional mural, and I could well understand why Neruda loved the work of Diego Rivera, the Mexican painter and muralist.

≡|||≡

Before moving on we have a drink and snacks in the restaurant. Against the background of the grey sea, pelicans swoop over the waves and we talk of art and writing. Jorge, whose natural good spirits have revived, suddenly remembers that he met the great man as a little boy.

'My mother took me to see "Tio Pablo". I remember only that he had a deep voice – oh yes, and that he wore a poncho! How strange that I had forgotten this until today; maybe it's because I am angry with the Foundation.'

Brian has picked up a brochure containing Neruda's self-portrait in words. Jorge translates it for us. It sounds good and yet, with the mix of feelings I have here, perhaps more pompous than purely honest. One phrase sticks in my head, though: 'a rust-proof heart'. I like that. A noble notion. Certainly the general adoration of Neruda nowadays makes him the nation's rust-proof heart. They seem to have jumped back to lionizing him while ignoring the intervening years that so devastated his ideals – indeed broke that heart. The accepted view appears to be that Neruda represents the real Chile: a place of poetry, freedom of spirit and international enterprise. The persecution and oppression was just an aberration, according to most. Timerman argues in *Death in the South* that this nostalgia allows people to deny the failure of the country and ignore the fact that the golden age of Chilean culture, the age of Neruda and others, was a precursor to the terror. Writing in 1987 he said that in order to understand and move beyond horror you have to dive into it, yet at that time Chile remained locked in a 'cultural blackout' where no artist was able to look beyond the banal aspects of the period of turmoil and create something profound. In an era of national tragedy, no one was writing tragedies. Perhaps this lack of emotional engagement is not so surprising given the trauma of the terror.

'Tomorrow I hope you will come to my house – I am having friends round for a barbecue. I think you will be interested in their view of these things,' says Jorge, adding, 'and they are all interested to hear about the Lebanese years.'

Suddenly, his eyes flashing from his handsome, bearded face,

Jorge speaks of his admiration for *An Evil Cradling*, becoming almost angry. 'I was really pissed off at the end. What happened after your release? You had taken us on this incredible journey and then left us high and dry.'

〜〜

I could understand exactly what Jorge meant but my book was a story about imprisonment. Life after incarceration is another story altogether. For a start, I had not been sure how to write it. After all, I had needed a few years of liberated normality before I could write the epilogue to my experience. My years in Lebanon had taught me one thing and it remains with me today: life is not a race.

'Things happen at their own pace,' I said to Jorge. 'Perhaps if you wait until we write our book about Chile, you might get some answers.'

≡Ⅲ≡

Valparaíso is a curious mix. The Navy Headquarters, where the '73 coup was given the green light, dominates the main square. You turn from its broad classical façade, see the monument to the heroes of the War of the Pacific and there, just a hundred yards away, large ships loom up beyond the low-level harbour buildings. This was a great port until the Panama Canal was opened and still there are the office blocks for the stock exchange and the big banks. The country's new parliament building is on the way out of town. A monster of a bunker, it looks more like a hideout for the powerful in times of unrest than a place where the people's representatives will plan a healthy future.

The city becomes more interesting as you rise up the steep gradients immediately behind the coastal strip. There are some monstrous 1960s blocks but also some elegantly faded colonial-style mansions. Up the steep hills the narrow streets twist and turn. The buildings are high and give the sense of a medieval hill town in Tuscany, though here the buildings are mostly con-structed of wood and corrugated iron. There are hardly any cars and there is a mysterious atmosphere. We came across the graffiti 'Muerte Romo' ('Death to Romo'). Osvaldo Romo was one of the Pinochet regime's most notorious torturers. Before the coup he was a left-wing activist in a shanty town. Then, suddenly, he switched sides and found an awful calling in destroying the minds and bodies of his former comrades. It is easy to imagine that this city would have witnessed furtive scurryings during the dictatorship: it was a place to disappear in and in which to be disappeared.

Now, though, the atmosphere feels friendly and I realize Brian is smitten too when I overhear him asking Jorge, 'So what sort of prices do you pay for apartments round here?' He turns to me: 'Wouldn't this be a great place to come during our winter and do some writing?'

Jorge had told us that the Valparaíso views are better as you get poorer. Certainly as you go up, the neighbourhoods descend towards the shanty level. High above all there is another ship of a Neruda home. I do not care that it is closed. It looks ugly and ostentatious amid the small dwellings surrounding it.

I was only partly aware of John's antipathy towards Neruda but I could not imagine a more suitable place for the poet to have built a home for himself than on this Valparaíso hillside. The whole corpus of his poetry was dedicated to the poor and oppressed of Chile. Indeed he had put his own life at risk by his poems of political condemnation. If he was self-indulgent and flamboyant, then so be it. Life was one long love story to Neruda and perhaps he did see himself as a type of Byron, a romantic hero fired with idealism. Perhaps his ship-like house pushing out of this hamlet of poverty was inspiring and gave the people who lived in the shanty town surrounding it something to dream about . . . or maybe it's me, maybe I'm the dreamer!

But Valparaíso had that effect on me. The name itself carries a hint of mystery and romance, like the name 'Scheherazade' or the music of Ravel's Bolero. I loved winding my way endlessly up and down the maze of street stairways and back alleys. They were everywhere, making a warren of the place, and each one ended in or opened out on to a different picture, a minute cameo of life and landscape. I felt I was walking through a picture book.

Neruda sometimes described his fellow Chileans as having about them 'the melancholy of a pain-haunted people' but I thought it was only a poet's fancy. In these side streets and open-air staircases you sensed life was teeming and that there was a story in every worn step.

I still remember the smells of coffee, black pepper, ripe tomatoes and cinnamon mixed with the aroma of old, stale wine and tobacco. It was an irresistible perfumery of human tales waiting to be told. Like the one of Gauguin's Peruvian grandmother who lived here for a while. What a tale she had to tell. And then there was Ben Gunn, the character in *Treasure Island* who first landed here after his long sojourn on the Juan Fernandez Islands. How well I remember that name! It was the first thing that McCarthy said to me in that Lebanese hell-hole.

But the harbour of Valparaíso must have as many stories salted into its stonework. It was the home port to those fabulous whaling vessels that hunted Leviathan and spawned such masterpieces as *Moby Dick*. From this harbour much of the wealth of South America was shipped. In return it received vessels laden with the treasures and spices of the Orient.

A statue of Arturo Prat, hero of the Chilean Navy, surveyed it all. From under his statue I look up on to those fragrant wooded hills. The shanty houses blur into a pastiche of colour, yellows and reds, cobalt and purple. The washing lines strung across the stair-ways and hung from balconies echo the ships' flags fluttering in the harbour.

This is a city of the muses. For poets, painters and composers. This is the artists' enclave. This is Venice and Florence waiting to be discovered. This is a dream city waiting to be explored, and I dream it still.

Jorge and Eunie have a great house in a shady street just ten minutes' drive from our apartment. It is quite a party with their children Martin, Santiago, Domingo and Maria Jesus, and other relations and friends there. As we enjoy the food and wine the conversation wanders between mountains and what they do to us, the mountains we find to climb in ourselves, and past terror and present forgetting.

One of the other guests, Rodrigo Jordan Fuchs, led the Chilean expedition that scaled the Himalayan monster K2 in 1996. Jorge has produced a film of this successful adventure. Rodrigo is delighted that we are going to get a taste of the mountains, albeit the lazy way, on horseback. Forever concerned about gear, I ask his opinion on our lack of *botas*: would it be a problem? Rodrigo has a very pleasant face with a big grin and, for a hardened mountaineer, a surprisingly light build. He, who has overcome the logistics of mounting a massive expedition into the wilds of Jammu and Kashmir, manages not to laugh at my curious obsession and gravely advises that, in all probability, it is not a great cause for concern.

As often on this trip we are fortunate that so many people speak good English. It gives us a chance to ask some of the many questions that have occurred to us as we have travelled. In captivity, when we so rarely had any sources of information, we often had to live in a land of accepted supposition. Whether this concerned our immediate predicament and Middle East politics or the development of the internal combustion engine, we sometimes just tried a good guess and carried on with our discussion of the topic on that basis. I always liked having access to reference books and now I feel at a loss without them.

Easily available research sources do not, of course, ensure an understanding of the world in which we live. *News Review* has been covering the current debate over Pinochet's retiring as commander-in-chief of the army and, as a former President, taking up a position as Senator for Life. Thanks to his own 1980 constitution, the senate already has guaranteed places for leading military figures. It seems astonishing that this old man, after the crimes of his regime have been made public through a national commission, can still have access to such power. Before that, in 1978, after five years of torturing, killing and 'disappearing' thousands of people, many innocent of even the mildest political thought, he instigated an amnesty law that absolved him and his henchmen from any charges of human rights abuse. Given that Pinochet is now old and that democracy has apparently returned strongly, it is extraordinary to an outsider that such laws are not overthrown and justice sought to heal the nation's wounds.

'You remember what I was saying about the Chaos?' Jorge asks. 'Well, many people still believe, as you have found in your travels, that Pinochet saved the country. For many he is a hero.'

'President Frei says he will not tolerate any interference with the march to full democracy,' I quote from an article I have been reading. 'So, if even the President thinks things need to be done, why can't his government just change the appropriate laws?'

'Well, on top of many people supporting Pinochet there is still the power of the military,' picks up another guest, a journalist. 'Many still worry that if we push too far too soon they will take power again. It is difficult, they weren't beaten in a fight. They had their time, then handed back to civilians after Pinochet lost a plebiscite.'

'But still, the torture and killing of thousands of people isn't seen as having been necessary, surely? Whatever the rights and wrongs of the initial coup, the subsequent abuses can't just be forgiven.'

'No, not by many. You see the debate in the papers and people keep working to get justice. But,' continues Jorge with a shrug, 'many who don't care for one side or the other often just don't want to remember. I have a friend. In 1974 he was walking in Santiago, beside the Mapocho river with his father. They looked down from one bridge and saw many bodies – all victims of the regime. Just rubbish thrown away. Both men were profoundly shaken, terrified of what was happening on their doorstep. Recently they were talking about the need for justice and the old man said that things were exaggerated, that they hadn't been as bad as all that. When his son reminded him of the walk by the river and the bodies he just said, "I do not remember that walk." Some minds, you see, become closed. Too difficult to deal with the horror and the guilt.'

'So you just have to wait until Pinochet and his cronies die off?'

'Maybe it will come to that,' agrees the journalist. 'When they aren't there to be tried, we can safely find them guilty.'

The talk turns again to mountaineering. Rodrigo tells us that they found many parts from the bodies of previous climbers who had fallen down ravines and then been torn apart by the ice.

〞〵〵

Rodrigo explained how a particular Japanese climbing team had simply left an injured climber to his fate – a lonely death on a snow-swept mountain. My admiration for the stoic samurai mentality quickly evaporated. I could not understand how the conquering of a mountain was more important than the life of a companion. Could such resolve obliterate the ghosts which would surely come to haunt the climbers in later life? Suicide and even sacrifice were comprehensible in some way but this act did not sit comfortably with me.

When Rodrigo told the story of having found the body of another climber who had been missing for some years, my interest revived. On occasions when the spring melt or an avalanche reveals a body, they ascertain the identity and leave a simple marker at the spot, so that other climbers may acknowledge the mountaineer in whatever way they see fit, perhaps passing in silence or saying a prayer. But they never inform the families of the bereaved. Rodrigo thought it was easier to live with the knowledge that those missing had been lost in the snow. Most of the bodies were beyond retrieval, and in any case it was rare to find a complete corpse. When he described finding the head of a climber with his face frozen in a grimace that was half smile and half scream, I could understand the rationale behind the tradition.

Later that night, as I tried to sleep, I remembered the frozen head in the snow and thought of the shock of that moment in our cell when I caught sight of my head and face reflected in the surface of a spoon, the first time I had seen myself in months.

≡Ⅲ≡

Although the expedition was ultimately successful, Rodrigo tells us of the appalling strain that came after four of his colleagues had finally triumphed and become the first Chileans on the summit of K2.

'We were all so happy, though worried that they make a good

descent. Then Cristián called on the radio to say that Miguel had just sat down and did not want to walk any more. We all knew that to stop there was to die – but with the exhaustion, dehydration and limited oxygen, Miguel had lost his focus. The other two were ahead of them but no one knew where exactly. Somehow Cristián had to find the oxygen Miguel had dropped, make him drink some water and get him back on his feet.'

'God!' I say. 'Trying to get through to someone who can understand what you are saying but no longer wants to see reason, that's tough.'

'Yes, I was shaking, but knew I had to appear calm. I was three thousand metres lower than these men and quite safe, but I had to ask Cristián to risk his life to go back and help his partner. I knew I might be signing his death warrant.'

This talk of getting to the very top of the world only to reach the depths of one's experience brings back sharply my own dark climbs. I recall how, in an underground prison in Beirut, Bri and I had to deal with our American fellows, Tom Sutherland and Frank Reed, when they were so depressed they thought they were about to be killed or, in Tom's case once, he had wanted to kill himself. They were alone in cells across a wide hall from ours. We could communicate only through hand signals, words spelled out using a cod deaf and dumb alphabet.

'My heart was breaking for them,' I say, 'but also I was angry with them. Their vulnerability was ours too.'

Rodrigo nods as I go on: 'I felt desperate and impotent. I was using the most obvious emotional blackmail to keep them going: "What about your wife, your children?" I felt sort of cheap waving my hand about saying things like that. Somehow I was demeaning them and their decisions.'

'What happened?' asks Rodrigo.

'They got through it. They hung on.'

Rodrigo nods again then his face breaks out in a big grin. He indicates Jorge. 'He gave me *An Evil Cradling* when we left Chile for the K2 expedition. I started it on a plane but stopped then passed it on to another in the team. He gave it back a couple of days later saying, "This is remarkable, but it is too depressing with the pressures we are facing now."'

Chapter Eight

≡ ||| ≡

'Holy fuck!' I hear myself murmuring through fiercely popping ears. 'We've got seven days up here!'

Our convoy climbs steeply up winding valleys. I have to sink low in my seat to be able to see the sky. We are very high already; there is still a long way to go. Brian, Tom and I had been getting slightly anxious about the seven days in the saddle given our extreme lack of experience with horses. Altitude sickness was also a concern, especially with Bri unable to shake off his cough. Some of our fears were allayed last night when we met up with our fellow trekkers. As well as we three there are Lian and Carmella (Mellie) who have known each other for ages and work in the City, and Marcus who has his own pottery design business. The man in charge is Nigel. We were hugely relieved that Mellie and Marcus had not ridden before. Tom revealed that while he had ridden in Bhutan, he had never mastered horse management as the beasts there grazed on cannabis plants and were pretty much a law unto themselves. Lian is an experienced horsewoman but not on the sort of terrain we are facing and has expressed an encouraging lack of confidence. Nigel is small, softly spoken and very laid back. I had dreaded that we might be locked into a week with ghastly macho egos but as we ate dinner last night the fact that, bar Nigel, we were all likely to disgrace ourselves, as Tom put it, by being 'a load of Wendies' was a great reassurance.

This commonality of inadequacy does little now to assuage my concerns about our first ride. Nigel said we might find traversing the initial wide scree 'a little hairy at first'. He seemed vague about the extent of this scree, how high we would be above the river at its foot, or how narrow the path was. He kept reassuring us, saying, 'The horses know the way well.'

Some wine and pisco sours gave us a little Dutch courage when Nigel brought out a sheaf of papers; they were disclaimer forms. 'Just a formality!' he laughed as we read the clauses that would surrender any right of redress should some disaster strike. We all tried to be casual, but there was a slight hesitation until one of us put pen to paper and then the others followed suit.

Naturally we all turned to Nigel as the wise one and asked, with nervous laughter, if he had ever taken such an inexperienced group before. What would happen if one of us had an accident or lost our nerve and couldn't go on?

'I don't think I've ever led a group quite like this before but of course . . .' his words deteriorated into a mumble, '. . . the time with the Colombian woman.'

'What's that?' we all demanded.

'Oh! Nothing really, just on one of the treks a Colombian woman developed such bad vertigo that she couldn't continue.'

'And? Is she still up there?'

'Oh no, no! It all worked out fine. In the end.'

We were just getting to know each other, so there was still a certain diffidence in the group. Eyes flicked from face to face with questioning looks. Those who knew each other already exchanged glances, hoping for some clarification. None was forthcoming. Marcus, with NHS black plastic spectacles perched on an aquiline nose beneath unruly black hair, had a straightforward, boyish openness about him, and had the advantage of knowing Nigel already. It was good he was there to take the initiative and ask the question that hung over our table like the close heat before a thunderstorm.

'Nigel! What the fuck happened?'

'Well, I had a word with her husband and he agreed that he'd put the bag over her head and then we'd both tie her across the back of one of the mules.'

'You tied her up and blindfolded her?' I asked, amazed.

'It was the only way to get her down.'

We mulled over this stark logic in stunned silence, then watched with something akin to horror as Nigel tidied and put away our signed disclaimer forms.

'You'll love it!' he said enthusiastically.

Last night's talk of bonds, blindfolds and forced, uncomfortable journeys had evoked memories of Lebanon but I am aware of a certain sense of déjà vu again today. Initially I cannot understand why, then realize that I am conscious of a feeling of tension in our motorized convoy as we approach our base camp. There has been much talk over walkie-talkies and fairly fast driving. I am travelling with Brian and Lian in a jeep. Earlier someone cut in between us and the vehicle carrying Nigel and Marcus. Our driver swerved around this interloper and cut back in and slapped on his brakes, virtually stopping the offending car on the curb. At first I thought this was just a bit of macho driving but then I remembered another of Nigel's pieces of information casually imparted over dinner. His Chilean business partner is married to a bank and newspaper proprietor. Some time ago one of their children was kidnapped and held for ransom. Although Nigel assured us that such threats were now considered a thing of the past, this style of driving was likely forged out of necessity.

I am aware that I am experiencing what I call 'remembered fear'; when a situation reminds you of something, a bad time, and you have a similar level of reaction: not exactly a flashback as you are still very conscious of the present, but the current experience is overlaid and informed by the past. I look across at Brian. 'Relaxed?' I ask.

He looks back through narrowed eyes and shrugs, then coughs and says, 'I'm more worried about my lungs. How much higher? By the time I get on a horse's back my head'll be scraping the sky.'

Far below are the brown waters of a river. The power of the floods here must be phenomenal; I see the remains of bridges that look like twisted little pieces of Meccano and vast moraines of soil and rock that appear to have been dumped by a colossal JCB. Nature can be intimidating. But then these mountains are not conscious of us. We are more like a bird on a rhino's back or picking at the alligator's teeth, just passing through, and irrelevant. I realize that my heightened nervous state comes from many factors – the curious reminder of kidnap is just one of a number of impulses. As we thread a dusty road ever higher I find the tension giving way to straightforward excitement. We are choosing to do this; there is no Jihad here.

At last we arrive at a camp. Don Ramon, an elderly man with white hair and a deeply etched and sunburned face, oversees the activity though he is not coming on the trek. Horses and mules are standing around. An old dog lies in the shade of a rock. We watch as the *huasos* load boxes on to the mules. Mauricio, the head *huaso*, is every inch the dashing horseman, lean and good-looking with a wide-brimmed sombrero at a rakish angle on his head. Cristián, who works the mules with Mauricio, is a chubby man with a gentle smile. Manuel is the expedition cook. It is clear immediately that his two colleagues enjoy teasing him. The loading is quite a performance. Each, very heavy load is carefully selected for balance before Mauricio and Cristián wrestle it up on to the mules' backs. There are many adjustments as the ropes are tightened. The beasts stay more or less still throughout the operation as one *huaso* holds a blindfold over their eyes.

Suddenly I feel at a loss, completely useless in this strange environment. There is a pounding in my chest that is not due to the altitude but to a serious bout of pre-match nerves. Out of the jeep one feels so much more exposed, and once on horseback I am sure I will feel even less in control. I pack and then repack my saddle bags.

Eventually they are ready to organize our mounts. I am not a judge, good or bad, of horseflesh. The only concern I can communicate to Mauricio is that I would like the animal to be *tranquilo*. He introduces me to a handsome, piebald creature with a brown coat and white patches on his legs and mane. I do not quite catch the name and am immediately preoccupied with adjusting the stirrups. It feels very odd up on the beast's back but I am relieved to find the saddle – the large western style, not the tiny English variety – covered in thick sheepskin. Once comfortable I feel ready to go for a spin. With my mind on John Wayne I move the reins, cluck my tongue and kick my heels and – amazing to relate – we move. I head towards Brian who is experimenting on his mount a little way off.

'Howdy, Pardn— aagh!'

My would-be casual greeting is rudely interrupted as my horse abruptly puts his head down to graze. My head and shoulders are jerked forward, my hands still gripping the reins. I lose the debonair attitude I had hoped to foster. Brian's horse backs away and he pulls on the reins.

'Whoa there, Milly, damn ya!'

'Milly? Milly?' I laugh, remembering, 'I thought it was meant to be Billy.'

Milly seems less threatening. My horse keeps its head down and goes on munching regardless of how much I yank on the reins.

'So what's your beast called, John?'

'I didn't catch its name.' A shouted conversation with Nigel and Mauricio elicits the information – Charlatán.

'It can't be,' I say, 'that doesn't sound too good!'

'Serves you right, I'd say. Charlatán, an impostor or quack! That Mauricio has got your number all right!'

Mauricio may have, but I am more concerned that the horse will too. Why would anyone give the creature such a name? What characteristics had the little foal shown that had made Don Ramon, Mauricio or whoever think that this one was going to be devious? More importantly, had the name proved suitable? Or, if not, had he decided that if everyone called him a charlatan then that was what he would be? Most importantly of all, why had they not given the nag to Bri? It would have been far more appropriate.

After some more backing and shunting, Charlatán becomes vaguely manageable. With guidance from Nigel, who, in a black wide-brimmed hat, battered old army jacket and very well worn, full-length leather chaps, looks entirely in his element, I join the line-up for a team photograph.

For the first hour or so we follow a narrow, tortuous trail. A river, the Colorado, flows in a muddy torrent far below us. Initially it seems terribly easy. The horses plod along as we relax in the western saddles with their reassuring pommels to cling to. Wearing his big boots and straw hat Brian looks every inch the explorer or prospector from a hundred years ago. He shouts, 'Butch Cassidy and the Sundance Kid, eat your hearts out!'

I am about to return an acknowledgement when my horse stops dead. I click my tongue and dig in my heels to no avail. Though not in any immediate danger, I am frightened, acutely aware that I have no idea of how to manage the creature. It feels as if I have woken from a deep sleep and found myself alone at the controls of a helicopter. Lian comes up behind me and kindly gives Charlatán a gentle tap on the haunches. He moves on.

For a while I just sit there, leaning back when the track goes downhill and forward when it goes up. Although I am doing nothing, the horse demands all my attention. Occasionally I risk a quick peek at the scenery, rocks of many hues, scrub, dust and occasional little valleys of green. There are moments when I am gripped by cold fear as the path narrows and I glance to my left or right and realize that there is nothing there, just a void extending maybe five hundred feet to the swirling river below. Just as unnerving is the steep rise above us. The scrubby scree seems to go up for ever, looking oppressively unstable. Although conscious of the others ahead and behind me, I am so preoccupied with Charlatán that I can give them little thought. Once or twice I think of trying to move up the line to see how Bri is doing but the narrowness of the path keeps me in my place.

On and on we ride, sometimes through rocky outcrops with stirrups clanging against the boulders. Remembering the way my mother admired the sheriff in the television series *Cimarron Strip*, I sit more upright, one hand on hip, the other holding the reins. I begin to feel more comfortable in the saddle, though my backside is soon tender.

When we stop to make camp, Tom, Brian and I walk down to the chalky stream to rinse the dust from our hands and faces. Although pleased to have overcome the first hurdle, we are not very talkative. Certainly the terrain was more frightening than I had expected and sitting on Charlatán was harder work than I had imagined. My body is stiff and aching and I picture a hot bath but, of course, there will be none of that for a week. The river water is freezing, apart from being laden with silt, so we content ourselves with a minimal splash.

⋀⋀

My cough had left the back of my throat like a rusty file. Foolishly, while John attempted to wash the dust off his face, I cupped my hands and swallowed long draughts of the cooling water. It was a mistake for which I paid later in the evening.

≡Ⅲ≡

The campsite is called Los Azules, the Blues, not that I can see anything very blue about it, the dominant colour being yellow, from the sulphur deposits that have created small terraces and pools a couple of hundred feet above us. The camp is a wide area of scattered stones and rocks with one large block in the centre which provides shelter for the fire.

We work out how to erect our little dome tent. Brian starts coughing.

'That still sounds bad. How are you doing?' I ask him.

'Not so bad, concentrating on the horse took my mind off it. I've got that medicine but it's not been as effective as I'd hoped. I'll get my head down for a bit once we've got this thing up.'

Given his cough and our shared fear of altitude sickness, neither of us has brought any cigarettes but I am relieved to find that Marcus has a stash. We sit around the fire Manuel is making from wood and dung, and have a cup of tea. The smoker's mentality is still strong in me so, after arduous exertion and feeling at one with nature, it is hard not to think of smoking as essential to the enjoyment of the moment.

'Marcus, I won't make a habit of it, but could you spare a fag?'

Grinning from beneath the brim of his very battered hat he hands me a packet. 'As you've given up, you ought to be able to make these last!'

What a very kind man. Like Nigel, Marcus seems to have travelled a great deal and often in difficult circumstances. Neither looks particularly rugged but I am sure that if the going gets tough, steely resilience will emerge from their quiet and shy demeanours. At least I hope so.

All around the mountains rise sheer to jagged peaks, only the highest still bathed in the evening sun. Though severe, there is a gentleness about them: as if they are the gnarled fingers of a giant's hand carefully cupping the pale blue sky and the white half moon.

As the light fades the deep blues, reds and purples of the high sky go grey. Strangely the rocks and vegetation seem more vivid and varied at dusk, out of the glare of the sun.

However much we are directly coping with the rigours of riding, we are certainly pampered in camp. Manuel has prepared a feast of chicken, salad and baked spuds and there is red wine too. Now I realize why there was so much to load on to the mules.

During supper there is talk of travels in other exotic places, Africa and Asia as well as South America. We are still getting to know each other but there is already a relaxed banter between us. Tom and I bicker about the relative merits of our multi-pocketed waistcoats but agree to share a pair of short chaps, not the fancy leather *botas* I had wanted but a pair of less glamorous canvas mountaineering gaiters, happily realizing that we will both appear ridiculous. Brian is quiet but not really subdued. Still under the weather, he chuckles often as he looks into the glow of the camp fire, a bright green 'Ireland' woolly hat perched on his head. Every now and then this gnomic, almost luminous head bobs back and forth as a joke, enjoyed too much, causes a fit of coughing.

I was unable to eat much of the meal. I was feeling desperately sick and stomped off into the darkness before the main course was served. I had wanted to throw up but couldn't at first understand why. Nigel had casually warned us not to drink from the river this far down. It was full of chemical sediments that our systems would not be used to, although the horses and the *huasos* could manage if they had to. I felt foolish as I stood behind a great boulder and offered back to Patcha Mama the little I had eaten, plus the river I had drunk. I retired to my tent from where I echoed the camp-fire laughter with my cracked coughing. I was feeling lonely and idiotic and embarrassingly pathetic. Before he retired, I saw John's pencil-like torch pierce the dark canvas enclosure.

'Can I get you anything, mate?' he asked solicitously.

'Some neck oil and a reconditioned stomach might help . . . No, not really, a good night's sleep might do the trick.'

In the darkness I heard John's voice again. 'Here, take this. It's the best we can do.'

I fumbled in the dark, finally locating John's proffered cup of herbal tea and a couple of aspirin.

The next morning I dressed and wandered over to the camp fire trying to look healthy. Our cook prepared a special brew made from some local herb, for which one of the *huasos* had spent the early hours of the morning scouring the hills. I was more grateful for the sympathy than the peculiarly flavoured tea.

≡Ⅲ≡

It was cold last night but at eight this morning, even though the sun has yet to penetrate the valley, the air is not too cool. Manuel dishes out a breakfast of toast, scrambled egg and melon. Under any circumstances this is a good way of starting the day but here it seems positively ideal. It has been a very long time since I did any camping and it was never anything like this. But the sense of being out in the open, having an adventure, has always inspired a whole raft of fantasies which are now coming to a sudden and perfect realization in the relaxed intimacy of this small camp in the midst of the brightening vastness of the mountains.

On the trail again, there are terrifying moments when the thin mountain air seems to stick to the back of your throat, as once more the reality of height and the unfamiliarity of being on horse-back touches you and vulnerability is all.

Moving from one valley to another, we find ourselves on a knife-edge ridge. Suddenly the land falls away for hundreds of feet on either side and one is hemmed in in front and behind by a line of horses and their nervous riders. You have to go on but you feel that every wild heartbeat will unsteady the horse's feet and send it, and you, sliding down the shale to the torrent below.

'Concentrate on the horse, fool!' I say to myself. Charlatán seems keen to show he was well named. I am following Tom on his imaginatively named black nag, Negra. Looking ahead it is difficult to believe a goat would feel safe, let alone a laden horse. Glancing down is horrendous in the extreme. Brian is coming up behind me on Milly. I want to tell him to back off and slow down, but realize that behind him is Marcus, then Lian, then Manuel, all relentlessly moving along the crag. I am frightened: almost to that crazy point where you want to jump. Here there is no remembrance of *Dharma Bums*; here it would not be impossible to fall off the mountain.

'Negra! Now don't be silly, dear!' I hear Tom crooning.

I see him disappearing round a pinnacle of rock as the path narrows to no more than a foot wide. I reach the spot. The path, such as it is, is so obvious I almost relax, then crazy Charlatán turns off and slithers a few feet directly downhill. 'No, fuck you!' I hiss, dragging his head back to the path. He comes round and we follow Tom. It is all over in twenty minutes but the experience will be there for life.

Pausing to gather our breath and share the terrors of what we immediately dub 'Death Ridge', we look across a wide plain to our campsite for the next two nights. The equilibrium restored by the prospect of a gentle trot over easy terrain is enhanced when we look up and see a pair of condors circling high, high above us. Having neither the appropriate tobacco nor a pipe, I enjoy the moment smoking one of Marcus's cigarettes with one leg hooked over the pommel of my saddle.

The feeling of limitless well-being is shaken slightly when we break into a canter to reach the camp. I find myself bouncing chronically near the point of no return on Charlatán's back. Grabbing hold of the pommel, I feel a stinging sensation as its metal rim cuts a finger before the horse slows and I regain my balance. Mellie is not so lucky. She comes unstuck. Looking remarkably graceful in a wide-brimmed *huaso*'s hat and jodhpurs, she somersaults perfectly off her mount. Nigel and Lian are there immediately. Amazingly, without any hesitation, she gets back into the saddle. As we ride on, more slowly now, we talk:

'When Lian spoke to me about coming on this trek, I realized I'd better have a couple of lessons. Seems mad now – I was taught by a woman who was a stickler for the niceties of riding. There I was riding around learning dressage in Hyde Park! Not very useful up here, but the hat was a good investment, I think.'

'Certainly was, this sun is intense. I'm impressed that you just got straight back on like that.'

'Well, I'm not too worried about the physical injuries, but I can get depression at high altitude.'

'Blimey, we're not going to have to tie you over a mule, are we?'

'No, the depression seems to focus my mind on survival, makes me a bit selfish.'

'Really?'

'Yes, I sometimes steal other people's food.'

I have not quite got the measure of Mellie yet. Working in the City she has to deal with a heavily male environment and is clearly well used to banter. I cannot quite decide whether she is winding me up but realize that I do not mind if she is.

I am sitting in one of the most perfectly empty spaces I have ever seen. A flat-bottomed valley, so wide it is almost a plain. A mile away to the west, rocky outcrops jut from a swathe of brown scree, suggesting human faces. This natural carving, far more eloquent than any Mount Rushmore, could be recalling the wisdom of something profoundly ancient. The valley is called El Museo, the Museum, so perhaps the shepherds and travellers in older times felt the same sense of antiquity that I am now experiencing. To the south the valley curves away upwards, losing its grassy cover and becoming a barren blur with the snow-capped tips of mountains in the very far distance. Sometimes a cloud moves over the valley casting its shadow, almost like the thought of a god. The air is cool in the breeze, though the sun is fierce.

There are horses grazing in all directions but beyond our party there is no sign whatsoever of humans. Brian lies a little way from me on dark green grass beside a narrow, very deep, clear and fast-running stream. Apart from the sounds of the *huasos* making camp, brought to me on the gentle breeze that occasionally sets my hat strings singing in my ears, the babbling and gurgling of this brook is the only sound.

The Museum was almost circular like a bowl and I thought I had arrived in our Elysian Fields. I watched several swallows skim along the surface of the deep narrow stream. They were feeding off tiny surface insects and their precision aviation was incredible. The river had its source not far from our encampment. The term 'water from the rock' was never more true as I took in the towering fortress of stone that enclosed us.

Reaching places like this makes the trauma of five or six hours in the saddle bearable. It is energy-sapping being on the edge of panic all the time and not knowing what hazards wait round the next bend. We climbed higher by the hour, along ridges so narrow you could measure them with a school ruler. Sometimes it felt as if the horses' hooves were treading across chasms of air! During the morning we crossed a terrifying pass. The thought of having to go back over 'Certain Death Ridge' frightened me. I comforted myself by remembering my equine friend from San Pedro. But the silence and sunlight were wonderfully calming. I lay back on the warm river bank and felt like I was sinking into the folds of a great soft eiderdown. I imagined I could smell my wife's perfume. My contentment in the valley was gnawed at by the desire for familiar things.

I wrote a note in my diary:

> I had found so many things in so little,
> in my own twilight discoveries,
> in the sighs of love, in roots,
> that I was the displaced one, the wanderer
> the poor proprietor of my own skeleton.

I reread the quote and underneath it, almost tearing the page with the weight of my words, added: 'WHAT THE FRIGG ARE YOU TRYING TO PROVE?!'

Some of us take an afternoon ride to see the valley of the Azufre, the Sulphur river. We pass through high pastures where they bring cattle and horses to calve and foal then drop down to a raging river which, after much kicking, Charlatán condescends to cross. Bizarrely the Azufre is a spectacular gorge of bare red rock, looking as if it has just been ripped out by a flood. All around are different angles and colours of strata and above everything sits a glacier.

Riding back I am happy and tired, pleased to have made the effort of the extra ride even though my legs feel only partially under control. The longer I sit on the horse the more natural it feels. Charlatán is tired too and keeps stumbling. Though we are spread out and rarely speaking, there is a peaceful camaraderie in the line of riders. The warmth of the evening sun as it lights the dust around the horses' hooves and constantly rearranges the mountainscapes as it goes down, reaches deep inside me. Cantering back across the valley to our igloo tents that look like a nomad encampment, I feel so lucky.

Beside the camp fire Manuel recites his poems by moonlight. Nigel translates for us gringos: verses on a lover, a drunkard and a journalist. Later we look at the craters of the moon through my telescope. Although the brightness of the moon blanks out many of the stars we learn to identify the Southern Cross.

The moonshine is reflected in the stream running through the camp. Its deep water, icy cold even at the height of noon, and its green grassy banks speak of a real life force. It springs from the base of the barren, five-hundred-foot scree just near the camp. There are strange plants growing in the water, long, bushy and thick. The effect is not sombre but caring, a widow's weeds perhaps.

I enjoyed the poetry reading Manuel entertained us with. The poems were romantic and wistful but Manuel, at least, took his poetry seriously and made me feel less guilty about my own obsession with Neruda.

I wasn't much company for anyone. My cough seemed to get worse in the evenings and now sounded like a piece of heavy-duty broadloom being torn apart. I thought maybe I could give some camp-fire recitals from Neruda, but then I suspected they would think me a weirdo rather than just an invalid.

Darkness fell very quickly, almost like a light going out. The cold came with it. I deeply regretted having sent home my warm jacket and woollen sweaters. Sometimes I curse the place I am in and cannot leave.

Frustration and fear seem to be the two constant emotions of this trek. Sometimes if the ride is particularly difficult or dangerous, I ignore them or accept the challenge of them with a torrent of abuse aimed at no one other than myself. I am sure the others think I am demented, and no doubt McCarthy encourages them in this belief.

But lately I have been trying to use these emotions. I am treading in the footsteps of my invisible companions, Neruda and O'Higgins. They too had to make this Andes journey. Outlawed and outcast, the liberators fled through these forbidding mountains on horseback: the Poet, liberator of the soul, and the General, liberator of the people, had both suffered from the most heinous of crimes, betrayal. O'Higgins had had to escape with a few followers over these mountains to Argentina after a defeat by the imperial forces at Rancagua in 1814. Similarly Neruda, after helping Gabriel Gonsález Videla win the 1946 presidential election, fell out with the new head of state and had to flee. The physical scale of the deserts in the north, of the ice and glaciers to the south and the ocean to the west, all such vital parts of Chile's identity, must enforce the sense of cruel finality for the exile.

Over the last few days I had been thinking about this: exile, the experience of betrayal, taking refuge in these mountains. Overcoming that experience in life and in art is what binds these Chilean heroes in my imagination. I could envisage their confrontation with constant fear and frustration in these hills. I had scribbled a note describing how the jagged edges of the mountains set against the evening crimson sky gave the impression of stone carnations, and beside it I had added: 'Red carnations, Neruda's symbol for betrayal of the nation – Bernardo's first bloody defeat, betrayed by comrades!'

My constant dipping into the *Canto General* as a kind of hymn sheet when I was feeling depressed, lonely or bored had given me the sense that the foundation of this mammoth work was one of betrayal. It sets the mood and the tempo of the text which is one of passionate outrage and the belief in promise and restoration.

But the betrayal of those men was not original sin. It was an evil act committed by men against their friends, comrades and ultimately the nation. And this act of betrayal enables a second beginning for both the politician and the poet.

Betrayal had engendered a fault-line in Chilean history and also in the value of words, the shared language of the nation and the promises that words had enshrined. Rupture and restoration necessarily became fundamental political and poetic acts. The recommitment by word and deed is a reconstitution of the bond of faith with the nation and possibly with the souls of men.

I had been developing this thesis on the more tedious rides or in the cold of the night to distract myself from coughing, snoring and generally making it impossible for John to sleep. In a way, it helped me focus on the journey itself as well as on my invisible companions and it also helped me displace the worry about my worsening health as we moved further into the mountains. I was anxious in case the combination of my chest infection and the altitude sickness brought me to a point where I could not carry on, and would have to turn back with one of the *huasos*.

But my contemplation on the poet and the politician and their journey in these hills had decided it for me. I had no choice. To turn back would be an act of betrayal. It would mean breaking the promise of friendship with McCarthy. It would be a surrendering of communication and understanding with Pablo and Bernardo and finally it would mean an irreparable break with my own instincts.

The following morning was cold but bright. We stood about the campsite with blankets wrapped round us and hoods covering our ears. We looked like ancient druids. John poured me a cup of Lapsang Souchong tea for my cough. I remember it had all the aroma and flavour of Sobranie cigarettes.

Meanwhile the *huasos* had gone looking for our horses, mainly successfully, although one small black mule refused absolutely to be caught and had our muleteers chasing him for hours. I had some empathy for the irascible black beast.

When we finally decamped and began our climb, I noticed that the trail was littered with the bodies of cattle which had died from eating poisonous grass. Seeing the way the dry air and the sun had stretched the flesh of their heads, giving their faces a horrific appearance, as if they had died screaming, I felt my new-found resolve slipping.

≡∥≡

I sleep well, possibly thanks to a brew from a sprig of a cactus-like plant (an ancient antidote to altitude sickness) that Nigel picked on our ride up the Azufre. Brian too is having a peaceful night – I have noticed that he is at his most polite when asleep. I nudge him when he snores: 'So sorry,' he grunts softly.

I wake at two o'clock and hear an animal stamping across the rocks and fear for a moment that it will stampede into camp. From the odd gait I realize it is probably Mauricio's hobbled horse. It wheezes horribly. The stars are wonderful now, filling the whole sky.

Up early, I go for a wash in the mystic river. I meet all three *huasos*, Mauricio, Manuel and Cristián, on their way back from bathing before rounding up the horses. We nod our good mornings and Manuel indicates he jumped right into a whirlpool caused by the stream's fast current and a series of bends: 'Jacuzzi!' He laughs.

I am not so sure. The pool looks ominous, the deep water black and swirling powerfully. Also, I realize, it will be very, very cold.

While I am pondering how best to get clean I hear their voices again and look to where they are now pointing. Far across the valley is a flash of white – a large bird on the move. I cannot make out what they are shouting.

After watching the bird disappear into the distance, I opt for straddling a narrower bit of stream and having a splash bath. There is a terrific sense of freedom in standing naked in this vast bowl of a valley and cleansing oneself. Washing my hair though makes my head numb and then, because the water is so cold, beyond numb into blinding pain. After vigorous towelling, however, I feel better for it.

As the warm morning sun creeps across the valley, I wander

down the stream's course and discover that it suddenly cuts away deeply to a gorge at the centre of the wide El Museo valley.

Back at the camp, I leaf through Marcus's bird book and say to Brian, 'Ah! Here it is, *Chloëphaga melanoptera* – it's commonly called the Andean goose but in fact it's a duck. Goose sounds better in this big country.'

'Goose, duck, nonsense!' laughs Bri. 'Take my word for it, it was an albatross!'

᠅

I stood watching its solitary flight through John's telescope. Goose, duck or even *Chloëphaga melanoptera* meant nothing to me. The great white bird moving effortlessly across the sky was Neruda's own great albatross. It was an omen confirming my resolve as the right one and that I was still on the route that had been somehow laid out for us. This was destiny's bird of promise. The others could call it what they wanted.

≡Ⅲ≡

After checking our belongings and, for the Wendies among us, bandaging our bruised calves, we set off. The business of riding, of checking stirrups and girths, is more routine now and conducted almost in silence. If Mellie is anxious after her fall she does not show it.

A gentle breeze wafts over our picnic ground, cool but welcomely so. Everyone is dozing after fat sandwiches of cheese, turkey and avocado, washed down with pisco sours. The horses graze around us. We are at 12,400 feet (3,800 metres) in a little meadow area surrounded by the most spectacular mountains. There are so many contours, types of hillside, and so many colours, it is staggering. Ahead of me are craggy bluffs, with a wide sweep of white and grey glacier on one side and on the other a bizarre patch of yellow and red scree. The meadow has little flowers: tiny, purple gentians; little, rubbery-leaved plants that hug the ground; and low bushes with delicate yellow flowers. There are no trees but a mix of soft and sharp grasses. There are birds too, plovers and Chilean swallows. We are very lucky to be in this place. The area is still controlled by the military and few people, especially gringos, are ever allowed here.

We had a magnificent ride up. Often there would be no sound save the clip, clop and clack of hooves crossing rock or their hollow thud on dried marsh. We went up and up in gentle stages, sometimes crossing screes; at others going through rich green pastures where wild horses and foals lazed about.

Much of the morning I was content to be a quiet part of our caravan listening to the squeak of saddles and catching the odd snip of conversation somewhere up the line – raucous laughter usually indicating Tom's involvement. It is easy to lose yourself in the images conjured by the ever-changing landscape: strange out-crops that look like massive anthills or ancient sphinx-like sculptures; smooth screes rising hundreds of feet with the odd swirl of white or green colour as if some massive brush has daubed a mighty canvas. The shades of rock and the shadows are confusing; what appears massive may well be shadow only. The combination of darkness and light denies a sensible perspective.

I stopped Charlatán for a moment to gaze across a wide valley. I found it hard to judge the distance to the other side of the ravine and remembered having the same difficulty after coming home from Lebanon. I spent some time at a friend's cottage in Wales which overlooked a big valley. At first I could only perceive it as a one-dimensional painting, unable to understand that the build-ings, trees and grazing animals were at different heights and distances from me. I was unnerved by this, fearing that so much time in tiny cells had permanently damaged my sight. Gradually the sense came back.

After lunch, the party stirs, especially Tom who begins taking many photographs in this wonderful place. Inevitably he takes many of Brian and me.

'Oh go away, Tom!'

'Now, now, poppet, don't be a Wendy. It's just part of the day's work!'

'He loves it really,' says Mellie, her dark eyes flashing.

She often says things that are quite sharp, though now we know each other I appreciate there is no barb there, just teasing observation.

Mauricio, looking perplexed, has a brief, muttered conversation with Nigel who appears to be reassuring him about something. Mauricio does not look entirely convinced and they talk a little more before Nigel turns to us all to say, 'Come on, it's another two and a half hours back to camp.'

The afternoon ride is a very hard grind down a different valley of endless rock screes. We make a couple of alarming descents and ascents early on, then jolt over endless shale, the horses' hooves making a sound like cracking pottery.

The main problem is that the shale is so large there is no obvious track so, once Mauricio and Cristián move out of sight ahead of us slowcoaches, one has to make the best line one can downhill. The scenery closes in and for the first time is unutterably dull, just shale screes everywhere. I am very uncomfortable in the saddle and can never see far enough ahead to get a sense of how long this torture must last. I am anxious too; it seems inevitable that a horse will lose its footing on the unstable ground and take its rider sliding to the bottom of the ravine.

Charlatán seems slower than ever and unresponsive to my kickings and on one steep hillside, stones slipping from his feet, he decides to take a different route from those ahead. I try to turn him downhill but he turns directly uphill instead. Very frightened, I hang on trying to regain my equilibrium but, because of the steepness, I am almost lying with my head beside the horse's neck. He seems as confused now as I am and I realize that we could be frozen here until something spooks him. It is a mighty relief when Nigel catches up and quietly tells me to turn the horse downhill again. This time he responds and on we go. Now I direct him constantly, watching his head and the path all the time. Brian points out a fox on the other side of the valley. It runs effortlessly down one side and up the other in minutes, but it is taking us hours.

Lower down, we ford a couple of streams which is a more enjoyable challenge but not enough to outweigh the anxieties of the afternoon. Tom rides up beside me, his face unusually serious.

'That was terrifying. I think we should talk to Nigel.'

'Yeah, I guess we could,' I reply.

'Now, John, you're my friend – you'll back me up, won't you?'

I am touched by this innocent appeal and realize that he was perhaps even more shaken than I was. We soon find that the others feel the same and decide to speak to Nigel.

'I'm sorry you found it hard,' he says, moving his head in the nervous way he does before answering a question, as if turning in his saddle or watching the skyline for a condor. 'I did mention it, I think, before we left the meadow.'

'No you bloody didn't!' comes the general reply.

Nigel is laughing. He seems to love winding us all up. 'Oh I think I did, but I know I mumble a bit sometimes. Maybe it wasn't too clear.'

He suffers some vocal abuse and it is agreed that we will steer clear of terrifying situations unless they are unavoidable or lead to something spectacular.

I have found that I quite like the frisson of fear, but only when one can see both the problem and the objective quite clearly. It is those moments when one loses concentration and the horse does too, that panic sets in. Suddenly you are in a different world, a parallel dimension almost, where you have no bearings and though things may still look entirely familiar nothing is certain and nothing, especially oneself, can be entirely trusted.

~~~

Nigel has made a first tentative mention of the Mal Paso, a particularly treacherous ascent and descent we will have to make. To lighten our apprehension, he suggests that we could walk the horses, and tells us that in any case the details he had sent us clearly stated that this trip was not for people who suffered from vertigo.

I rounded on John, 'You didn't send me those details!'

'Didn't I?' he answered, barely concealing the smirk on his face. I spent the night much disturbed by the impending Mal Paso.

≡ ||| ≡

Two mules prove determined to avoid moving on to another camp so we have a delayed start while the *huasos* try to catch them. I go down by the mystic brook for a last wash. Walking back, my shadow is long in the early sun and I feel at home in this huge, free landscape, a place that would lift the spirits, however badly depressed. I cannot help thinking, though, of Nigel's warning, that this afternoon we have to go up something that the *huasos* call Mal Paso, Bad Pass. It must be bad given that they did not deem 'Death Ridge' severe enough to warrant a particular name. Later, as the sun reaches its zenith, one will feel less confident, cut down to size as one's shadow shortens and then disappears.

The sun is well up when we face 'Death Ridge' again. Having focused on Mal Paso, the surprise of coming to it out of the blue distresses me and I become more anxious as we start debating whether we should follow the *huasos* who have taken the mules down an alternative but steep and longer route, or go straight across the top. I hate dithering like this. It seems we are just making ourselves more anxious. I realize that I am losing my cool. Luckily we move out – across the top – before my anxiety turns to panic. It is not nearly as bad as the first time; I am actually enjoying it and manage to look down often and at one particularly exposed slab of bare rock. I stare down the almost sheer drop to the churning river and say, 'Fuck off!' It makes me feel much better, good enough to get through a wait halfway across the ridge while the mules' loads are checked.

We plod on gently for a while before making another steep, dusty descent. As we tack back and forth down to a river I find, for the first time, that I am simply riding the horse. Casually taking in the scenery as we manoeuvre hairpin bend after hairpin bend, I enjoy another special moment of feeling at one with myself and this environment.

Ironically the rest of the morning's ride is a slow, tedious slog across a wide, scrubby plain with vast brown bluffs ahead. It reminds me of scenes from the many westerns I watched with my father years ago. We used to sit at home on Saturday afternoons watching the old black and white films. Most of them were of the 'brave white settlers take on depraved Injuns' school and I would sit on a sofa with cowboy hat on and six-shooter at the ready. Once, as I was taking pot shots at the marauding Apache from the cover of a cushion, a particularly fearsome warrior came running right at the camera. I blasted away desperately and was amazed when he fell back and lay motionless. I turned wide-eyed to my father who said, 'Nice shooting, cowboy!'

I felt very tough indeed. So it is with an expert eye that I recognize this place as being just the spot for the wagon train to be attacked by the Red Indians. However, the only attack today is of boredom and soreness in my backside and thighs. As the pain intensifies, I try to tell myself how lucky we are to be seeing this from horseback – on foot or bike one would be working so much harder, while in a car or train it would be gone in a flash and there would be no sense of the air or sounds of silence. This attempt at positive thinking fails. I am increasingly uncomfortable and bored as the weather turns cold, threatening rain.

I stop Charlatán for a moment's rest and look back. I am surprised to see Tom and a couple of other riders far behind. Small and indistinct save for Tom's white hat, I wonder what it would feel like if those distant riders were pursuing me, harrying me into the mountains and exile as Neruda and O'Higgins had been. Such reflections on battered dreams and lost homelands take my mind off ennui and sore limbs until we stop for lunch.

〰〰

After we had been an hour or so on the trail I spotted a large low-flying bird which Marcus confirmed was a buzzard. I reined my horse back to where John was and pointing upward stated, 'Low-flying buzzard – death on the Mal Paso.' Our laughter could not disguise our anxiety. My heart was in my mouth and my knuckles permanently white. Eventually we reached a shepherds' campsite and having unsaddled my mount for lunch I remarked to John, 'Well, the Mal Paso wasn't that bad.' His answer was distinctly demoralizing.

'You're right, but that's largely because we haven't done it yet!'

≡ ⦀ ≡

Despite the heavy cloud and rumbles of thunder there are only a few spots of rain. Nevertheless the dreaded Mal Paso looks bad – a grey cliff with the narrowest of trails snaking up it. As we make a sliding slalom ride down the scree on the opposite side of the valley, we watch the *huasos* guide the mules up.

〰〰

'Bad Pass' does not sufficiently describe what confronted us. I looked towards John to confirm that he was sharing my panic. He sat silently staring at the ascending mule train. I wiped the nervous sweat out of my own eyes and studied the sheer face of the bad pass.

There was no direct ascent. Instead the slope had to be traversed several times, each zigzag elevating man and beast maybe another ten feet. There was one dangerous hairpin turn which, Nigel informed us, the horses had to be driven into and out of quickly before they stumbled or bolted in another direction which would be impossible to get out of, and potentially fatal.

I was last to make the ascent and much relieved that I wouldn't have another horse behind me spooking my own. I had watched John getting snarled up behind a stalled horse as he was about to set off up the trail. Cristián skittered down to assist Mellie whose horse had refused the last, incredibly steep section.

'Is problem?' I heard his voice carry across the canyon. It was a dangerous situation for the riders banked up on the narrowest of step ledges. Cristián was well intentioned but I could see he had not really helped matters by loosening all sorts of rock and debris as he descended. John's voice carried over to me: 'You're the problem, pal. Move out of the way.' The nervousness in his voice was audible. It didn't encourage my own rapidly wilting self-confidence.

But no prevarication could stop me having to face Mal Paso. It was now my turn.

I scrambled up, stopping at each intersection before negotiating the turns in fear and trembling. Gravel and rocks were kicked out by Milly's urgent movements. It seemed to me as if the whole mountain path was collapsing under the animal's weight. She clambered upwards, splay-legged, grunting and huffing.

The last ten feet seemed almost sheer. I could not believe the horse would make it. Instantly the *huasos* gathered behind it with scarves to frighten it over this final hurdle.

I accepted Nigel's proffered flask of pisco and tasted nothing but my own adrenaline-fuelled panic. My first thought was that we would have to go down this again, followed quickly by a realization that playing cowboys at my age was seriously suicidal.

But it was time to press on. A few moments gloating over our heroic efforts was all that was permitted. One fixed rule had become apparent over the last few days. The pace and duration of our riding was always determined by the absolute necessity of reaching fresh water before sunset.

After a few hours we had almost arrived at our high-altitude camp. I looked at my companions and noticed a change had occurred. Until this point we had travelled in single file behind the *huasos* and our guide. But now we had simultaneously and unconsciously fanned out and were riding abreast. I looked to my right and left and saw the hardened faces of real pioneer trekkers. The Mal Paso had not been so bad after all.

≡Ⅲ≡

The flush of success after the perilous ascent of Mal Paso somehow imbues me with a clearer understanding of Charlatán. I have been kicking him along all day but this has ceased to be effective and I have been getting very frustrated at not keeping up with the horse in front. It adds to the tension of sore and tired legs. I experiment, whirling my leading rein close to his head, and find he responds immediately. Less frustrated and not needing to kick him, I feel my aches and pains subside.

We have been joined by two shepherds, Marcello and his young son. As well as looking after their sheep they guide and run supplies to mountaineering teams climbing Tupungato, the 21,500-foot (6,570-metre) extinct volcano that dominates the area.

It is amazing to see that Marcello and the boy have so little with them. They were expecting to be out in the mountains for a night or perhaps two, but had brought no warm clothes and just some bread and cheese. Once we have set up a new camp, the pair sit round the fire drinking tea from a length of cowhorn. Tom immediately leaps into action, cameras dangling round his neck, light meters being checked and his enthusiastic Spanish tumbling over itself as he explains that he would love to capture this terrific image of mountain life.

There follows a lengthy muttered conversation between our *huasos* and Marcello. The boy looks on intently. Every few moments these untypically sombre faces turn to study that of Tom, beaming expectantly back at them. Nigel, who had been on the other side of the camp erecting a tent, comes over and joins in the conversation. He alone seems to find it funny but evidently reassures them that it is fine to let Tom do his work. It occurs to me that maybe Marcello does not want to feel that he and his son are being treated as freaks. Or could it be that they feel that if they are to be scrutinized for Tom's and our benefit they should receive some payment? Whatever, Tom starts taking the shots and with his usual style manages to get everyone to relax and move about a little to get the angles he wants.

As he does this, he is also taking photographs of Manuel, Cristián and Mauricio as they tend the fire and prepare supper. Mauricio, who normally looks dashing under his wide sombrero, is wearing his evening headgear – a woolly hat declaring his allegiance to Arsenal.

As ever Tom cajoles and banters as he works. For some reason he decides it is hilarious to tease the quintessentially macho Mauricio.

'*Todo equipo Arsenal es maracoñes*,' he says, a broad smile on his face.

I look at Brian. 'I think he is implying that Mauricio's heroes are all gay.'

Brian nods. The other *huasos* seem to find this extremely amusing and Nigel is doing his best not to double up. Mauricio cannot quite decide what to do and continues posing as directed by Tom. When his persecutor finally wraps up the session, he struts off to do something manly with the mules, saying – and even I, with my limited Spanish, grasp his meaning – 'Well, Arsenal may be pooftahs, but I'm definitely not.'

Before supper Brian and I wander a little from the camp to have a wash. This site is not the best, as the nearby river, the Colorado, is so full of the red soil that gives it its name that washing in it would make you dirtier rather than cleaner. Nearer the camp are some shallow, stagnant pools, sufficient only to rinse one's hands and face. As we squat beside the inky water, our silhouettes are reflected beside the moon. The moonlight plays on wisps of cloud drifting around a high ridge across the valley.

'It is so peaceful,' I say. 'No sounds beyond water running over rock, the wind, a few birds, sheep, and the horses. Apart from us lot we've only heard the voices of a couple of other humans. We haven't seen a machine since leaving the cars at Don Ramon's camp. It's funny, apart from that little camping gas light Manuel sometimes has on while he's cooking, the most sophisticated technology up here is my Swiss Army knife and my Psion.'

'And the light's amazing,' says Brian. 'We are so far from everything there's no light pollution.' He pauses and, looking up, turns full circle. 'Aye, it's a strange place. No one lives here. A few pass through, like us and the shepherds, but no one ever stays. What happens when we're not watching?'

There is an otherworldly atmosphere here. I think of Mervyn Peake's novel *Gormenghast*, which I read in captivity. The opening scenes create a terrific sense of being in another dimension where time and place are distorted. As the book progresses, it lapses into a fairly mundane story and loses some of that magic. But this place is so alien, its proportions so different from anything I have seen, that the potential for magic seems to remain. Weird and wonderful things may be happening all around us. It might be a home to spirits and dragons.

The sound of laughter brings us back to the here and now. As we draw close to the company round the camp fire Tom is speaking.

'Oh my God, no! What is it?'

We sit as Nigel starts explaining: 'Mauricio and the team have been pretty confused by Tom taking all those photos of Brian and

John. And up at the meadow where we had lunch yesterday, they were really perplexed. You know: John has an after-lunch smoke – Tom gets up to within a foot and shoots off a roll of film; Bri looks pensively at a mountain or reads a poem and there's Tom, snap, snap, snap! Then he gets the two of them together, an arm around a shoulder and takes another thirty pictures.'

'But surely everyone takes loads of photos up here,' says Brian.

'Sure, sure, but not quite so many and people mostly take shots of the views, not endless close-ups of a couple of blokes.'

'Fine, but surely they understand that for a book a professional snapper's going to take hundreds of pix?' I observe.

'Well, I'm sure they would understand if they knew you were writing a book.'

'You mean you haven't explained?'

'Well . . . No, not as such.'

I remember the muttered conversation between Mauricio and Nigel before we left the meadow.

'If that was all about Tom's photos and you didn't bloody tell him why he keeps filming us, what does he think?'

'Oh, he just thinks the three of you are incredibly gay.'

We are all roaring with laughter and Marcus splutters, 'They think these three are gay and Tom then starts telling Mauricio that Arsenal are a team of pansies! God, did he think he was making a play for him?'

'I think he was a bit worried,' says Nigel, his head waggling furiously and his speech descending to a mumble, 'and of course the fact that he keeps calling John um, well, you know!'

'I keep calling John what?' barks Tom.

'Wendy,' says Nigel.

∾∿∾

The night was bitterly cold, and the supper of stewed lentils and meat was more than appreciated. Our campsite banter was limited by the chill and the wildness of nightfall. I retired early while there was still some light to update my diary.

I note that in a curious way this trip is like captivity. Fear and tedium are something we constantly have to deal with. Incredibly

I resort to the same strategies in the saddle as I did on my prison mattress.

During long, boring stretches of our journey, I sit perched on Milly's back and compose detailed lectures on academic or esoteric subjects. In the evenings or during afternoon stops, I have taken to reading Neruda's love sonnets in much the same way as I read the psalms each day in captivity. Both the psalms and the sonnets have the same force in them. Both are composed out of desperate hunger and longing and the best of both styles conclude in a joyful encounter with either God or a moment of experienced love. I don't really know why but this mountain landscape seems perfectly suited to such writing. Maybe it's simply that the emptiness and vastness of the place makes one's mind focus in on things that are really important, or maybe I am just lovesick.

If I am not concocting elaborate theses on some obscure author or poet, then invariably I am thinking of my wife and unborn child. There are no telephones or post offices up here. I have only my notebook and Neruda ... and pages scribbled with Spanish names for my unborn son!

There is no music up here. I would love to have a tape of Ennio Morricone's soundtrack to *The Mission* or even the soundtrack to Scorsese's *Last Temptation of Christ*. The raw passion in both pieces seems entirely appropriate to this brutal landscape. Both soundtracks deal in different ways with betrayal and suffering which have been in my thoughts throughout the trek.

≡Ⅲ≡

The shallow pools around the camp are covered with ice in the early morning as we prepare for a long ride. Today we go to Argentina and will climb five thousand feet in four hours. Before we start, we are treated to an impromptu display of virtuoso horsemanship as Mauricio races bareback across the rocky hillside rounding up the mules. When the first Spaniards arrived, the Indians, who had never seen horses, thought that man and mount were one beast. Watching Mauricio now one can understand their mistake. His skill is stunning.

Perhaps inspired by Mauricio's display I feel really at home in

the saddle this morning and although Charlatán shows no indication to move over shale at anything more than a stroll, my
relationship with him has shifted from one of subjection to one of
proprietorship.

〰〰

Twenty minutes or so after setting out, we rode cautiously over a
huge sloping plain of stone and then progressed upward following
a washed-out river bed. Soon we were in blue-black cinder
country. The whole place was littered like a burnt-out ash pan, the
detritus of volcanoes. I remembered that these mountains were
formed out of cataclysmic eruptions. We seemed to be surrounded
by 'exploding rock' terrain. Beneath us the river had a covering of
ice.

When we came upon the base camp of some mountain
climbers, John and a few others went to chat. When they heard
we were continuing upwards, one of them remarked, 'You guys are
nuts, horses aren't supposed to go higher than this.'

The landscape was becoming more harsh and brittle. There
were few rounded edges up here and the air was icy. Like the idiot
McCarthy is always telling me I am, I had forgotten to put on my
long johns and my legs were becoming more numb by the minute.

At this point Nigel had kindly procured the loan of one of the
huasos' ponchos for me. Though I was glad of it I had ominous
premonitions about shrouding myself in this voluminous black
cape. At first it made the ride cumbersome as it flapped wildly like
a banshee in the wind. I remembered having referred to demons
the night before and for some reason I associated this cape with
them. But I soon adjusted to it and was content to have it around
me. For an instant I glanced back to see where John and the others
were. The sight was splendidly terrifying.

My first impressions at such altitude may well have been
informed by the illusory effects of low oxygen. Everywhere the
land was falling away from me, making it seem as though
the mountains were being thrown up even as I looked at them. I
was in the entrails of an immensely powerful landscape that awed
me. I was being swallowed up by a pandemonium of stone.

We moved on, making a long, slow, steep ascent, then rounding the top to look out on an unending vista of mountain peaks and glaciers.

≡⦀≡

Nigel points to a glacier high above us across the valley. 'See those little pinnacles of ice? They're unique to the Andes. They call them *penitentes*, like repentant sinners on their knees.'

We go on up, aiming for a ridge high above us. The track is steep, winding forever upwards on barren rock and dust. Suddenly we are level with the *penitentes* and come across some on this side of the valley. It is a very odd sight, like something from a sci-fi film set. Dotted over an area about a hundred yards square are little pyramids of snow, the biggest about six feet tall. The ground between them is totally dry and rocky like everywhere else.

'On your knees, sinner,' I say to Brian.

He remarks with a scowl that they look more like those old-fashioned gents' urinals you find in underground lavatories 'I'll strangle Nigel from the bollocks upwards,' he fulminates. '"Steady climb; not too difficult," he told us but this is just boring and tiring.'

Clouds begin to mass over the summit for which we are heading. Although we are still riding in sunshine it is cool. I move up beside Nigel who is looking skywards, blissfully unaware of how close he is to a garrotting from Keenan.

'Are we going to get bad weather?' I ask.

'I don't know. Normally the clouds gather later in the day.'

'It's getting colder.'

'Most of that is just the morning downdraught from the glaciers. In the afternoon, when the land's heated up, warm air will be coming up.'

I enjoy picking up titbits from Nigel; he knows so much about this environment that we have imaginatively nicknamed him 'Mountain Man'. He has climbed some and seems to have been everywhere, once earning his living as a shepherd in Argentinian Patagonia.

'It's on those thermals that the condors glide. They never need to beat a wing, just leave their high perches and soar up on the land's heat. They each watch a valley and each other. They eat carrion and if one swoops down the others follow, assuming that food has been spotted.'

Looking down it is hard to believe we've climbed so far – I feel I am peering back to another world.

'Are we nearly there?' I ask.

'Almost there. It's easy now.'

I continue looking, watching the others coming up, a line of riders working their mounts back and forth across the steep hillside. On the far side of the valley and rising yet higher the mountains are covered in snow. This trail used to be used by smugglers and rustlers. I imagine that at this point they would have paused and felt elated like me. I am achieving a lifelong dream; they were nearly on home ground and safe from pursuit. I turn Charlatán's head uphill once more.

〜〜〜

Leaving the airless, immobile ice sculptures we were off for lunch in Argentina as if it was a Sunday school outing. I found it hard to believe that we had come so far or so high. Loose shards of stone were dislodged by our horses' hooves and then tumbled into oblivion below us. I stopped looking down for fear of following them. As I rounded a section of the path to come up on John, I was forced to stop suddenly.

≡Ⅲ≡

Nigel has disappeared, Brian and the others are behind me, and suddenly I find myself riding another knife-edge ridge. But this is so high, the wind is strong and I cannot see that there is anywhere to go on the other side.

Lying bastard, I think.

Just last night Brian, Mellie and I were talking about how we deal with fear. We all tend to displace it by getting angry with something or someone. Nigel is going to be it.

Once across there seems to be no room at all: the land stops and just drops away in all directions. As I dismount I am certain that one false step would see me falling thousands of feet. Off the horse my instinct makes me crouch low. Here at the top of the world one feels certain to be toppled.

When my turn came I sat, half frozen in the saddle. From somewhere in front of me I heard Nigel call out, 'Don't hesitate or pull her up. Keep her moving!' John's voice joined his: 'Come on, Bri, you can do it.' My head was too full of words and my heart was in my mouth preventing them from escaping. I repeated Nigel and John's advice: 'Don't pull her up, you can do it.' Then I whispered to myself, 'I'm gonna do both you bastards when I get over this.' Get over what? I asked myself. There was nothing there except another chasm of air for me to gallop over. I sat poised on a knife-edge of loose stones with a sixteen-thousand-foot sheer drop on either side.

'My horse is not a fucking tightrope walker!' I screamed at the top of my voice so that every stone in the Andes could hear me. Immediately it's out, I hear myself say, 'Learn a song, or a few verses of several. You'll need something to occupy your time when you are falling.' It was something one of the K2 climbers at Jorge's house had said to me. 'K2 Keenan, that's me,' I quipped. As I threw the black poncho around me, I noticed Milly's great big soft eye roll back to look at me. 'OK, sweetheart, I'm all yours,' I whispered as we both stepped off into the Andean air.

I didn't know how to describe absolute terror because I don't remember it. I only know that Milly became Pegasus and flew me to safety, for which I will be eternally grateful.

Landing on the other side, I dismounted to put the horse out of the wind. How could I have thought, even for a second, that this black cape had an ominous significance? Even if I had fallen out of the sky up there it would have flown me down to earth like a fallen leaf. The thought calmed me for no longer than a nanosecond. I looked around me. We were on a ledge barely able to accommodate one man and horse, never mind three, with another equine astronaut about to land any minute.

I looked briefly at Nigel, and he will never know, until he reads this, how close he came to forcibly encountering the Japhy Ryder/*Dharma Bums* mountain descent experience – first hand, with my right foot starting him off.

≡|||≡

Last night Tom specifically quizzed Nigel about the 'vertigo factor' from which he suffers. I watch him now coming across the ridge on foot, like me keeping his centre of gravity low. The cameras around his neck must feel truly like a millstone at tense times like this. He gets across and sits down with Brian. They are both scared and very angry. Brian scowls and curses. He nods towards the narrow little path, a rock bridge really, to the level area where Nigel and Manuel are laying out lunch.

'You don't have to go over there with them, John. We can have our lunch here!'

Tom, every inch the Englishman, finds it hard to express his anger. Like me, a shock moves him to nervous laughter rather than angry outburst. 'I have to say that this is not my idea of a great picnic spot. Don't anyone mention the word earthquake!'

We begin to laugh.

'Look, while no one's looking we could have Nigel and Manuel over the cliff. Then the swine couldn't torture us like this again,' says Tom.

'OK, but be careful of the food,' I say. 'I'm starving!'

'Typical bloody McCarthy,' snorts Brian. '"Where's my eating?"' he squeaks in a childish tone, remembering me telling of a childhood picnic in an English summer's downpour. Mothers and children trying to get dry in some shelter but the boyhood me jumping up and down in a petulant rage for the abandoned sandwiches.

I was vaguely conscious of passing a tall iron post on the ridge but had been too frightened, too concerned with where Charlatán would put his feet, to look at it. I look back at it now and realize it marks the border between Chile and Argentina. Mellie appears at the far side. My heart goes out to her; she must be going through the same nightmare that I had had, not being able to see where the track leads. My concerns for her are suddenly overwhelmed with selfish anxiety. There is not enough room for any more horses and people, I think, I must go and turn her back.

Fortunately my saner self intervenes and I decide to sit with Brian and Tom and get acclimatized to our immediate surroundings.

After a little while I realize that though this area is tiny, it is large and stable enough to hold us all. Once the rest join us, we consume smoked salmon sandwiches at over fifteen thousand feet. As ever, Nigel just laughs when we subject him to a barrage of finely chosen insults.

The drop to Argentina is as colossal as that we have climbed, of course, but from our eyrie I can see none of the gentler gradients to allow any form of trail. Every descent looks sheer. The mountains and valleys are orange in the sunlight. Far away a clear blue lake glints. Once more, any sense of perspective, any ability to judge depth and distance, goes completely. There is nothing to give one an ordinary sense of scale: the whole is once again distorted, surreal and fantastic. Who knows what other dimensions of reality could be conjured here?

Tom decides that he must take some photographs. He enlists Cristián to hold on to him, '*In serio, Cristián*' – seriously.

Fulfilling his professional duties clearly puts him through hell again. He is unusually muted when he sits down, his back to the mountain. There is no trace of a smile on his face as he looks levelly at Nigel and says, 'Nigel. You are a bastard.'

We mount up again, all of us tense. The wind has stiffened in the past ten minutes, bringing with it an icy chill. We are wearing all our layers and our hats are tied on fast. Recrossing the ridge I feel that Charlatán and I are little more than a feather buffeted by the whistling devil of the wind and that we will be hurled into the abyss. Hard snowflakes come snapping at us as if they are the agents of another, minor demon willing us to lose both heart and footing. Nevertheless soon we are all safely across and begin the long ride down. Ten minutes later we look back and the ridge has disappeared in a dark cloud as if it were a place of fantasy after all.

The change in weather and the long ride back to camp bring home the true nature of this experience. This is now no holiday outing, it is a survival course. The suddenness with which the mountains can become unfriendly is far more alarming than saddle sores and aches and pains. As with sailing the special nature of trekking is of being in a wild place, learning to respect it, and realizing that you can gain an expanded sense of wonder and purpose.

⌃⌃⌃

The snow, wind and sleet were like savage razor blades. I huddled underneath the *huaso*'s great black poncho. Nothing can overcome me. After my flight on Pegasus and protected by this huge Chilean cloak, I am unassailable.

I instinctively knew we had achieved something and wanted to relive the moment. Above us the sky was a clear, clean blue, behind us the mountains were reds and browns, dappled with white snowfalls. John's pinto horse seemed to have been cut out of the landscape.

We had both made it to that mythic mountaintop the Psalmist had written about. I was filled with the same sense of muted elation that is the culmination of the Psalmist's art. Having struggled through loneliness and despair with the enmity of the whole world thrust against him, the poet finds peace and comfort in the blissful contemplation of the glory and majesty of God. I had the same sense of things. Perched here where the mountains pierced the sky, we had made the journey of our captive imaginings into a reality. We had overcome and gone beyond and now stood God-like looking down on the world, quivering with fear, adrenaline and the kind of joy it is probably only possible to experience a few times in one's life.

≡ ||| ≡

I wake feeling refreshed from yesterday's dramas. Last night the *huasos* all slept in the open so Bri and I had a tent each. When I poke my head out after waking, Tom is passing. He comes over to exchange good mornings, nodding to where his tent sits beside Brian's. 'I had no idea anyone could snore that loudly,' he says.

'Oh yes! It just happens that I have a spare set of earplugs. I could let you have them for, shall we say, fifty quid?'

'It was very loud, even fifteen feet away and out here in the open. What was it like in a cell?'

'Well, loud enough. But we got used to each other after a while.'

He smiles down at me then his face grows serious. 'How long was it?'

'Four years for him, five for me.'

'My God. My God!' He staggers off, looking appalled.

We break camp in warm sunshine and head off on a leisurely ride to a new base. After the drama of yesterday even Mal Paso has lost its terror. It seems quite small in scale and I relish guiding Charlatán round the tight bends, my free hand held out for balance as he slides on the steeper sections.

I feel more at ease in the saddle now and realize that even though my legs are permanently knackered, I am growing stronger and fitter. Although I cannot swing into the saddle as the *huasos* do, without putting a foot in the stirrup, it is now no effort sliding on and off Charlatán's back.

At the new camp, I help rig the windbreak and realize that with the growing fitness my head is clearer than for a long time; knots long unpractised suddenly form themselves in my hands. Having found a sense of place, I seem to have recovered a sense of purpose. It is hard to define, but it feels as if some unspecified weight has been lifted. Perhaps the physical exertions have eased psychological stresses.

After lunch some of us go to explore a fossil field. As soon as we move off I have doubts; all I can think of is my aching backside and how I could have had a pleasant afternoon bathing in the river and reading and snoozing in the sun. However, it is only an hour's ride during which the spectacle of steam rising from Volcán Tupungatito (the younger, smaller but still active neighbour of Tupungato) eases my pain. The fossil field is an extraordinary sight. Acres of mounds and hollows, as if someone has been sifting for treasure. Yet everything looks like cement and in a way it is: countless shell shapes bonded together into rock – thick seabed at over ten thousand feet.

᭡᭡᭡

While John and some of the others hunted for fossils, I stayed behind, daydreaming about our conquest of the Andes. The descent from Argentina reinforced the spectacular dimensions of the mountains we had crossed. Normally my logic would insist that there is nothing in reality that is unbelievable. But I now hereby declare my logic inadequate.

We had overcome terror and fear. We had recognized them as ghostly apparitions from the past and shunned them. We had defied our own animal instincts. We had achieved no great feat in the world's terms, but for myself I felt that to overcome my own inadequacy and fear was earth-shattering enough. I remembered Tennyson's words echoing Homer which I had imprinted somewhere in my psyche during our captivity: 'To strive, to seek, to find, and not to yield.' It may be an old time-worn motto, but unconsciously I seem to have carried it with me into the Andes.

During that descent I remember I wanted to scream something utterly inarticulate that only the mountains would understand. I was still afraid, sometimes terribly so, but I was moving in a fantasy in which the fear could not survive.

The many poems I had read on our way to that angel-fearful place were echoing out of the ether of my still-fevered imagination. But it was merely a kaleidoscope of images and impressions to which I could give no form or shape.

≡ⅼ∥≡

Nigel, Manuel and Cristián start looking about with experienced eyes, hunting for good examples. Cristián teases Manuel who is clearly something of a fanatical fossil collector. Searching too, I begin to see the expression 'as old as the hills' in a new light – that perhaps it should be taken out of common usage, reserved for something more profound; something speaking more to the very core of nature and man.

Alone in my own little well of discovery I look, with my novice eyes, over the mass of shapes and swirls of shell. I want to find something. A perfect fossil certainly but more it is the desire to express how it feels to get so close to the beginning of time. Head down low, scrutinizing the squiggles and lines on the little rocks, the musty odour of the earth takes me back to the pottery at school. Yet as the dust of this dry clay runs through my fingers, I realize that it was once the floor of the oceans from which life first crept. This was the 'primordial ooze' that started it all.

I come across Tom sitting on his haunches in a dip between two banks of fossils. Behind him a mountain rises sheer. His face is bright with smiles.

'I am a little boy again.'

That is just how he looks, tiny compared to the landscape, and as I come closer I see that he has filled his jersey with fossil trophies.

We spend our final night back at Los Azules camp. Despite all the joys of gaining confidence in the saddle I was delighted to get out of it at last. It had been a gentle day's work, just three and a half hours, but my legs were still dying. Crossing the river just before the camp I could hardly move them to kick Charlatán on. For the first time, we had done a fair bit of trotting and cantering. For a few seconds I believe I was actually galloping, an exciting and liberating moment, during which, albeit briefly, I felt at one with Charlatán; a vital part of his fluid motion. At one point, as Bri turned Milly, I charged past, unable to resist a cow-boy 'Yeehaa!'

Moments later, as I slowed Charlatán, he came steaming by, shouting, 'My testicles are in the back of my throat.'

After that it was a slow jog to camp. It was great to see Tom, having decided he had all the pictures he needed, getting to grips with Negra. He was trotting and galloping everywhere. One minute he would be off to the right, the next a blur on the horizon, identifiable by the black mass of the horse and the white flash of his sunhat.

I feel so tired this morning it is a relief that it is only two and a half hours to Don Ramon's camp. The ride, though, is much hairier than I had remembered – it just shows how nervous I was then. My spirits are buoyed, often to the point of out-and-out laughter, remembering Marcus at the camp fire last night. We had been looking back over our week of rough riding, recalling the good and bad moments with equal relish. Marcus had become almost hysterical at one point and it took him a while to calm down enough to let us share the joke. It turned out to be one phrase he had heard Brian endlessly chanting all the way up the mountains on the great ride to Argentina. 'Focking bastard, focking, focking, focking bastard!' had been the mantra.

After a week experiencing the joy of being free of man's pollution of the environment with waste, noise and light, it is ironic that the first sign of modern man is a hydroelectric plant. The one thing we can get from this place, untouched by electric light, is electric power.

While we have a final lunch at Don Ramon's, the horses roll in the grass and lie down to sleep, knowing that they will not be called upon for a little while. Charlatán is as I first saw him, a blur of brown and white on the far side of the meadow. Brian is sitting near the small hillock where we had first lined up for our team photo before setting off. It seems so long ago. After taking his own final photo, he sits scribbling in his little red notebook. He seems preoccupied and I leave him to it. I understand. It is a time for reflection.

〜〜

I was watching the camp as the mules and horses were unsaddled for the last time. John lingered for a while with Charlatán before the animal trotted off into a small meadow.

I wondered what this expedition had meant to those who had suffered and laughed through it. There were so many impressions and memories I wanted to seal in my mind before our departure and final goodbyes to companions.

In my notebook I was busy trying to cobble together my own 'memoriam'. I had the uncanny sense that old Pablo was whispering every word into my ear.

I have infiltrated the stone walls of icons
and ice ages
I have stood in the blitzkrieg and the broadside
of elemental siege
I have known the neck of Pegasus grow numb
beneath the stone cold impress of the night
I have felt raw muscle in man and beast
quiver in every ascent
But I know the end of the gallop in the
footless mist
For me there is no God but this
The end long spine of stone and light
and the advent
of the beast man taking eagle flight.

Chapter Nine

≡Ⅲ≡

Standing in the shower at Frank and Noni's flat as the water gushes over me is an exquisite luxury. The water drains anti-clockwise, a miniature of the torrent of the Rio Colorado as the accretions of Andes dust sluice off. I wash and shampoo repeatedly and change into fresh clothes. Tom, Bri and I lounge in the comfort of the sofas drinking cold beers. I think we are all pleased with ourselves at the completion of the great adventure. Also relieved – our bodies are exhausted.

Sadly, Tom has to return to England. His sense of fun and boundless enthusiasm will be sorely missed. However, in some of the places on our itinerary he will still be with us in spirit as he has given us introductions to more of the friends he and Katie made when they were here in the mid-eighties. After checking we have all the addresses and phone numbers we need, our last sight of him is of his spectacles flashing on his ever-beaming face as his taxi pulls away outside the apartment block.

〜〰〜

Before setting out on our journey to Patagonia in search of yaks and long-dead Irish revolutionaries, we had planned to have a few days' relaxation in an old colonial hacienda, Los Lingues, some eighty miles from Santiago. To get there we once again took to the Pan American Highway, that famous road on which the intrepid traveller can journey from Alaska to Patagonia. In our many captive fantasies both John and I had often talked of exploring this mythic highway.

Everything seemed to suckle off this concrete artery. The section that we travelled now was lined with fruit stalls, small cafés and open-air workshops all ablaze with colour and teeming with life. I could imagine how decades ago this same population would have been strung out along the great rivers of the continent eking out the kind of precarious existence that is the lot of rural people dependent on the geography of their country. Certainly this motorway had injected a new dynamic, but carried with it its own debris from North America. Fast food bars and a few factories stood out glaringly, among the otherwise impressionistic haze of colour. But one particular feature caught our eye. Every few miles we would find astonishing relics, vintage cars and trucks that would be the dream of any collector. Some of them had their year and make chalked on the windscreen: a 1928 Dodge, a 1936 Ford. Amazingly, in some of these backyard workshops we spied small steam locomotives that could have been the original Stephenson's *Rocket*.

'Wow, what if we bought one of these, fixed it up and then motored down to Tierra del Fuego?' I was in tune with what John was thinking. I had in mind the epic motor journey that Jack Kerouac wrote about. A trip down to the bottom of the world in one of these quaint industrial dinosaurs would certainly have appealed to him. It did to me. We could sign the declaration of the independence of Patagonia on the bonnet of that 1928 Dodge. Now that would be something monumental and historic.

Los Lingues sat back a few miles off the road in the foothills of the Andes. It was part of the Angostura estate given in 1599 by Philip III to the then mayor of Santiago and had remained in the same family for four centuries, preserved in all its colonial splendour. Its native gardens were filled with many trees and flora that had disappeared from much of the rest of the region. Los Lingues itself was named after a tree, the *lingues*, almost extinct in the rest of Chile, though the hacienda retained a few.

But this air of colonial preservation was not restricted to the buildings and flora. German Claro (pronounced 'Herman') and his son German Junior were our hosts. The senior German was full of aristocratic charm and wit, most of which he seemed to lavish on any female guest. It was inevitable that, as the owner of such an establishment and descended from such old Catalan stock, he should have such manners.

German Junior still retained the vestiges of his Catalan breeding. He enjoyed socializing with his guests and, if you were game, he would be more than willing to join you over a few drinks in the regal salon. In the afternoons German Junior could be found wandering the grounds in sneakers, light canvas trousers, a loud colourful shirt and a panama hat. He could have been a character straight out of *Our Man in Havana*. In the evening he donned a suit and tie, slicked back his hair and joined us in the small private drawing room. It was full of reds and golds and the rich dark browns of furniture that had been built by craftsmen's hands centuries before we sat there. Shadows of his father's elegance were visible, but he laughed too much, occasionally pointing out a piece of furniture or a painting and describing its history as if mocking its archaic significance. In one corner was a large hand-scripted and embossed charter from England declaring that German Claro was in direct line of descent, through his mother, from the royal family of Scotland. Maybe it was the Celt in German Junior that tarnished the aristocratic grace his father displayed. There was a sense of pathos behind all his camaraderie. For a moment I thought of Charles, Prince of Wales, a king forever in waiting.

During dinner I asked German about the large painting that was the central feature of the room. It was a full-length portrait of an old, severe-looking woman. Age had already darkened the oils so that it seemed her face and huge hands were the only points of light. Her austerity was almost frightening. Our host had no hesitation in proclaiming his distaste for this ancient aunt. She had owned a great amount of shares in Chile's massive copper mine, but had been very ungenerous in her dying bequests. German strongly suggested that he had not fared as well as he believed he should have done. I looked again at her huge, manly hands and wondered if the artist knew what German had told us. Her expression was disapproving. It was without doubt the most severe Scottish puritan face I have ever seen.

≡Ⅲ≡

We sit out at a table on a lawn as a cooling breeze stirs the lush trees and plants. In this palatial environment it seems entirely natural when a peacock wanders by. Germans Senior and Junior join us for a drink. We chat about our mutual friends, Tom and the Hickman family, and our plans. After a while German Senior asks, 'Why did you choose to visit Chile rather than another country in the region?'

Brian and I exchange glances. He nods at me, so I make a brief mention of kidnaps and captivity before moving on to explain how escapist fantasies had kept us going. Brian is about to take up the story with details of the yak scheme, both of us anticipating laughter, when the older of our hosts raises his hand very slightly with an apologetic dipping of his head. Brian pauses. I notice that German Junior is sitting on the edge of his seat as his father asks, 'How long were you held hostage?'

'I was in for four years,' says Bri.

'And I was there five.'

Brian takes a breath and is about to continue with the yak tale when he pauses again.

Both men are weeping.

I think we both experienced a number of such moments when we first came home, often with complete strangers. People would be overwhelmed for a little while as their minds raced and threw up memories of news flashes, prayer vigils, campaign events and film of us walking off an aeroplane to freedom. After collecting themselves, this last image was often their first talking point. Strength coming back to their voices, they would wipe their tears and begin smiling and tell us where they had been and who they were with and what they had said and done on those days. These impromptu emotional exchanges were remarkable. To mean so much to a passer-by is an extraordinary privilege. Apart from the warmth of the moment, it also did much to alleviate the sense of isolation that had so dominated our lives. We had never really been alone. One might almost say we had never been away. Unknown to us we were in the hearts, not only of family and friends, but of thousands and thousands of others who cared for us.

It has not happened for a while so it comes as something of a shock that these urbane and powerful men, totally at their ease in an environment that has been theirs for ever and probably will remain so, should be so moved by our story. We sit quietly and sip our drinks. Within a few minutes our hosts regain their natural conviviality and we chat on as the shadows lengthen across the lawn.

〰〰

Every room in Los Lingues abounded with stories. In fact the whole house was a history book waiting to be reread. The ornate splendour of the interiors and grounds was counterpointed by a simple chapel built in the centre of the estate, once the farm workers' place of worship. Its cool minimalism was a relief from all the opulence around it. The only concession to the Baroque was a magnificent crucifix hung quietly on one side wall. Every detail down to the faint lines on Christ's fingernails was apparent. The creamy whiteness of the ivory figure blended almost imperceptibly into the stark decor of the tiny church's interior, almost invisible until your eyes alighted upon it. This was more than a work of art. It was a work of impassioned love.

The majesty of it more than equalled anything in the hacienda. I left the chapel enthralled and too frightened to photograph the sculpture. I asked German about it. 'It's by Cellini,' he said nonchalantly.

On our second night we joined the other guests around a great formal dining table. Among the diners were an American heiress, a wealthy Belgian lawyer and his American wife, and a trio of Chilean folk singers called Los Parakeets. I had a feeling as the meal progressed that the after-dinner drinks in the salon were going to be an interesting affair.

It was only as we all sat around the huge, magnificently carved table that I began to feel uneasy. The table was arrayed with so much silver and crystal that my 'meat and two veg' attitude was quickly wilting. This was in every sense a royal feast and I furtively looked to Don John, signalling my total confusion about the etiquette for such an occasion. John's head nodded imperceptibly to acknowledge my concerns. Then he lifted his hand casually to his face and tapped his nose as if to say, Don't worry, watch me.

It wasn't long before Chile's fine wines began to loosen everyone's tongues. It was obvious from the heiress's attitude that German Senior had informed all his guests beforehand of our previous experiences. While the other guests politely avoided making reference to our hostage years the heiress jumped two feet first into the situation and fired a salvo of questions on the subject across the table towards us. John made every effort to answer her without going into much detail but the woman had the infuriating habit of not listening to his answers and always interjecting another question before he had finished. As this banal interrogation continued John threw me a silent glance, as if to say, what am I supposed to do with her? I fixed my eye on his and tapped my nose in reply.

Once the heiress had tired of asking questions, she began to make ludicrous statements about American foreign policy, including suggestions that President Reagan should not have dealt with the terrorists but would have done better bombing Lebanon instead. She went on to point out the worthlessness of the Arab and Islamic world. I listened, thinking I had heard similar idiocy before – only then it had been from the mouth of an impoverished, brainwashed Shi'ite and the object of his zealous dismissal was Reagan, American foreign policy and the 'terrorism' of the CIA.

When I probed her understanding of Irangate and Reagan's bloody flirtation with certain South American 'terrorist' organizations, it was as though she hadn't heard the question and had already begun talking to the table as if I wasn't there.

Some minutes later she attempted to analyse the mind of an Islamic terrorist and question our treatment. When she deliberately posed the question to 'the Irishman, who will no doubt have his own view of things', Sancho Panza rose to the bait.

'It's difficult to talk in such specific terms. Surely the problem is really that privilege and wealth obscure one's understanding of the world, just as poverty might. Only the poor's struggle is for survival while the wealthy struggle to maintain their privilege. It's an unequal equation and has seriously to limit our ability to respond to the worlds we inhabit.'

Fortunately our host had been following the conversation intently. As the heiress was about to ask another insensitive question about torture, he quietly but forcefully turned the conversation in another direction. It was a royal dismissal and everyone knew it. The woman shut up like a scolded child and we all breathed a sigh of relief.

Later when we returned to the salon for drinks, one of the other American guests approached me and apologized for her fellow countrywoman. I smiled and told her there was no need as I'd rather enjoyed the joust. As we spoke, I watched the woman in question drop a glass of wine to the floor. Fragments of the exquisite crystal goblet scattered everywhere and everyone turned at the noise except the heiress who continued talking to her companion as if nothing had happened. It is the habit of the privileged to shatter things and not their inclination to pick up the pieces. I helped clear up the detritus, placing the shards in a napkin before setting it on the ancient sideboard near the heiress, thus enabling me to have another chat with her.

'You know, Irishman, you have a bit of a mouth on you, but I like you. I genuinely like you more by the minute.'

My answer was out of my mouth before I could stop it. 'Well, I kind of fancy you for exactly the same reason.'

And for the rest of the evening, when we weren't being serenaded by Los Parakeets, the heiress and the Irishman chewed the fat in amicable accord.

≡ ⫼ ≡

After the meal we take coffee and liqueurs in the great salon. The heiress sits at the grand piano, which she plays very well, and calls on people to sing to her accompaniment. She bellows at me, 'John, you're English – gimme some Vera Lynn!'

I manage a passable 'White Cliffs of Dover' but when she calls for more, some subconscious self-preservation system stops me remembering 'We'll Meet Again'.

᠕᠕

We had to leave this paradise and move on. There were still three thousand miles in front of us. After a night in Santiago we left by train for Chillán, birthplace of Bernardo O'Higgins.

Everyone we spoke to about our plans told us we were unwise to travel by train. They were dirty, noisy, they didn't run on time; why didn't we take the bus or fly? Our answer was simple. We believed the best way to see a place was by train. People simply shook their heads as if to say, poor deluded fools. But we were determined and the next day found ourselves at the railway station.

The train lurched out of the station in Santiago like a great drunken whale, rolling from side to side at unbelievable angles. Suddenly I was beginning to believe all the stories. Five and a half hours of this reckless rocking was not something to look forward to.

≡Ⅲ≡

As we hang on to our seats, eyes rotating with every violent lurch, I say, 'D'you reckon you can get seasick on dry land?'

Holding his stomach, bulging his eyes and puffing out his cheeks, mimicking someone on the verge of throwing up, Brian replies, 'If it's like this all the way to Chillán – how long is it? Five hours? – then yes, it's almost certain!'

However, once clear of the station sidings with their mauve and yellow signal boxes, we level out and it is plain sailing.

There are occasional small shrines beside the track, presumably marking the spot of a tragic accident. In the warmth of the spacious carriage we enjoy that pleasant, comfortable drowsiness that comes when you are free from the bustle of others and from any responsibilities. We watch advertising hoardings flash past, most with Spanish names. The occasional English one, like 'Chadwick and Sons', a garage in the middle of nowhere, comes as something of a shock. Their names are probably the last vestige of any Englishness.

‧᠕᠕᠊

The tidy shanty-like suburbs gave way to acres of bright-coloured containers being loaded with acres of fruit, in preparation for their long journey to the supermarkets of North America. Speeding past, these packing yards looked like an abstract cubist canvas, each square of colour melting into the next.

Pushing further into the open countryside, the small shacks of the farm workers looked like ghostly throwbacks to Steinbeck's dustbowl country. The rural stations were dilapidated, peeling pastels of blue, orange and Amarillo yellow. Behind them the dry scorched earth of the Andean foothills sprang up and lost themselves in the heat haze.

As the train bullnosed southwards, we sank back into the armchair-like seats and talked about the pleasures of Los Lingues and how it seemed that train travel was not as woeful as had been suggested. The carriage might not have been spotlessly clean but it was highly comfortable lying back in the huge leather seats and planning what to do in Chillán. The train had a stewardess dressed in a neat black uniform piped with yellow. She was extremely solicitous and helpful and neither of us could understand why people were so critical. We were soon to find out.

In the meantime we watched the changing countryside. So many of the rivers we crossed were dried up but still seemed to be of immense width. We passed more stations than we stopped at, and at each of them two or three lean mongrels lay dozing, hopeful of an occasional titbit. The whole countryside seemed paralysed by languor. I watched, infected myself by the lazy drag of the train. Every twenty minutes or so the refreshment trolley would come trundling down the carriage. The attendant's squeaky voice sang out, 'Bibedas, sandwich, café, cola, cerveza.' Hour after hour the squeaky vowels of his Spanish diction ground its affliction on us. But we were forced to put up with such irritations and before we knew it we were offloading our luggage in Bernardo's Chillán.

We knew little about the place apart from the facts gleaned from a book. The original city had been destroyed by an earthquake in 1833 and its replacement was similarly destroyed in

1939. It had also been the home of Arturo Prat, the renowned
naval hero, also of Irish extraction. I laughed and said to John that
perhaps the fates would be grateful and Bernardo and Arturo
would delay any intended earthquakes until our homage to the
heroes was complete and we had moved on.

We booked into a hotel in the town square which was named
after Bernardo's mother, Isabel Riquelme, and after a quick shower
and a beer decided to visit Parc O'Higgins.

We walked through the town laughing: Bernardo was everywhere. Banco O'Higgins stood solid and imposing at the corner of
the square, and even the cabs had roof signs declaring Taxi
O'Higgins.

Chillán was laid out on a grid system. Getting around was uncomplicated but there was really little to see. Earthquakes had
obviously destroyed whatever history had been here. Even the
statue of Bernardo in the square was hoisted on a huge Nelson-like
column. He might be able to look over the land but no one was
able to look on Bernardo. The town was lively and full of young
people. Even well into the late evening they could be found walking in couples and groups. This sudden press of people made me
think of how empty the countryside we passed through had been.
Santiago is said to contain one third of the total population of
Chile and I could well believe it. What I realized I had missed as
we drove to Los Lingues, and here also, was the roadside art and
craft stall. The bric-à-brac of ethnic and local culture was entirely
absent. Perhaps Chile's was an urbanized culture and the long-
established mix of diverse immigration had eroded any artistic
expression in the form of keepsakes such as I was looking for.

At the Parc O'Higgins we found a small museum. It was filled
with artefacts that some local dignitary had donated to the town
and the four walls of the upper gallery were lined with paintings
by a celebrated local artist. They were executed in the French
Impressionist style, and well worth the space that had been
afforded them.

Finally we found Bernardo's bronze statue. It was cast in the
customary pose of the great general leading his armies into war.
His horse reared up on its hind legs, defiantly pawing the air.
Bernardo's sword was thrust forward, calling the charge. But it was

somehow disappointing, reminding me of the little lead soldiers I had been given as a child.

The long, fifteen-foot-high, stone mural depicting the history of those first years of liberation was, however, a real work of labour and art. Large lumps of rough local stone, carefully selected and positioned, made up the relief of this brutal mosaic. The centre-piece was, again, the Liberator's charging warhorse. The animal's snorting mouth was set with pebble-sized shards of uncut marble and flint, its terrified, screaming expression caught perfectly in those broken stone chips. I had never seen such a mosaic before and its simple ingenuity informed me that here was an artistic ability far superior to the kind of local craft work I had expected. This marriage of labour, art and history was something Neruda was teaching me. I knew if he had ever seen this memorial he would have heartily approved. I remembered that on his own sea-facing wall at Isla Negra there was a mosaic made of local stone and glass from his empty bottles and pieces of wood and shell that he had casually picked up.

As we walked round the park, we discussed the strange paradox of a land liberated by the radical intellectual son of an immigrant Irishman who remained so obviously part of the history and folk memory of the people, compared with the disastrous and appalling years after Allende. There were many parallels and many contra-dictions that our ill-informed minds could not resolve. But these were the tantalizing questions that a stranger asks. Outsiders, after all, see history as one simple clear projection, a list of events and incidents in time. I was trying to understand things from Pablo and Bernardo's emotional perspective, wanting to get inside their skins, or rather to allow their ghosts to enter mine so that I might 'feel' their response.

≡Ⅲ≡

We find a fine statue of Bernardo in the park. On rearing horse he waves his cocked hat at the adoring masses. Every town in Chile has solid statues to national heroes and most of them are good. But what makes this park special is another monument. A wall, sixty metres long, carries a mural depicting scenes from his life in a mosaic of Chilean stone. This tribute to a native son is more powerful than any European public statuary.

Born here in 1778, Bernardo was sent at seventeen to London for his education. There and later in Spain he became involved with South American revolutionaries. Given his father's position as Spain's Viceroy of Peru, Bernardo's politics must have seemed remarkable. This aspect of the man's life – apart from his being half Irish and a liberator – greatly intrigues Brian.

'Didn't you used to say that you wanted to write something about him, the great Irishman freeing the South Americans from the European yoke?' I ask.

'Damn right! And we Irish are still trying to throw off the imperial millstone today, aren't we, Englishman? But that's only a little part of it. Think of it: your father runs an entire region – Chile and Peru – but you grow up determined to destroy all that he stands for. Why?'

'Yeah, it makes great drama. He hardly knew his father, according to my books.'

'That's true – he used his ma's name until after Ambrose died. Then he came back here and lived on the old man's estate, very happily it seems, till the independence movement got going.'

The early nineteenth century was a period of extraordinary upheaval. North America had won its independence from Britain, the French Revolution had toppled the monarchy there, and then Napoleon conquered Spain leaving her colonies, including Chile, in a state of limbo. Although swearing allegiance to the deposed king, most grasped the opportunity of greater independence with alacrity and governed themselves, paying only lip-service to the Spanish crown.

In Chile, local leaders formed a junta in 1810. By 1813 they had a firm grip on the country and had even written a constitution. When the Spanish king Ferdinand was reinstated after Napoleon's defeat in the Peninsular War, he looked to re-establish his rule over the colonies and backed an invasion of Chile. In October 1814, General O'Higgins's Chilean patriots were decisively beaten at Rancagua.

We walk along the mural, studying the scenes depicting the Rancagua debacle and the subsequent flight over the Andes to

Argentina. Just over two years later, O'Higgins returned with the Argentine general José de San Martín and their 'Army of the Andes', numbering some 3,600 men. At the Battle of Chacabuco in February 1817 the Spanish army was routed. A new government was set up and O'Higgins was named Director Supremo.

'You'd like that, wouldn't you!' I say. '"As Supreme Director I, Brian Bastardballs Keenan, devise a new ruling . . ."'

'Quite right too. From now on all Brits will touch the forelock and call me El Big Supremo!'

For months on end during our captivity we had no books and only a set of dominoes to pass the hours. Dominoes is a great game but when you have played it a thousand times, it loses some of its appeal. With nothing to do and so much time to fill, we invented games to get through the days. In a cell just large enough for two mattresses we would sit crosslegged, facing each other. Having begged a bit of old cardboard box and the loan of a pen from a guard we would try to remember games from childhood and reinvent them. We drew a winding path marked out with spaces and obstacles, a customized version of snakes and ladders.

'That's good,' I said, 'but how can we make dice, we've nothing heavy enough.'

'No problem,' said Brian, carefully shaping a piece of card into a hexagon with the nail clippers. He marked the edges 'one' to 'six' and put a dead match through the centre. He spun it and the improvised dice came to rest on 'six'.

'There you are, six to start, so I'm off!'

He was highly imaginative and could overcome difficulties that would have me giving up. But he had the infuriating habit of foreseeing a problem in the first few rounds, calling a halt and, with the immortal phrase, 'I have devised a new ruling', changing the game and usually eradicating my advantage with it.

Reading more about O'Higgins I feel that our jokes about El Supremo might suggest more substantial similarities between the two men. He and Brian both grew up in places of civil conflict, both became keenly political in their youth and both developed a liberal view of how society should be run. I imagine that Bernardo shared some of Bri's charisma, perhaps also some of his eloquence, yet I have a strange idea that were they to meet they would find it hard to communicate; their clear-sighted stubbornness provoking what to an outsider would be a mystifying tension.

O'Higgins was Supreme Director for six years. Though he introduced many liberal social reforms, ultimately he fell foul of public opinion because he was undemocratic. He alienated the church and landed aristocracy by raising taxes to promote his liberal reforms and trying to rework rules on land ownership and inheritance. Threatened with an army revolt, he resigned in 1823 and went to live out his remaining years in exile in Peru.

'What a strange thing,' I say. 'The man who seems now to be synonymous with Chilean freedom only lived in the country for twenty years, and died an outcast.'

'I wonder what made him tick? How would he have lived those last twenty-odd years? He had a farm in Peru – the great general turned homesteader. Seems he never married but, like his dad, fathered children with local women. It would be a tough job bringing him to life.'

'Yes. But I think you should try – takes one uppity bugger to know another!'

That evening we went in search of one Enrique Schuler. Our guidebook informed us that the banks did not give a good exchange rate and we should ask for this character at the Café Paris. It all sounded a bit dubious but we had no alternative. It was evening, we had run out of cash and we were leaving the next day.

Eventually, with only the vaguest of directions, we found our man after trailing around the back streets for some time. In a tiny shop selling nothing but balls of knitting wool, the mysterious Enrique stood talking to the lady owner. He quickly ushered us in and changed our traveller's cheques. He was pleasant, polite and not the least bit seedy, with something of the look of a parish priest about him.

As we returned to the town centre, the evening streets were still filled with young people and disco music was everywhere. We settled at a pavement table at the Café Paris and ordered brandies while we sat and watched the nightlife pass by.

≡Ⅲ≡

I wake next morning, my mind full of only one thing: is John Bruton with Fianna Gael or Fianna Fail? I am perplexed for a moment at this odd concern so far from home, then realize we must have been talking politics last night. After eating we spent a couple of hours at a pavement café. Dimly I recall drinking cognac and suddenly I have one of those alarming 'morning after' flashbacks. Brian is sitting grinning at our table. I am standing with my back to the café wall preparing to demonstrate the gait of the younger German at Los Lingues. Why I wanted to do this I cannot imagine. After a while, though, I became aware of the waiter giving me odd looks so I returned to my chair. It must have been then that, illogically, we turned our attention to Irish politics.

After a restorative breakfast we head for the market: aisles of stalls spread out from a hub, specializing in everything from flowers to spices, foods to hardware, even saddles. Brian is keen on a saddle, but settles on an elegant poncho in the colours of County Mayo. We wander around, buying some water and snacks for our next expedition on the train, to Temuco.

〜〜

The market was a delight, teeming and symphonic, full of people and voices shouting and laughing and calling out their wares. It was like walking into a huge aquarium of colour. John bought a hat which made him look like Harrison Ford, or so he thought, and I bought some special riding gear for a young horse-fanatic niece. I snapped pictures like a maniac and began to understand the paintings that we had looked at the day before.

On our return to the station, we discovered our train had either left or never arrived or perhaps was not even running that day. It was difficult to tell. In the absence of any reliable information about its replacement, we decided to take the bus.

Chapter Ten

≡‖≡

Chilean bus stations are like those the world over – a large hall where the various bus companies have little offices, usually no more than dingy cubicles. You book your place and then wait for the departure to be announced over the tannoy. Beyond a few seats and a newsstand there is rarely any comfort on offer other than a couple of kiosks selling a sad-looking array of sandwiches and drinks.

It is a banal process. People wander about rather aimlessly with bags and bundles until their destination is announced and they move to the stated departure point. Although often there is quite a send-off for a family member, being Chilean these are fairly subdued affairs, even the children letting out only the odd yelp.

We queue for our bus – then, at the last minute, my stomach threatens revolution so I nip to the lavatory. This too is basic. I have to pay to get in and for loo paper too; not advisable when you are in a hurry and do not have the time to search Berlitz for the right phrase. In any case, would it have the Spanish for 'I'm desperate, pal, get out of my way!' Within seconds of surpassing the various hurdles, I hear Brian bellowing.

'∿∿

As the bus pulled out, I jumped up.

John, John . . . he's not here! Tell them to stop, I kept telling myself. Where is the stupid bollox?

'Stop the bus!'

I tried to squeeze past a very elderly lady fussing in the aisle. '*Mes amigo*,' I said, panicked by the bus's apparently imminent departure.

'*Mes amigo*,' I said again, pointing to the bus shelter. Everyone looked perplexed at the demonstrative gringo shouting, 'Stop, stop.' Fortunately my panic and insistence paid off. The bus stopped.

Everyone seemed genuinely concerned as I jumped off, but they started laughing when Harrison Ford dashed out of the gents', buckling and zipping himself together, as I shouted, 'For frigg's sake, John, come on. Come on, will you!'

≡III≡

'Is John Bruton Fianna Fail or Gael?' I ask when we finally settle down.

But I am clearly destined to remain ignorant on this matter. Brian has already adopted his favoured travelling position: head on chest, eyes closed.

Once on the road you will be entertained with music or, very often on the longer runs, with a video. Here, as elsewhere, the popularity of the movies of Sly Stallone and Bruce Willis is clear; I guess grunts and expletives are simplest to dub. Brian can – or at least he makes every attempt to – sleep through this when he wants to. I can only do it with my earplugs screwed in. Despite feeling groggy I decide to remain awake and watch the world rolling by.

The warm morning sun burns off the mist from last night's rain – and smoke rises as the fires in the small houses are rekindled for another day. Every now and then we take a detour from the main road to drop people off outside the bus companies' wooden chalets in one of the small towns. Once off the Pan American Highway the farmsteads and villages are fewer and farther between and many of these places look run down. While the buildings and streets are shabby, you do not get a sense of real poverty as the people appear healthy and are well dressed.

At times the road peters out into a single-lane dirt track at roadworks. At one such place I get out for a cigarette and am struck by how precarious civilization can seem here. Looking at the tree-covered hillsides, often shrouded in mist, I feel an air of the primeval, of raw nature close by. If one wandered far from this ribbon of communication one could easily be lost to the modern world. Then the sun breaks through and everything is reassuringly pretty again. This region is called La Frontera. It seems appropriate.

A light rain begins to fall and it gets cooler as we move through an ever more verdant landscape. We cross the wide Bio-Bio river, the old border between Spanish control and the wild country of Araucania, home of the Mapuche people, 'people of the earth'. They were never defeated by the Spanish, and were not finally broken by the independent Chileans until 1881. They were clearly great guerrilla fighters but not, as often portrayed, a naturally violent people. I am reading *The Happy Captive*, the true story of a conquistador held hostage by the Mapuche. He came to love and admire his fiercely independent captors.

After the last uprising in 1881 their lands were taken over by the state and settled by immigrants from Germany, Switzerland, Italy and many from Croatia.

I slept until John woke me up. 'This is the Bio-Bio!' I looked out sleepily. In half flood and marked contrast to the dried-out river beds of the north, the Bio-Bio was a broad river. Huge stones which would normally have formed its bed now sat exposed. They were massive and round. This was big country. These stones had arrived before the waters rounded them and their bulk and weight clearly expressed the power of the river that moved them.

We crossed another wide, more slow-moving river. I remembered my feeble attempts at fishing with my father. We would never have left a river like this. It sat waiting and, I imagined, full with fish. A road sign informed us we were entering the land of the Mapuche Indians.

Beside us a young woman and her child were sleeping. The baby could not have been more than a few months old. It looked like the Eskimo babies I had seen in Alaska. The mother slept with her hand in her child's, its tiny fingers wrapped tightly around hers, and in each ear a gold stud glinted.

I have never been to Canada, but I imagined that this landscape of deep, wet, green forest was similar. The houses, set here and there among trees, looked like 1950s seaside bungalows or tiny Swiss chalets. But the occasional faces of the people along the roadside declared quite clearly where we were. We were the gringos and this was their land. Their faces were round and silent like the boulders along the Bio-Bio. They had been here as long as those stones, tumbling and rolling in the river bed. There were no apples, oranges, peaches, tomatoes, pumpkins or grapes growing at the side of the road. The sunny north was far behind us. The windows began to steam up. Outside the temperature had dropped.

Here and there, the tight forest opened up to small hills. For a moment, looking through the misted window, I felt I was in the drumlin country of my own homeland, or even the Wicklow hills near to where I now live.

I looked out on the forest and the timber yards, the black heaps of charcoal, the rusty-coloured stumps and rings of trunk-wood set against the painted clinker-board walls of the houses. We were going to Temuco and I read Neruda's poem about his first journey there.

> I don't know when we came to Temuco.
> It was vague, being born, and a slow business,
> being truly born,
> and slowly feeling, knowing, hating, loving.
> All that has both flowers and thorns.
> From the dusty bosom of my country
> they took me, still an infant,
> into the rain of Araucania.
> The boards of the house

smelled of the woods,
of deep forest.

From that time on, my love
had wood in it
and everything I touched turned into wood.
They became one in me,
lives and leaves,
certain women and the hazelnut
spring, men and trees.
I love the world of wind and foliage.
I can't tell lips from roots.

From axes and rain, it grew up,
that town of wood
recently carved, like
a new star stained with resin,
and the saw and the sierras
made love day and night,
singing away,
working away,
and that sharp chirp of the cricket
raising its plaint
in the unyielding solitude turns into
my song, my song.
My heart goes on cutting wood,
singing with the sawmills in the rain,
milling together cold, sawdust, wood smell.

≡Ⅲ≡

I consult the guidebook for a place to stay in Temuco. It recommends the Continental Hotel.

'Here, Bri, this sounds like us: "excellent restaurant, the bar is popular with locals in the evening, clean, friendly, colonial-style wooden building".'

Brian laughs, showing me the Neruda poem he has been reading. 'The Continental it has to be,' he agrees.

∿∿

Temuco was a special place for me. For it was the major city of the Mapuche and it was the place where Neruda grew up. I am a firm believer in the saying, 'find the child and you will discover the man', and his childhood memories of Temuco had infiltrated his poetry and formed part of the intricate symbolism of the work.

Neruda identified and sympathized with the indigenous peoples. Maybe his sensitivities were heightened by the fact that his father distanced himself from his children. I hope that Temuco will bring me closer to him.

In his *Memoirs*, Neruda is scathing about what was called the policy of the pacification of 'Araucania'. He writes:

> Every kind of weapon was used against the Indians, unsparingly; carbine blasts, the burning of villages, and later, a more fatherly method, alcohol and the law. The lawyer became a specialist at stripping them of their fields, the judge sentenced them when they protested, the priest threatened them with eternal fire. And hard spirits finally consummated the annihilation of this superb race.

In another part of his *Memoirs*, he declares,

> Temuco is a pioneer town, one of those towns that have no past, though it does have hardware stores. Since the Indians can't read, the stores hang their eye-catching signs out on the streets: an enormous saw, a giant cooking pot, a Cyclopean padlock, a mammoth spoon. Farther along the street, shoe stores, a colossal boot.

In a sense, Neruda wrote with an Indian's eye. If you 'saw' his poetry the way the Indians 'read' the shopfront symbols, the work became less obscure. And as in Neruda's poetry, rain was everywhere, patient and falling endlessly from the grey sky.

Having spent his childhood on the frontier, he never lost the sense of wonder he felt while observing the Mapuche and exploring the dense, majestic forests that surrounded Temuco. He later recalled that when he travelled back and forth to the city as a student, 'I always felt myself stifling as soon as I left the great forest, the timberland that drew me back like a mother. To me, the adobe houses, the cities with a past, seemed to be filled with cobwebs and silence.'

Our rain-soaked arrival in what seemed a dismal city did not encourage me to share Neruda's sense of wonder. As I stood bedraggled and a little cast down by my first impression of Temuco, the great cartographer McCarthy was still working his magic and pulling all the right things out of his bag of tricks.

'OK, Sancho, just a few blocks this way and we're home and dry!' Don John declared.

'You're a little late with the dry bit,' I answered, shuffling after John's rapidly disappearing figure.

The hotel squeaked and creaked as we were shown to our room. Wood was indeed everywhere, polished and glowing. Nothing much had changed here since it was built. It had the feel of the frontier about it. As I stood on the landing overlooking the foyer I could imagine it in busier times, buzzing with ranchers, travellers and businessmen.

Before dinner we decided to change and go for a walk. The deafening roar and explosion of the pipes in the bathroom made us laugh. Outside it was lashing down, and inside the plumbing gave every indication that it was about to join in.

As we walked through the dark wet streets I saw again those enigmatic Indian faces staring out from the shadows of doorways. I remembered a photo I had looked at as a child in an old encyclopaedia. A sepia-tinted group of South American Indians had intrigued me and somehow locked itself away in my memory, only to emerge as I contemplated this city. The strangeness of their coarse ethnic faces. The women in their pork-pie hats drawing heavily on short, crude pipes. They were posing for the camera and yet they weren't. There was something very distant about them, and here they were back with me again after thirty-five years. These were the same faces. Some of them were sheltering from the rain; others were packing up the woollen sweaters they had been selling. As we ventured further into the back streets I expected to see more of them and to be accosted for money. But

I was wrong, there were no beggars here. I suppose I had an idea of a marginalized people, drinking in doorways or sitting wrapped in an old blanket, a hand outstretched.

But I remembered that the Mapuche have never been defeated at any point in their history. Not even the imperialism of the Inca or the Spanish had subsumed them. Colonialism and modernization had never broken or pushed them to the sidelines. I had expected to see pride and perhaps even arrogance in the faces. But no, there was only quiet confidence that this was their town. I thought again of the sleeping mother and child on the bus and remembered how they clung to each other, even in sleep. These people needed no one but themselves. That evening I ordered a meal of vicuña meat which was a staple of the Mapuche people. I didn't want to make myself feel any more alien.

Our walk through the rain-filled streets had revealed the last remnants of those giant shopfront symbols that had so intrigued the young Neruda. On our perambulations I had spied huge shoes, scissors, knives and cooking pots, and I had been drawn into the fascination of the Mapuche Indian with something of the same curious admiration as Neruda.

The poet tells a story of how, as a timid child, he was playing in the back of his house when a hand reached through a hole in the wooden fence and placed a small toy lamb in his palm. Neftali quickly ran into his house and retrieved one of his favourite treasures, a pine cone, and handed it to the unknown child on the other side of the fence. He later wrote about this experience that 'maybe this small and mysterious exchange of gifts remained inside me also, deep and inexhaustible, giving my poetry light'.

In a strange way I could understand that story. I was glad we had come to Temuco in the rain. It had made me look harder. In a way I can hardly explain, encountering those dark, passionate, ageless faces, I too had received a 'mysterious exchange of gifts' which I know will remain with me and provide a light into Neruda's poetry and the Chile I was only now learning to see.

Our time was short and we had to leave the next day but we had pencilled in another stop on our return. Perhaps by then I would be better prepared to uncover the secrets of this city at the edge of the green forests.

≡Ⅲ≡

From Temuco we want to drive south through the Lake District and take a look at the island of Chiloé before catching a ferry down to Patagonia. Patagonia: the name holds such mystery for me that it takes on the mantle of a sea-level Shangri-La. Yet we are going there after all, no longer just dreaming.

We set about organizing transport. Before entering the first car hire office I consult the phrase book and rehearse my lines. We go in.

'*Quisiera alquilar un coche para seis dias con devolución en Puerto Montt, por favor!*' ('I'd like to rent a car for six days and return it in Puerto Montt, please.')

Brian stands beside me nodding wisely. The man behind the desk nods also, smiles and replies with a rapid burst of Spanish.

'Ah,' I say, 'um. *Habla usted Inglés?*'

No, he does not speak English.

'OK. *Seis dias, bueno?*'

Six days is good.

'*Devolución en Puerto Montt es OK?*'

That is OK too.

'*Bueno. Cuánto?*' ('Good. How much?')

The man gets out his calculator, does an elaborate series of sums, then shows us the result glowing on the small machine's LCD. He gives us a solemn nod and says, '*Muy bueno, señors!*'

We go through an increasingly fluent version of this exchange at the various hire companies around town, and settle on a Toyota Tercel at 450 dollars all in. It is no great roadster but then there are no great roads so we reckon it will suffice.

〰〰

At first the landscape looked like how I remembered Tipperary, but there the similarities ended. Lonache, Lanco, Los Lagos, Rio Reno, Osorno. They all seemed lifeless and forgotten. But at about ten o'clock the streets and roads came to life. It was the Easter Festival and throngs of people arrayed in their Sunday best were walking to church, clutching bunches of palm leaves.

☰⚏☰

Sitting on the balcony of a cabin on the edge of Lago Villarrica in the evening sun, I look across at the perfectly conical peak of Volcán Villarrica and the twin peaks of Volcán Llaima glowing pink above the dark green hillsides across the water. We had a gentle drive here through open country of pasture and woodland. There are some fantastic houses in the middle of nowhere; from mansions that look like they should be on the set of *The Addams Family* to romantic, turreted, modern whimsies. Churches in particular seem often to be remote from any settlements, to cover as wide a catchment area as possible. We passed a tiny, wooden Mormon church with a few faithful sitting outside it and others, more intricate, with the onion domes of east European and Russian orthodoxy.

This cabin is a great find. We did some shopping at a supermarket and Bri has elected to cook tonight's supper. I begin browsing through the guidebooks thinking of where we should head for the next day. Brian appears with a bottle of red wine to top up my glass.

'I'll throw those bloody books in that lake!'

'What?'

'Jesus, John, you drive all day, we stop in a fine place and all you can think is, where next? Give me a break! Instead of where are we going tomorrow, think about where we are now.'

'But there are still so many places to see!'

'Yes, but you know most places are like the last place and anyway we can't see everything. Take it easy, soak up the atmosphere a little.'

'You want to stay here tomorrow night then, loaf about a bit?'

'Sounds good to me.'

I take a deep sip of Tarapaca, feel the sun warm on my face as I look at the lake and volcanoes.

'Bugger it! You're right – I'll go see the manager and tell him.'

'Now you're whistling Dixie! The steaks will be ready in five minutes.'

*

On our way out the next day we bump into the manager, a nice, middle-aged gent who speaks good English. He tells us he originally came from Santiago but has made a good life here in the tourist business. 'You still want to stay, my friends?'

'Sure, we're having a grand time,' says Brian.

'So you are not worried about earthquake?'

'Should we be?' I ask.

'You didn't notice it last night? The tremor?'

'No, we must have slept right through it,' says Bri.

As we walk on I feel cheated.

'One tremor and we completely miss it! How?'

'Very strong red wine, that Tarapaca.'

We saunter into town down the wide, calm and friendly streets of Villarrica, one of the most popular resorts in this, the Lake District. As with our cabins, much of the architecture could have been transplanted from the Alps and there are Germanic names over many shopfronts. We buy some basic supplies. The bread shop is far more confusing than one would guess. There are three ladies working in it, all standing around the till. The many loaves, cakes and rolls are on open shelves around the walls and in a central unit. Plastic bags are available from dispensers. An elderly couple meander about pointing out delicacies to each other. Bri is across the road buying some water so I swiftly decide on some rolls, take a bag and pick up a pair of tongs.

The three ladies all start squawking at once. I turn to them as one descends on me, earnestly shaking her head, to take the tongs from me. Her colleagues become calm again and the old couple, visibly shocked too, also relax and turn back to their perusing. I do not move. I feel as if I have just been halted by airport security; guns might even be trained on me. Without making any sudden movements I nod slowly in the direction of the rolls and cautiously raise four fingers with what I hope is a winning smile. All goes well and the rolls are tonged into my bag. Lady Number One nods kindly and gestures towards her colleagues at the till. I murmur *gracias* a few times and go to Lady Number Two, behind the till. This time there is no outcry, just laughter and much shaking of heads. Clearly they have realized that I am not dangerous or malicious but merely a very simple gringo.

Wreathed in smiles the old folk tut and nod benignly. The wife, very elegant and dripping gold, steps up and gently, hand on my elbow, guides me to Lady Number Three who checks the bag and writes out the cost on a sticker which she fixes to it. I feel I am getting the hang of this insane job-creation scheme and turn to Lady Number Two, still smiling by her till, and make a gesture to offer her my bag with a questioning look on my face. The whole company nods effusively as I master my first shopping lesson. I pay and leave hurriedly, almost flattening Brian who is clutching bags of bottles.

'Look where you're going, fella!'

'My God, what a palaver! Did you get the Idiot's Guide to Complex Shopping?'

'They were up to something or other, so I just ignored them, got what I wanted and gave the man on the till a few banknotes and let him work it out.'

'You devised a new ruling!'

'Correcto!'

Smug git.

I fancy heading back to base and chilling out on the balcony. Brian has other ideas and convinces me to look at the *artesanal* or craft market. He seems insatiable for these tatty arcades. As far as I can judge they are all pretty uniform, usually pricey and not offering much that is different from what you would find in Switzerland or Camden. We do not buy anything and head back for a pleasant lunch looking over the lake. The afternoon is spent dozing and reading. I lose myself in the magic of Isabel Allende's *The House of the Spirits* which has lain hidden at the bottom of my bags since Arica. Having thought to ignore this resort, I happily admit that Bri was absolutely right about staying here.

A couple of days later, we wait for breakfast after an overnight stop in Liffen. We are on the shores of Lago Ranco which is supposed to be very beautiful. It may be, but the sky is low and overcast and it is very cold and windy outside. Indoors, smoke pours from the fireplace in the lounge area. The owner, a smiling, nervous man, seemed quite amused when we pitched up here after ten last night, though I cannot imagine why. Our late arrival I righteously blame on Brian who did not believe we should take the turn we should have taken. This added an hour of rather hairy driving in order to rejoin the correct route. We found ourselves on a single-lane gravel track with ridges of stones on either side and down the middle. The Toyota Tercel is just too low for such roads and its undercarriage played a frightening bongo beat. We were hemmed in on either side by tall grasses and felt we were heading down a tunnel of no return. Occasionally the road would widen to reveal a couple of houses looming in the dark, sometimes a glimpse of people on their verandas. We kept moving, my anxiety over the likelihood of ripping off the exhaust on the road encouraging wilder fears of meeting *Deliverance*-style hill- or rather lake-billies. I ended up feeling so spooked I nearly put the car right off the road when a vast pig raced out just in front of us.

After checking in, we went to the bar and had a couple of beers and some chips. It was full of locals. Four men sat round a table drinking a jug of pisco and beer. They looked like they were in for the duration.

Normally these backwoods dens are like a magnet to me. I tend to sit in them for hours trying to look impossibly inconspicuous, hoping that by remaining long enough the 'locals' will forget I'm there and then I might discover that 'exotic moment' that sums up the whole experience of travelling or else opens up a line of thinking about somewhere that I hadn't considered before.

The problem with this place was that it was so tiny and so packed with people that it was impossible to merge into the background. We were definitely in the wrong bar and attempting to brass it out was merely becoming uncomfortable. When I went to the toilet and realized that the woman in the next paper-thin cubicle was having the noisiest session I have ever heard, my discomfort became unbearable. I returned to where John was sitting and suggested we drink up and leave. He gratefully agreed. As I washed down the last gulps of beer, I saw my next-door neighbour emerge from the toilet. She was a pretty native woman, but our brief intimate encounter in the lavatory shattered all my illusions.

≡Ⅲ≡

As we drive along the road – excellent surface, no pigs in sight – that we should have taken yesterday, I realize that I must be emanating smugness. I am sure that most people enjoy being proved right, but I have been told before that the levels of unspoken 'told you so' I generate might lead others to homicidal thoughts. Excellent!

‹〜〜›

As it is generally acknowledged that the mindset of the domestic servant is not given to homicidal tendencies, Sancho Panza simply considered Don John's smugness to be an aristocratic idiosyncrasy. Pity was the proper attitude, Sancho Panza thought, but pity was not an inexhaustible quality. And while Sancho pretended to sleep, he plotted the most hideous revenge.

≡Ⅲ≡

We continue on in silence past wide flat fields of maize and pastureland dotted with clumps of trees. The fields roll away to the hills and the copses become forest. We stop at Frutillar, a very German resort looking across to the perfect, snow-capped Osorno volcano on the far side of Lago Llanquihue. But the place seems so dead and sanitized – you probably get shot for littering – that we decide to head on further round the lake to Puerto Varas.

A fiery sunset turns clouds purple, black and magnificent. On the other horizon a forest fire on a mountaintop mirrors diurnal nature. Presumably such fires are just left to burn as they are so inaccessible. The frontier is never far away despite the main roads. This place is civilized but can so easily turn primeval.

‹〜〜›

As the light faded we became lost. Fortunately a group of college students were doing a road survey, accompanied by a policeman.

He approached us and, sensing our dilemma, gave us directions. Both John and I thought how, not so many years ago, a traveller might not have found the police so accommodating. He assured us Puerto Varas was a beautiful place and hoped we would have a good holiday.

He was right. It was a picturesque little village built around a sweeping bay. Its one striking feature was a large, ornate church built entirely of corrugated iron by German Jesuits in 1918. Our hotel was luxurious compared to Temuco and the food was a lot different from vicuña steaks. It had that comfortable end-of-season feel about it.

We decided to relax in preparation for our four-day boat trip to Patagonia. As we walked through this very European enclave, we noticed signs advertising an amazing range of activities: horse-riding, canoeing, water sports, boat trips, rafting, fishing, even volcano-climbing. Supper, a few drinks and a game or two of cards were as much as we were up to.

≡ Ⅲ ≡

At supper Brian orders shrimps in something called Pil Pil sauce. We are merrily tucking in when he suddenly shouts, 'This sauce would roast the tongue out of your face.'

The Belfast emphasis on the last word, 'fayess', and his look of outrage have me helpless with laughter.

〜〜

We talked endlessly into the night about deserts, horses, the Andes, our forthcoming trip south. In a way, our excited conversation reminded me of other discussions long into the night when we had only our imaginations and dreadful hope to sustain us. But that was another time and another place, a long way from the delights of Puerto Varas.

In a few days we would be in Patagonia's never-never and beyond that, the final extremity, Tierra del Fuego, and the long shadows of our captivity could not dull our enthusiasm.

≡⫴≡

The following morning I wake early. The sky over the lake, towards the distant hills, is very black in the first light of day. I shiver, thinking ahead to the boat trip out into the Pacific we will be making in a few days. Yet, as I watch, the sky over my head begins to clear, and soon, as if it is a roller blind, the whole black mass disappears to the south, revealing first the far shore and the hills, then the snow-capped peaks of the volcanoes beyond.

After breakfast we walk along the lakeshore. The sun is out and there is a fair breeze. Then within a couple of minutes we are forced to seek shelter as the wind turns bitterly cold and hailstones come flying at us across the lake. A frightening change. Twenty minutes later and the sky has cleared again.

En route to Puerto Montt we drive past miles of flattened earth. Japanese businesses have bought up thousands of acres of primitive rainforest and are systematically stripping it, chipping it and then shipping it home to make wood pulp for the paper industry. Our English-language newspapers reported on the efforts of a growing ecological movement in Chile, but apparently the lure of big money has been irresistible for government ministries and so the rape of this virgin forest goes on unabated. In Puerto Montt we see the vast mountains of steaming wood chips with huge trucks crawling across their backs: another man-made horror like the slag heaps of Chuquicamata.

We dine at the Club Alemán which is, not surprisingly, very Germanic in style with lots of pine. Modern and more upmarket than most restaurants outside Santiago, it gives us a good meal. A certificate on the wall was signed by the Commandant of the Chiloé Naval Region, one Carlos Mackenney Schmauk: a history of Chilean immigration in one name. We try to imagine what he would look like.

'Tanned face with jet black hair and bandito moustache,' I suggest, 'wearing a kilt and—'

'Simultaneously clicking his boot heels a lot!' Brian raises his left index finger to make a mock moustache, while jerking his right palm to his shoulder and grunting, '*Jawohl!*'

Puerto Montt does not have a touristy air about it. The main shopping street is busy but a little shoddy, with the unfinished feel that most towns have here. Wires hang listlessly from telephone and power lines and there are strange little potholes in the pavements, which may be for drainage but are possibly intended as junctions for electric, water or gas supplies. I get my boots shined by a guy on the street and wander into some of the big chain stores, such as Johnson's and Ripley's, that are holding a *liquidacion*, a sale. I buy a couple of shirts for a fiver each.

⌃⌃⌃

Sancho Panza never ceases to be amazed at his excellency Don John's sartorial consciousness. The purchase of shirts was not unusual but having one's boots shined before entering the Patagonian wilderness spoke of a truly blue-blooded being.

≡ⅠⅠⅠ≡

We brunch at a Pizza Hut which is a surprisingly reassuring outpost of Western imperialism. We must be tired – next we will be looking for a McDonald's in Patagonia.

We wander down to the port at Angelmo from where we will be departing in a few days. This is where the wood chips are stockpiled before a giant vacuum device funnels them by the ton into a ship lying alongside. Brian spots an antique shop next door to a restaurant. After a while we twig we can only get in there by going through the bar so have a beer en route. The stuff is mainly junk but much fun and from all corners of the globe – at one time many ships must have called in here, stopping off between the Horn and Valparaíso and the other ports up the coast. I am quite tempted by a wonderful brass and copper diving helmet.

'Excess baggage?' observes Brian.

'You're telling me. I already have you to worry about!'

The road is full of cars and buses heading for the Estadio, so there must be a big match on. Grudgingly I follow Bri through yet another *feria artesanal*. It seems the place is bustling with locals

'Your money or your life!'

Man and horse
in perfect harmony.

TOP LEFT: Temporary settlement in the Museo valley.

TOP RIGHT: Non-stop tapping. Road-testing the Psion.

BOTTOM LEFT: Tom in the fossil field: 'A little boy again.'

BOTTOM RIGHT: Ireland greets the dawn.

'Nigel, a word if you please.'
Imminent terror on Death Ridge.

Sancho Panza struts his stuff.

LEFT: Nigel's life hangs in the balance, 15,000 feet above Argentina.

BOTTOM: The most comfortable way to sit in a saddle. Don Ramon's camp.

ABOVE: Bernardo, Brian and the Brit, Chillán.

TOP RIGHT: Checking out the lifeboats. Ferry to Patagonia.

BOTTOM RIGHT: Another extreme, Tierra del Fuego.

TOP: Tranquillity in the archipelago.

BOTTOM: Yak country. Alfonso's farm, Patagonia.

Compañeros, Chillán.

rather than tourists. He steers me into a shop selling saddles and checks out prices with the sweet old man running the place. After much sign language and use of the phrase book we work out that saddle, stirrups and reins would cost around £250 all in.

'Yes, but think what that would cost back home,' says Butch Cassidy, dismissing my reminder about excess baggage.

'Be that as it may, do you really see yourself trekking off into the Wicklow Mountains on a regular basis?'

'Sure I do!' Brian is endlessly optimistic.

We walk past Puerto Montt's imposing fire station. Ironically there is the burnt-out shell of an old wooden building right next door. In fact there are about three blackened ruins in the vicinity so either the developers are moving in and working insurance scams or there is a fire bug in the city. Then again perhaps the *bomberos* are keen on overtime within walking distance of the office.

We cruise in the trusty Tercel towards Paguar to catch a ferry to Chiloé, the large island that lies between the Pacific and the channel leading to Patagonia. This is flat land and although some houses are built of aluminium siding, most are wooden with shingle roofs. The land is divided up into neat square plots but there are large swathes of burned wood, now grey and petrified looking.

'You'd think they'd clear out all that dead wood and use the land,' I say.

'Maybe there's too much land and not enough people to farm it – this is frontier country, remember.'

The trip across the Chacao Channel takes twenty minutes over smooth water. As we go I read a little of the history of the place. The Spanish colonists held on to the island even when the Mapuche regained sway on the mainland. During the seventeenth century the small colony was supplied by a boat from Lima just once a year.

'Talk about waiting for your boat to come in.'

'How long did they last like that?' asks himself.

'Well, the book glosses over the seventeenth and eighteenth centuries but in the nineteenth, with the rise of the independence movement, the last Spanish governor did a runner here and, in despair, offered the island to Britain!'

'My God, they must have been in a bad way. I mean, a *really* bad way.'

'I don't know, shows remarkable good sense in my view. But the Brits turned it down anyway.'

'Lucky for the Chilotes, but amazing for the Brits!'

'We get some things right. Anyway it was another nine years before Chiloé capitulated and joined the republic. So this place was isolated from Chile proper by more than water for a hell of a long time – they're meant to be a bit different here.'

'I've been telling you that about the Irish for years.'

Soon after reaching the island, we come over a rise to see the Pacific, magnificent and sparkling below us in the distance. We are both grinning and Brian turns up the tape player so that the Hothouse Flowers' cover of 'I Can See Clearly Now' booms out for us, words and music echoing our surging spirits. A bright, bright, bright sunshiny day indeed. It was a song with special significance. We used to sing it in dreadful harmony as we paced round our cells in Lebanon.

Chiloé's swooping hills are covered in woods and pasture. Squinting against the sunlight across the valleys I imagine the buildings as Tuscan *castelli* but, as my eyes adjust, the castles become small, shingle chalets.

We wander around the main square of Castro, the island's capital, where there is an extraordinary cathedral painted orange and lilac. Given its surprising exterior, the inside of San Francisco's comes as a delightful contrast. Everything is in natural wood: pillars, panelled walls, statues and roof.

❧

I loved this wood cathedral. It was in complete contrast to Eiffel's iron monstrosity in Arica. Wood softens the most austere structures – but perhaps I was still under the spell of Neruda and his homage.

The heavy, bold limbs for the ceiling and walls looked like they were whole trees, carefully crafted into shape. They say that the stonework of Inca temples is cut with a precision that only the most up-to-date machine could achieve, and the tight, snug fit of the cathedral timbers informed me that the craftsmen who had constructed this magnificent structure owed much to their Inca predecessors. The minutely carved Stations of the Cross would have drawn the admiration of an Albrecht Dürer. The wondrous tracery of the altar and private chapel could well have been the work of a Latin Grinling Gibbons. Everywhere the sense of time-less patience, art and love permeated the building. It was warm and inviting, seducing you to prayer and meditation. The ancient Irish druids had a belief that God inhabited the trees and in here I could believe it. You could almost hear the age-rings of the timber's heartwood sing out to you.

≡⦀≡

Down a steep hill we find the harbour area. The front is lined with *palafitos*, buildings on stilts. From the land side they look like any other building in town but from the water you can see the large drop left at low tide. At high tide fishermen bring their boats right up to the back door. It seems they are being preserved these days and certainly they add a romantic dimension in the run-down atmosphere.

There is a large *feria artesanal* here. I spot a woollen jacket I like, ask the elderly stallholder the price and successfully haggle with her to get a reduction. Bri tries on a few hats. He is looking for something sturdier than his straw one as rain rather than sun is likely here, according to all reports, and especially in Patagonia and Tierra del Fuego. He settles for a stylish black number with a wide brim and colourful band.

We try out a few, progressively more basic bars, all with matt blue interiors, a couple of chairs and committed locals. Most of the men wear hats, not sombreros but Tyrolean-looking trilbys. The last bar we try is on the first floor and has a balcony over-looking the water. It is populated by a lady barkeep and three drunks. One, enormously fat with a trilby perched on his head, picks up an accordion but seems unable to play. Two other men engage us in conversation despite repeated statements that we do not understand a word. A particularly irritating man, short, fifty-ish with white shirt and blue cardigan and greased-back hair, keeps on and on. Nodding and winking, he comes up whispering in my ear about things he had seen, something to do with Argentina and the Malvinas during the Falklands conflict, I think. He reeks of stale wine. I would like to hit him. The glasses are filthy so after a couple of sips of wine it is a relief to get away.

We head off for the very south of the island, to the fishing village of Quellón. On the outskirts of Castro we stop to look at a boatyard. The craft under construction are crude skeletons at the moment but these forty-foot fishing boats should be extremely strong, judging by their massive timbers.

During our long incarceration we had built many boats, precisely working out every meticulous detail. Although neither of us had any knowledge of seamanship whatsoever, we imagined ourselves master craftsmen. Confronted by the reality, I was amazed that the keel and ribs of these vessels were still hand-hewn out of naturally bent timber.

On the road to Quellón, we see oxen drawing sleds loaded with logs, driven by ancient-looking men. Surprisingly we have hardly seen a horse, nor as many sheep as expected. There must be a lot somewhere to make all the hats, jerseys and ponchos that we saw at the market.

The old, weathered wood, plank and shingle farmsteads are strangely complemented by the many brightly coloured houses and churches that appear out in the wilds as well as in the towns. These have a Caribbean flavour to them and perhaps the colours lighten the spirits on dark days.

We come up behind an old truck lurching along with a load of rough planks. An old fellow snoozes on top of the pile, blissfully immune to the jolting. The road is quite good but there are many treacherous potholes which Brian slaloms through with gusto.

Sancho Panza's perfidious ponderings are finding an outlet. He darts a knowing eye at the ill-composed Don and smiles quietly to himself.

In Quellón, the unpainted corrugated-iron roofs blink blinding bright in the late afternoon sun as we drive down to the front. On the beach and in the shallows are a motley collection of fishing boats, many very Heath Robinson-looking with strange little cuddies. We watch a small boy struggling to get his minute rowing boat off the mud. Brian is angry for him.

'Why don't those other guys help him?' he says pointing at some other kids in a bigger boat. 'They should be ashamed.'

He is delighted when the boy eventually frees himself of the ooze and rows off with panache.

For once, Brian is looking at a guidebook. '*Mish mahoul!*' ('That's amazing' in Arabic.) 'What do you say, tomorrow we ride horses in the Pacific surf?' he asks, turning the pages.

'Yes! How, where?'

'At Cucao. You can rent them by the hour, according to this book, and ride along miles of sandy beach as the waves pound the shore.'

'Wonderful, let's do it.'

Looking at the map I realize that Quellón marks the very end of Ruta 5, the Pan American Highway. We have followed, crissed and crossed it all the way from Arica.

Like our expectations, I suppose, mythic highways always end in some backwater somewhere. But we were pursuing a dream bigger than the route ways of American imperialism. We had had enough of that hydra and its hideous tentacles in another life and we intended travelling beyond its confining grasp.

≡Ⅲ≡

We look out at the channel, the Golfo de Corcovado, where we will be sailing in a couple of days. We have heard tales of furious storms making this passage perilous. Although it has been a hot, mainly sunny day, dark clouds have hedged the horizon all the time. The weather is volatile here so I just hope it holds.

In the near distance we see the low islands of the great Chilean archipelago and, farther off to the east, the Andes. The sky at sunset is a confection of yellows, blues and pinks unlike anything I have seen before. These hues blend into a reflection on the water that is pure burnished copper. As the sun sinks further to the west the water turns black and the clouds, a palette of gold, copper and silver, take on a thunderous, menacing edge of charcoal. The islands in the channel begin to blur in the fading light so that they appear to be floating, like low clouds. Above these miasmas, on the mainland far to the east, the snow-capped mountains shine bright in the sun's last rays. One of Chiloé's many myths tells of the lost city of the Caesars: a place of fabulous wealth, of streets paved with gold and silver. The story goes that mists and sacred rivers protect the city from the sight of man but that all will be revealed at the end of time. Watching now it is easy to understand the genesis of such a tale.

The next day we leave the main road for Cucao, a long drive over a rutted track and a continual crunching of metal on stone as the car tries to cope with the terrain. The track threads through forest which opens up now and then around a lonely habitation in a patch of cleared land. This part of Chiloé has only recently been colonized and certainly the A-frame houses look basic. We pass women and children carrying home buckets of water. A tough life, clearing the forest for a vegetable patch and some pasture for the sheep and cattle. But what a beautiful place to hide away in, with the perfect Lago Huillinco always glistening deep blue through the trees.

∿∿

The track to Cucao was never a road, though it was the only means of reaching the village. It had never been levelled or reinforced against flooding which was a constant hazard. In many places the 'road' ceased to exist because of this problem. Instead one was forced to negotiate holes, mudbanks, huge boulders and fallen trees. Sancho Panza's simple mathematics declared that the quickest way between two points on a map was straight ahead! The road had to end at Cucao – or else Cucao would not exist. Anything in the way was an obstacle or a tedious hindrance to be negotiated, bulldozed or slewed round accordingly. To turn back would only mean doubling the hardship already endured, whereas reaching Cucao would mean dancing and prancing on horseback then galloping into the sunlight with the Pacific heaving and rolling beside you. I had this weird but very real dream of becoming a horseman in liquid mercury. At least reaching Cucao and doing the business would make the horrendous return drive all the more bearable.

Apart from this fantasy, it really was possible to emigrate here with a gift of land and some grants. Perhaps you could even set up a yak farm. The fact that Cucao and many small settlements along the coast had been completely obliterated by tidal waves several times in the past hundred years made the place and my fantasy ride all the more challenging. After all, what was a tidal wave to a mule-brained Irishman?

≡Ⅲ≡

Cucao is just a collection of houses, stores and a church around the outlet of the lake to the ocean but it has a special atmosphere. We sit in warm sunshine outside a little restaurant across the river from the settlement. It is very peaceful, the soothing sound of the ocean breakers brought to us by a gentle breeze across the dunes. A man and boy play chess on the verandah as they wait for their lunch.

We hear the clip-clop of hooves on wood and turn to see two horses being led over the long suspension bridge from the village. There are horses grazing just beside us, but Bri has commented on their being 'too small'. The ones coming now are slightly bigger. They all look pretty careworn. We head off to find the 'bigger' horses, still happily anticipating trotting along the beach. We find another place where we hire two mangy nags, no bigger than the others we have seen and with the worst saddles and gear you could imagine. The stirrups are barely held together with raffia. We are attended by a man of indeterminate age. He gives us a bit of old stick with imprecations to hit the beasts: *'Fuerte! Fuerte!'*

We try this but to no effect, they want only to walk, so we lead them across the suspension bridge, a hundred yards long and quite narrow. We have planned on a two-hour expedition and there is a picnic in my rucksack.

We kick and hit the horses but to no avail. Mine starts bucking so I pull its face round to mine and scream at it. Presumably it speaks only Spanish but it seems to get the tone and trots for a hundred yards before easing back into a stroll. After a while we decide that the frustration and sweat are not worth the candle and head back. Even if we had been able to master them I would have been loath to gallop with tackle like that – too dangerous. We take them back, pay for one hour and go and find a pleasant spot on a bluff looking out across the wide beach to the ocean.

'I'm really disappointed,' I say. 'It would have been wonderful.'

'Look, John, the horses hadn't been trained right – it's just the farmers trying to make a few quid. I don't reckon even Mauricio or Nigel could have done much better.'

As he finishes the sentence a little girl trots past on a horse as easy as anything; she is riding bareback. Butch and Sundance munch moodily on their cheese and tomato sandwiches.

Ancud, Chiloé's second city, is not as smart as Castro but still has bustling streets and a museum that gives some insight into the life of the colonizers. The next day we talk to a friendly old man making boats and learning English. He points out the replica of the *Ancud*, the little sailing ship that ventured through the islands and fjords to reach the Magellan Straits to reaffirm Chile's owner-ship of the region in 1833. There had been concerns in Santiago that one of the European powers might try to gain a foothold on the straits, in those days a vital stopping-off point on the trade routes. He tells us that he sailed in a similar vessel from Puerto Montt to the south in his youth. The passage, in boats that were often no more than twenty-five feet long, was very arduous, the weather conditions frequently terrible. Talking to him I feel close to the pioneering age and share a sense of conquest.

In the museum's lower courtyard I discover statues of Chiloé's mythological creatures and of a *brujo*, a witch doctor. There are craft shops in turrets around the courtyard. From the most remote stall, one easily overlooked, a mad little man appears, jabbering at me. I tell him I do not speak Spanish so he scuttles back into his cave and returns with a Spanish/English booklet on Chilote myths. In his grotto, with his light but raspy voice, he could be a *brujo* himself. The booklet tells me the *brujería* is a brotherhood of male witches that may still function, despite persecution. The initiation rites sound grim and the powers unclear but it seems likely that this underground group also worked as a force for resistance against the Spanish.

Brian buys a very fine saddle for five hundred US dollars from a stall in Ancud market. He negotiates well and gets *botas*, bridle, stirrups and reins thrown in – very impressive. I would have agreed a much higher price. This goes a long way to compensate for the riding disaster at Cucao yesterday.

〜〜〜

I had searched everywhere on our journey to find one keepsake that would sum up and be a receptacle of memory for our epic journey. John, I knew, was fed up to the eye teeth with me dragging him into every craft and curio shop my eyes lit on. The problem was I didn't know exactly what I was looking for, but I knew that when I found it I would know. I *had* found it and was going to enjoy the pleasure of bargaining to obtain it. I think it adds to the ownership of the thing. Bargaining makes the buying part of the experience rather than simply a purchase! Somehow I knew this saddle was mine. It had been made and placed there for me to come for it. I could do no other thing than take it away with me. It was part of myself. It was not a matter of having to have it, it was rather a matter of being incapable of not having it. For me it encapsulated more than all this trip was about.

For me this saddle designed
like a heavy rose in silver and leather,
gently sloped, smooth and durable.
Every cut is a hand, every
stitch a life in which the unity
of forest lives, a chain of eyes
and horses, lives on.
Grains of wheat shaped it,
woodland and water hardened it,
the opulent harvest gave it pride,
metal and wrought morocco leather:
and so from misfortune and dominion,
this throne set forth through the meadowlands.

≡Ⅲ≡

As we leave Ancud for the ferry back to the mainland we notice
that the Costanera, the coastal road, has been renamed Avenida
Dr S. Allende. It is the first time we have seen his name among
the litany of Chile's heroes mapped out on street signs.

Part Three

Puerto Montt

•

Patagonia

•

Tierra del Fuego

Chapter Eleven

᭢

Chiloé had softened us. I liked the place. It was as though we were on holiday from the compulsion of the compass, a place apart. Leaving meant knuckling down to the journey, but I didn't mind so much: I had my saddle, and the weight of it would keep me on track. It was to be my throne even if I had to carry it to the ends of the earth and back.

We arrived at the ferry port of Puerto Montt at 8 p.m. and the darkness had already fallen. Why we had to be in the terminal four hours before our boat left was never explained. The other voyagers were already there, all European, in their thirties, every one looking the epitome of the seasoned traveller with expertly packed rucksacks, stout walking boots and brightly coloured raingear. We made an odd accompaniment to our fellow passengers and I noticed one or two of them eyeing our appearance with more than a little curiosity, followed by sniggers.

It was to be a four-day, thousand-mile run down to Puerto Natales. The boat was a relatively small ferry plying the Chilean archipelago with its odd cargo of misfits, eccentrics and dreamers, all disguised as travellers. Joseph Conrad would have loved this boat.

≡ꟽ≡

Brian and I are wearing our usual travelling outfits: jeans, light sportscoats and reasonably stout shoes – and of course our Chilean trilbys. Preoccupied with finding the check-in desk, we realize after a few minutes that people are standing around openly laughing at us. We look hard at them. They are all wearing Antarctic gear, their luggage made for mountains and ice-fields, with odd pieces of kit, vicious-looking little axes and so forth, hanging from their belts. I have a kitbag and Bri his haphazardly packed trolley. We must look as though we are heading off for a weekend in the Cotswolds rather than the end of the world. After sloping into the gents and donning a thick jersey and anorak I feel more appropriate. I try to keep a distance between me and Bri's ridiculous luggage.

When the desk eventually opens we confirm our cabin and, bizarrely, surrender our passports. This is, I guess, just another element of Chilean bureaucracy – after all we will not be leaving the country and there is only one scheduled stop, at the romantically named Puerto Eden, which, being a tiny village on an otherwise uninhabited island, with no airstrip, let alone road or rail connections, seems an unlikely place for anyone to want to jump ship.

∴∿∿

Neither of us was too bothered by the glances of our fellow travellers; we were more anxious about whether we could get some food when we boarded the MV *Eden*. A few enquiries of the terminal staff informed us that there would be no food until breakfast. John and I decided to search the waterfront to see what we could find.

One of the other travellers, an American called Fred, offered to join us. His family was Argentinian, so he had excellent Spanish. He asked us to wait while he collected his cycle. He did not want to leave it unattended in the dockyard. Fred quickly arrived back wheeling his machine. It was loaded to the gills with baggage and equipment and with the added eccentricity of an attached trailer, equally laden. Our amazement turned into subdued laughter as Fred informed us that he intended cycling through southern Patagonia on this juggernaut. As we explored the back streets in search of food, I pondered this seemingly foolhardy quest; in many areas of his intended journey, roads were non-existent.

After some minutes we found a small but sadly decrepit waterfront café. A chalk sign read '*Pollo con fritas*'. John offered to stand guard on the fantastical contraption as the demon cyclist and I went to negotiate our chicken and chips.

The proprietor of the ramshackle restaurant informed us that, yes, he had chicken and chips but could only serve it on the premises. Although we explained that we had to be back on the boat, he was adamant he could not sell us chicken and chips to take away. However, if we wanted steak and chips, he could oblige. We agreed. The proprietor smiled widely. As he turned to go and prepare our supper, Fred called out in Spanish for two bottles of wine. '*Si, si,*' the café owner called back. But when we asked him to prepare the food in separate portions he suddenly stopped in his tracks, turned and came back. 'Impossible, cannot be done,' he informed us. His face was marked with urgent apology, but he could not explain why such a simple task was so difficult. Frustrated and hungry, we left.

John's laughter at our story did not relieve the necessity of finding some food. Persistence won out and eventually we found a supermarket where we stocked up.

≡III≡

I stand alone outside a supermarket. Somehow the place seems rougher than in daytime. Not that I am worried about being mugged so much as being ridiculed. I am happy to guard Fred's bike, it is the trailer that goes with it that bothers me. This two-wheeled device, loaded with bags, looks to me as if it would be more trouble than it's worth. So many of Chile's roads are little more than tracks that it seems likely one would spend the greater part of any day at a standstill, putting the thing straight again. There is also the matter of the US flag which flutters over it on a whippy metal mast, as a result of which I am receiving some very strange looks. This is not unusual: we are gringos after all and have drawn stares before, so I am used to that. It feels much worse appearing to be responsible for a bit of kit that is not mine and that looks faintly ridiculous and imperialistic to boot. I stand close enough to the machine to make sure no one tampers with it but far enough away, I hope, to convey the idea that I am in its vicinity purely by chance.

Eventually, having bought some supplies, we return just in time and sweat our bags across the deck area where there are a variety of trucks and cars chained down. One truck is obviously transporting cattle; both the noise and the smell are powerful. A small, smiling steward greets us in the saloon, checks our tickets and gives us a key to our cabin. We lumber up another steep flight of stairs and find our quarters for the next four nights. The cabin is quite small but, with its own tiny bathroom and a porthole, will suffice. Few cabins seem occupied, most of the passengers having taken berths in the dormitories in the depths of the vessel.

As the ferry slips out of port, we meet up with Fred to eat. He is tall and skinny with dark, thinning hair and a beard. His eyes shine brightly behind metal-rimmed spectacles. He is one of those very eager, enthusiastic Americans. We talk over our plans.

'So, Fred, where precisely are you going on that amazing machine?' I ask.

'I want to get right down to Tierra del Fuego,' he says, his voice bubbling with high-pitched excitement, 'then back across Patagonia and north on the new road, the Carretera Austral, to Puerto Montt.'

'How long will that take?'

'Well! Boy! I'll have to do it in two months – that's all the vacation I have!'

'You know, Fred,' says Bri, 'according to our books, the wild winds of Patagonia often reach speeds of a hundred miles an hour. Will you not spend most of your time flat on your back – or flying?'

We talk more about our various plans but have to conclude that, though Fred is a lovely fellow, he is clearly barking mad.

'ᴧᴧ·

My abiding memory of Puerto Montt was the sight as we left: mountainous heaps of wood chips piled up in the harbour. They were so massive that huge trucks drove to the top of them and unloaded. Having driven through the spectacular natural forest of central Chile, this sight was deeply depressing. Twenty-four hours a day every day these trucks arrived to deposit acre upon acre of wood chips en route to the processing plants of Japan. I thought of Neruda's love of wood and his constant reference to it in his poetry. He writes of 'the smell of wood with me always now'. I thought he might feel that all the poetry in the world was not worth these mountains of destruction and the memory of that wonderful cathedral in Chiloé made this hideous waste seem all the more blasphemous.

The next morning I stood on the prow of our boat as it moved placidly through the calm waters of Chile's archipelago. There is something almost hypnotic about travelling through strange waters. Like a dream that possesses you, everything seems to move in slow motion. The cry of a solitary bird cuts through the silence like a scalpel. Your sensory perception becomes finely tuned and only part of you feels human. Other parts seem to be melting and merging with the elemental landscape.

For more than an hour the landscape repeated itself like the wheel of an old projector that has jammed and keeps flicking up the same slide. Mountains evaporated into the mist, the implacable swell of the cold sea and the dark forest echoing endlessly at you.

In such places the monotony can repel you. The eye is forever scanning to find something recognizable, a feature or a landmark that might somehow reveal the place to you. Impatient for stimulus, you want to turn away. But that is the wrong way to 'see' things. Such landscape as we were moving through reveals itself at a different, more emotional level. Neruda had isolated the feeling for me in his poem 'The First Sea':

> I, in the prow, small,
> hardly human,
> lost,

> still without mind or voice,
> or any joy,
> transfixed by the movement of the water
> flowing between the receding mountains –
> mine alone were those solitary places,
> mine alone that elemental pathway,
> mine alone the universe.

I understood this. As I surrendered myself to the world, I seemed to be moving at dream speed. It was an echo of what I had sought in the desert and couldn't find. Perhaps the passion of the poet's words here was less urgent and hysterical than his desert adoration. The movement and imagery of 'The First Sea' were in perfect tempo with what I was seeing and feeling. It was only when you surrendered and allowed a place to receive you that you began to 'feel' it. Perhaps that was the answer which Pablo, like myself, had had to wait to discover.

≡Ⅲ≡

We awake to a beautiful sunny day and wolf down breakfast from the now operational galley. There is no explanation as to why there was no food last night. We are at the southern edge of Chiloé and, as we look westwards through the channel towards the Pacific, a slight swell reminds us of the mighty ocean out there. Now we are on the water, thoughts of the rollers coming into the beach at Cucao are not so reassuring. Fortunately there are not too many people on board so we presume there would be plenty of room in the life-rafts, if it comes to that.

We explore the ship. At the rear is the car deck, above which a gangway stretches around the ship. There is a sheer drop to the sea some forty feet below and the narrow passage is completely fenced in. We carry on towards the bows, going up and down various companionways until we reach the bridge, where we exchange salutes with the captain and his officers who are snug inside, radar screens and banks of other navigational equipment flickering on consoles around them. Looking aft, we see the heads of other passengers high above us. After a few blind alleys we discover an internal companionway that takes us on to the uppermost deck through a heavy steel storm-door that swings alarmingly, threatening to crush one instantly. There is a large flat area on the port side and we stop to take in the views of mountains and islands, then move around the large funnel to look at the rocky outcrops between us and the ocean. We forget them when we encounter a completely unexpected sight. There is a giant chessboard marked out on the deck. The squares are painted green and white with pieces, two feet tall, to match. It is like something out of Lewis Carroll. It seems quite mad but maybe here, going to a place where physical nature can show great beauty as well as awful strength, human beings need to show off one of their great intellectual achievements. Antoine de Saint-Exupéry wrote in *Wind, Sand and Stars* of coming to wild Patagonia, 'the most southerly habitation of the world . . . born of the chance presence of a little mud between the timeless lava and the austral ice. So near the black scoria, how thrilling it is to feel the miraculous nature of man!'

The ferry ploughs on, the mountains to the east rising timber-clad and magnificent, and to the west the great Pacific Ocean. What must it have been like for those sixteenth-century crews on their tiny square-rigged ships, after months at sea, facing land like this and having no idea what the interior might contain? A land shrouded in cloud and mystery.

What sort of people would you find here and what sort of people would come? I look at our shipmates and wonder. We have met a couple of young fellows from London, and two Scottish women on their university vacation, but most seem to be travelling alone. Are these seeking escape, recuperation from some other loss, in this wilderness, or are they misanthropes, or outcasts?

〰〰

During the second day, the captain delivered a lecture on safety and progress so far. Apparently we had been sailing in exceptionally fine weather and making good time. He informed us that all reports suggested that the weather would hold until we entered the open sea of Golfo de Penas, the Gulf of Pain. The midnight navigation back into the shelter of the archipelago promised to be more challenging and we were advised to take whatever seasickness pills we had.

The diminutive officer did not inspire confidence, particularly when one of our travelling companions pointed to one of the narrow channels on the wall chart and asked him where it was in relation to our present position. He answered that he didn't know and bent down to study the map. I decided to take comfort from the fact that throughout our voyage the land had never been too distant.

It was raining heavily now, and between the squalls a cold wind blew. There wasn't a lot of sense in going on deck; the landscape was repetitively brutal. I guessed why the sailor had not known where the particular channel was: there was no reason to, for no one lived there. All the names along the archipelago were only survey points, not the names of real places. Their existence was ephemeral.

I sat back in the lounge and began catching up on a book I had borrowed from John, *The Happy Captive*, written in 1629. Unpublished until 1863, it was the true story of a young Spanish soldier and his experience as a hostage with the Chilean Indians. Among his tribulations as a captive he describes a journey through the landscape which I could now look out on. He told of savage rain and hailstorms and how he was made to swim across turbulent, rain-gorged rivers; in all this he confirms 'that the natives are born to water. In its wildest and most dangerous state they have no fear of it.' I hoped things had not changed since 1629 and that our little officer and his crew had inherited the qualities of their ancestors. However calm the weather might be now, we knew it could change in a moment, and these waters were a notorious ships' cemetery.

I soon finished *The Happy Captive*. It was a slim volume and I noticed that the author's name was longer than the book was thick. Francisco Nunez de Pineda y Bascunan.

To pass the time I looked in the small glass case that served as a library and games store. There were a few boxes of chess and ludo and a couple of sets of Dama, a game which John and I had learned to play while we ourselves were captives. I was tempted for a moment to take it out but the notion passed.

Among the books I found several in German, two in Japanese and five in Russian. Among the English were titles like *I Met a Gypsy*, *The Holyman and the Psychiatrist*, *The Small Gardener* and an esoteric work on Eastern religion. I wondered about them and the kind of travellers who had left them behind. To occupy myself I tried to match the books with those who were sailing with us.

Intrepid travellers make poor conversationalists, I thought. The two dozen or so who were on board seemed a dull lot generally. But as I looked over the faces around me I thought that there were two specific problems that beset us as a group and made for such poor communication. The first was a thoroughly boring and opinionated Englishman who most people avoided like the plague having indulged him once. Anyone he struck up a conversation with soon made an excuse and left. The second problem was obvious: a noticeable lack of alcohol on sale – but then again, as our Englishman considered himself an authority on Chilean wine, no one wanted to be seen drinking any in case he joined them.

≡Ⅲ≡

The sun sets behind the archipelago shielding us from the Pacific. Overhead there is blue sky and a full moon shining in the east. The islands are dark above the ominous black of the sea. It is more comforting to look eastwards where the green, timber-covered islets flicker brightly in the late afternoon sun and, on the mainland, the hills rise green to the snow-covered mountain peaks. I experience a feeling of loneliness walking on deck in the cold breeze. But I am also invigorated – excited by the unreadability of the climate.

A sea voyage had never figured in our dreams about the end of the world, yet somehow it seems right that after horses, planes, buses, cars and trains we should be making this leg of the expedition by ship. It has been a very long journey to get to Patagonia, from the captive fantasy through the readjustments of freedom: we have crossed many more horizons than we had ever thought or imagined.

We turn in around midnight as we approach the ocean. A little more swell now but with virtually no cloud and a full moon the sky is magnificent – the islands snug and low. The weather is almost too good to be true. This leg of the journey into the ocean will take some twelve hours and, aware that this area is well known for its foulness, every lurch has me worrying in my bunk that a storm is about to attack. The ship dips and rolls unpredictably and doors in the unoccupied cabins crash back and forth. For someone who wants to be a lone yachtsman as I do, this should be less disconcerting, but perhaps because of some experience of boats I know how quickly things might change. I am aware also that I should be calmer, knowing how lucky we are. To confront the demon that denies me sleep, I go up on deck.

Up high on a foredeck I encounter a young man I have not seen before. He stands, feet splayed and body swaying with the motion, his long dark hair blowing in the breeze as he looks forward.

'Isn't it beautiful,' I say.

He starts a little and turns to me, taking in the newcomer for a moment. He does not smile but says, 'Yes, is magnificent!' and turns back to gaze.

I move to lean on the ship's rail and look down at the white water bubbling back from the bow far below. I turn my body to make a windbreak and light a cigarette. When I straighten, the young man has gone.

The sky has clouded over but enough light remains for me to see the swell and feel the rhythm of the ship's passage, which is re-assuring. Suddenly off to starboard, a wide circle of silver appears on the water: a cloud break letting the moonlight through, like a natural searchlight.

The next morning, the air is fresh and the sky is clouded over as we start across the Golfo de Penas.

The ship's company is coming to terms with the inevitable bore. An Englishman in late middle age, retired, travelling alone, he descends on the solitary or unwary with unwanted observations or 'facts'.

At lunch he spots Bri and me drinking some red wine. We have already noticed that he has been carefully managing his own bottle of white. These wines are not expensive and naturally we have shared ours with Fred and another traveller who is sitting at our table. Bob the Bore has conspicuously not done this. Fair enough, like many he may be on a long trip and a tight budget, yet he has made much of sipping and sighing as if he is enjoying some rare vintage.

'Ah! I see you have the red variety,' he says loudly to us.

'Yes.'

'I am intrigued to discover how the quality varies between the red and the white.'

'Oh.'

He stands there expectantly, grey hair, grey beard, grey shirt and those trousers that unzip just above the knee to convert into shorts which even I, with my passion for travelling gear, had dismissed as being a crime against fashion.

Brian has a gesture to express pounding rage. He holds his hands as fists close in to his neck. He tilts his head back and flexes the fingers open and closed, describing a goitre of pulsing fury. An effective image, which in years past sometimes made me anxious of an imminent explosion of feeling that might lead him to take on the guards. I can still anticipate the volcanic moves of his emotion and know now that he is tightly coiled. He stares at Bob then suddenly stands up, pours wine into my glass, his own, Fred's and our neighbour's. The bottle has a little left and he holds it looking at Bob's bland face. He moves towards him but continues on round to the next table and graciously offers it to an older man who nods and smiles as his glass is filled. Bri returns and sits beside me. He plonks the bottle down and stares at Bob once more. Bob's face flickers with something, though he seems unable to realize the slight. He opens his mouth to speak, stops and wanders off.

'Cheers, Bri!'

'Arseholes!'

We plod on through the grey day back into the channels between the islands, but there is little to see through the steady drizzle. Boredom sets in as wildness loses its romantic appeal. I turn to a guidebook and find some big facts. This trip from Puerto Montt to Puerto Natales, which will be the start of Patagonia for us, is 1,460 kilometres – more than 900 miles. It is the distance between London and Algiers. The lands south of Puerto Montt, the regions of Aisén and Magallanes, represent a third of all Chile, but only

3 per cent of the population live here. So far this is not surprising. Though it can be beautiful, it is so remote that life must be very basic.

My geographical musings are interrupted by an announcement over the tannoy. People start drifting out of the saloon on to the deck. I catch up with Brian and Fred.

'What's going on?'

'The captain has just alerted us to a ship nearby – a Panamanian vessel, the MV *Captain Leonidas* or something,' Fred explains.

Sure enough, when we join other passengers at the rail there is a small ship off to starboard. People are taking pictures and chattering animatedly.

'What's the big deal, Fred?'

'The ship's aground! It's been there for thirty years. It looks fine from here, doesn't it?'

It certainly does. Looking again, I see there is no bow wave but the ship appears complete. I am amazed that it has not broken up in the storms it must have experienced. It gives us all pause for thought – these are treacherous waters. I find Brian watching some crewmen greasing the winches on a lifeboat.

He says, 'That'll be my boat! It might be OK for Francisco Nunez de Pineda to explain how Indians were born to water but I'm no Indian.'

We soon lose sight of the stranded vessel and return to the dry saloon. The steward puts on a video for us: *Silence of the Lambs*. Just what you need as you go beyond the pale.

Within an hour or so we were anchored off the tiny village of Puerto Eden. This was the first habitation we had seen in days. A line of multicoloured shacks was strung out along the water's edge. They were barely visible in the mist. Soon a small flotilla of about five yellow rowing boats pulled through the mist and rain towards us. The whole scene could have been a set for *Riders to the Sea* or a location for one of D. W. Griffith's bleak films of island life in the 1900s. The harsh monotony of the place was unbearable to imagine. As the rowing boats approached, a massive bull seal rolled through the water between them. I could not imagine living here, and it took too great a mental leap to understand why anyone had called this place Eden!

While we waited, the small boats unloaded half a dozen new passengers and took on supplies.

After dinner everyone seemed to liven up. The new passengers asked us to join them in a game of bingo. At around 10.30, the three feeble disco lamps lit up and Spanish rock-and-roll pumped out at us. The weather had closed in and I feared we would be rocking and rolling all night, one way or another.

I woke at about 7 a.m. and looked out of the porthole. I was exhausted after spending the night clinging to the side of my top bunk. All I could see through my sleep-hazed eyes was a grey sea merging into a grey sky. The emptiness outside and the droning hum of the relentless engines confirmed we were moving towards the end of the habitable world. I lay back to try and find some sleep. I thought of the ancient mariners' belief in a world's end, and ships and crews toppling into oblivion.

≡ⅲ≡

We are all pleased to arrive in Puerto Natales, our first sight of Patagonia proper, a little town spreading out from the anchorage. There are some large, new, drab buildings but the majority are small and brightly coloured. After days of mountains rearing high from the water, the flatness of the landscape here is shocking, as if it is the unfinished end of a canvas where the artist has painted in the sky and water, the whites and lighter blues but has only just started on the heavier tones of the foreground before filling in the hills.

We have arranged for a driver to take us to Punta Arenas. We were told, when we did so, that he would not speak English. First we reclaim our passports from the ever-smiling steward who gives us a scrawled note. We cannot work out how this has arrived but there are enough letters of the name McCarthy present to suggest that it is indeed meant for us. We study the rest of the scrawl and work out that this is a communication, of sorts, from Tom and Katie's friend Alfonso Campos whom we hope to meet in Punta

Arenas. Fortunately we already have a phone number for him so do not have to rely solely on this hieroglyphic fragment.

We lumber away from the ship, Brian's wheelie-bag looking far more comfortable than the mountainous rucksacks of most of our shipmates, and bid farewell and fair winds to Fred as he mounts his machine. Suddenly we are approached by a large man in a stetson.

'Brian Keenan? John McCarthy?' he asks, beaming.

We nod, smiling back.

'I am Tomislav Goic, your driver! Call me Tomi.'

'Great. How are you doing?' asks Bri. 'We weren't expecting an English-speaker.'

'So you have a good luck! Hahaha!' cries Tomi.

A big and powerful-looking man, he sports a shooting vest with many pockets ('my office, hahahaha!') and the thickest, blackest beard I have seen outside the Middle East. He would be the archetypal bandit in a spaghetti western. A descendant of Croatian immigrants, Tomi has a farm on the edge of the Torres del Paine National Park as well as being a tour guide.

He drives us round Puerto Natales, 'Just to get the feel for it!'

There is little to get the feel of. A small town laid out on a grid pattern, with nothing much to note beyond the few hotels on the shoreline. Then we head south for Punta Arenas. As we drive in his vast, ancient and battered Chevrolet pick-up truck Tomi tells us some local history. Pointing to a large spread of farm buildings, he says, 'That place has twenty-six thousand acres. Before it was one farm, but in the Sixties and Seventies the government changed things – they broke up the big estancias and made co-operatives. This one had twenty-six families.'

'How are they getting on? Was it a success?' I ask.

'To start, yes. But then many children, like everywhere, see another life on television, what?' He turns to catch Brian's query about communications from his perch on the back seat.

'Oh yes, they have telephone, TV satellites. So the first um, generation, worked well but more and more of the kids are going north to the big cities. Some farms are being taken back by the old families, or big business is moving in.'

'It must be a hard life.'

'Yes, it is. This is special place, special people!'

They must be. The landscape of Patagonia dwarfs even the giant scale of Chile that we have already seen. Jorge had said in Santiago, 'In Patagonia you will see the planet curve.' The expanse of sky and rolling brown, green, yellow pampa is breathtaking and I am moved. As we drive up an escarpment and look over the vastness in front of us, the clouds break to allow in light at either end of this wide horizon, revealing many shades of colour but leaving some areas dark and mysterious. I feel my heart beating fast with both empathy and anxiety.

As if to further compound the mixture of feelings – the infinite smallness of myself and the surge of optimism that the bleak, vast land inspires – a rainbow appears, forming a perfect arch across the entire plain. It seems that we are going right under the apex; through a gateway into a land of wonder and enigma.

Strange patches of decaying woodland add to the unsettling atmosphere. Beautiful splashes of red and yellow are blighted by swathes of trunks and branches bleached grey and white by the weather. Some trees, in their death throes, are draped in hanging grey-green moss – a veil of decay. It looks like a petrified forest.

'These woods used to be much more, bigger. Forests!' Tomi explains with what is clearly his customary explosive delivery.

The drama of his speech is enforced as he swerves abruptly off the single lane of tarmac and runs on at undiminished speed at a perilously uneven angle. Another car approaches but neither vehicle slows. The drivers exchange salutes. I duck as the Chevy is spattered with fast-flying gravel thrown up by the other car. Tomi swerves back on to the tarmac roaring with laughter as I reappear from below the dashboard.

'You think they are shooting! Hahaha! So, the trees! Much was burned for sheep farms. Now many die from disease. It will take long, long time for recovery.'

The scarcity of trees was, as Tomi explained, due to a parasite which attacks them when they are mature. The gnarled stumps of these trees gave the landscape a post-catastrophe appearance. While John and Tomi chatted, I took up the *Canto General* and dog-eared the poem 'Oh Earth, Wait for Me' which could almost have been written in explanation of this bitter wilderness, Neruda's words echoing the desolation in front of me.

> Return me, oh sun,
> to my wild destiny,
> rain of the ancient wood.
> Bring me back its aroma, and the swords
> that fall from the sky,
> the solitary peace of pasture and rock,
> the damp at the river-margins,
> the smell of the larch tree,
> the wind alive like a heart
> beating in the crowded restlessness
> of the towering araucaria.
>
> Earth, give me back your pure gifts,
> the towers of silence which rose
> from the solemnity of their roots.
> I want to go back to being what I have not been,
> and so learn to go back from such deeps
> that amongst all natural things
> I could live or not live, it does not matter
> to be one stone more, that dark stone,
> the pure stone which the river bears away.

Tomi's lava of information poured forth. Before Allende's government the farms were probably four times their current size. 'We must find a way to make the communes work or the economy will not survive,' Tomi said. As we drove along the single-lane road that snaked for four hours to Punta Arenas, I thought how departure from the land was too often a one-way affair.

Tomi also complained that the land here was too poor to support more intensive farming. We thought the farms were huge but when I was informed that it took about a hectare of land to feed one sheep, the size suddenly dwindled. John turned and told me to 'note that statistic for the yak enterprise!'

As it was a public holiday, Tomi explained that Punta Arenas

would be all closed up. Suddenly the two nights we were intending to spend there did not seem so appealing. I thought then of
the shepherds' huts that Tomi had pointed out. The men lived
alone here, with only a horse and dog for company throughout the
bleak winter. Their wooden huts clung tight to the land, miles and
miles away in the low hills. I found it hard to imagine their
existence, locked in against the wind and wet and snow for
months on end. Our trek over the Andes was a kind of splendid,
luxurious indulgence by comparison with this lifestyle and I
wondered how they endured such deprivation.

'What do they do when they are not counting sheep?' I asked.

Tomi laughed as he replied. 'They stay until they have been
paid, maybe every four months. Then they disappear for weeks,
spending all their money on drink! It is a good job to do if you
have much stress in your life!'

I asked Tomi what he did when he was not acting as a tourist
guide. His mouth widened in a great grin and mischievously he
said, his eyes rolling, 'I count sheep.'

I thought of our guide over the Andes, Nigel, the definitive
Englishman who climbed mountains, had glaciers named after
him, led people on treks in the most remote parts of the world. For
two years he had worked here in Patagonia, as a shepherd. He had
spoken of them as the best years of his life and of Patagonia, out
of all the remote places he had lived, as the one he loved most.

As Tomi drove through this blasted landscape, I thought long
and hard about the isolation of shepherding in such a region.
Could we really farm yaks here? You would need a skin tougher
than that beast's hide to survive! I could understand local
Patagonians doing it for a living, the only living they knew. I
could understand their going on an alcoholic bender for several
weeks after being snowed in with no form of human companionship for months, especially when they found that during their
enforced hibernation they had lost all capacity for normal human
communication. So they drank themselves into oblivion, only to
return when the money ran out.

But what about those men who choose solitude, men like Nigel,
or those mountaineers we had met at Jorge's, men much younger
than myself? I was reminded of some monks I had briefly come to

know at Glensal Abbey. Everything about them was outwardly composed, yet there was in them a fire greater than any furnace. I am drawn to such men, and that is, in part, why I am drawn to this, one of the most solitary of all parts of the world. Aloneness is something we carry with us at all times, yet how do we understand it and, more importantly, how do we value it? Most of us hardly know where to begin to unearth this part of ourselves. All our lives we are told that love, sharing, human community, is the ultimate source of all happiness and well-being. I am convinced that this is not wholly true, and that human happiness is heightened when human beings learn to cope with aloneness; when they learn how to navigate without love, companionship or the trappings of religion. Aloneness is not a dreadful place once we understand how to be with ourselves on our own. It may not be the cup that is given to all of us, but part of me, I know, craves it.

≡Ⅲ≡

I follow our route on the map, trying to identify the occasional rivers. One appears to flow to the Atlantic while another empties in the Pacific.

'Yes, yes!' says Tomi. 'This plain of Patagonia gets smaller between the great oceans. We are nearly to the bottom of the world! Hahaha!'

The clouds close in, reducing the wide horizon. But it is still vast as we go on and on and on, the drumming of the rain on the windscreen combining with the monotony of the ride to deaden one's ability to think.

The wide tree-lined boulevards of Punta Arenas are flooded under the dark grey sky as we enter the town at dusk. From nondescript suburbs we are quickly into the centre of smart squares and large stone buildings. Tomi drops us at our hotel, the Cabo de Hornos – Cape Horn. We bid him a fond farewell with warm feelings in this cooler climate. Our last sight of him is of his tall frame swaggering out through the glass swingdoors of the hotel foyer into the darkening street. He turns round, raises his stetson in salute and roars, 'Have a good luck! Have a good luck!'

Before turning in we call Alfonso Campos. Tom and Katie had

recommended that we try to visit Alfonso's estancia at San Gregorio, east of Punta Arenas on the Magellan Straits.

'An unforgettable place,' Tom had said, 'quite remarkable, it'll knock you out. Alfonso is an interesting character.'

Intrigued by this comment, I am eager for Brian to get off the phone. The call is lengthy and Brian's expression keeps changing from perplexed frown to delighted grin. Eventually he hangs up.

'Right you are, Alfonso ... Yes, OK ... That'll be grand, Alfonso! Bye!'

'So what's happening?' I ask.

'Alfonso and his wife Isabel are coming to join us for breakfast – I think!' he answers, beginning to chuckle. 'It all seemed very complicated.'

'So what do you make of this Alfonso?' I ask. 'What's he like?'

'Excitable!'

The following morning, Alfonso and Isabel cross the hotel dining room with a confident, almost proprietorial air. She is a handsome, dark-haired woman, he a tall, lean man with dark hair shot through with grey. His face is intense; Isabel too looks preoccupied. We greet them and, as they sit down, relate news of Tom and Katie and a little of our Chilean experiences to date. They both speak good English, Alfonso with a high-pitched staccato delivery.

'You want to see my home at San Gregorio?'

'Yes, please, we'd like to very—'

'You must hire a car – the buses are not good!'

With this he jumps up and races out of the room. Brian and I exchange glances, wondering what this means. Isabel smiles, somewhat wearily.

'I think he talks to um, reception? Yes, reception, about your car.'

'Oh, I see,' I say. 'Shall I go with him?'

'No, let him go. To drive to San Gregorio is maybe two and half hours – maybe more. You have a map? Good. I think you will be OK. We must go soon to speak to our *abogado*, lawyer, about the farm.'

'About San Gregorio?'

'No. Another – in Torres del Paine.'

'Ah, we are going there in two days' time,' says Brian.

Alfonso is back with us in a blur.

'They will try for your car.'

'Thank you very much,' I say. 'We will take care of it now. But we must let you go, Isabel says you have a big meeting with lawyers.'

'I am in dispute with the people I own the place with there. We do not agree. I think they are fools! You want to see my farm at Torres del Paine?' The last word, pronounced 'piney', comes out almost as a squeak.

'Well, perhaps – it all depends on how much time we have up there before going to Tierra del Fuego. But it is kind of you to offer.'

There is a pause now. Isabel looks from her husband to us and then around the dining room with the same tolerant, tired smile. Alfonso, hunched forward, stares at his clasped hands. He looks up smiling.

'My dispute in Torres del Paine – it supports whole families of lawyers!' He follows this statement with a high, whinnying laugh. Isabel draws in a deep breath and looks at her watch.

'Alfonso, we must go.'

For a couple of moments he stares at his hands again, seeming not to have heard his wife. Then he looks at her with a warm smile, nodding gently, and turns back to us. 'You will come to the estancia for supper tomorrow and stay the night. It is easy to find – there is nothing else there!' He laughs, and stands up. He and Isabel head off for their meeting.

'Very nice,' observes Bri. 'Excitable?'

'Excitable.'

We set out to explore the wide tree-lined boulevards of Punta Arenas under a dark grey sky. Our hotel is on the main square – inevitably named Plaza de Armas – a large area filled with trees and statues surrounded by fine nineteenth-century mansions. The main statue is dedicated to Magellan. There are two Fuegian Indians at his feet. Brian pauses long, looking at the face of the Indian man.

'What a great face, so noble,' he says, 'and all wiped out by the people who followed the big fella on top.'

'Yes, it seems there are very few, if any, pure blood Fuegians left,' I reply, leafing through a guidebook. 'Aha! It also says that if you rub the big toe of the Indian it means you will return to Punta Arenas.'

Brian touches the bright brass toe pensively.

'I like this place, sure it would be good to come back – though this fellow's people never will.'

Reading on, I see that the city was founded as a penal colony. Seeing Bri so moved by the statue I stifle a desire to crack a joke about him feeling at home in such a place.

The shopping streets are the familiar mix of clothes and shoeshops that seem little different from those back home and general stores with plain window displays of cookers, chainsaws, fishing rods, cutlery and furniture, reflecting the frontier nature of the place. Yet the large mansions and scale of the boulevards testify to the city's one-time importance. In the second half of the nineteenth century Punta Arenas was one of the world's busiest ports, a stop-off point for vessels exporting the technology of the Old World's industrial revolution and trading across the oceans. The city became the natural centre for the export of wool after the introduction of sheep from the Falkland Islands in the late 1870s. Vast estancias were set up, to be dominated by the union of the empires of the Menendez and Braun families – antecedents of Alfonso. But in 1914 the Panama Canal opened and ruined Punta Arenas as a port of global significance. After the Great Depression of the 1930s, wool too saw a steady decline although it is still very important to the region. As Tomi had told us, the land reforms of the 1960s and early 1970s saw the break-up of many of the great estates.

〜〜

There were two churches in the main street of Punta Arenas. The largest was gothic and ornate, awash with bleeding Christs, effigies of the apostles and long-dead bishops and priests. It seemed to me that these dead artefacts and images were pushing the living out of the building. There was hardly room to breathe, literally or metaphorically.

The other church was plain and not unlike the chapel at Los Lingues. It was certainly not devoid of images but neither was it suffocated by them. The walls were painted white, enhancing the burning colour of the stained-glass windows. From somewhere, Latin plainsong and Gregorian chant warmed the silence of the place. I sat for a moment to let the voices wrap themselves more fully around me. I was in no rush to leave. But as other penitents took up prayerful positions around me I got up to go, and walked quietly towards the entrance doors.

At the rear of the church I was stopped by what confronted me. An Indian woman, perhaps in her early sixties, stood motionless in front of a life-size carving of a nun. The statue was standing on the floor so that the Indian woman and the wooden nun looked deeply into each other's faces. The Indian was draped in a blue-black woven shawl and a rusty red dress that reached her ankles. Her long black hair hung in strands that disappeared like snakes into the folds of her shawl. Her feet were encased in a pair of rough workmen's boots that were too large for her. The two women stood toe to toe and eye to eye, both impassive, yet some-how the face of the Indian was more knowing. But perhaps it was only her fleshy reality that made it seem so. The flesh is always more illuminating than gilded plaster saints.

I wondered what held this Indian woman transfixed. Why did she venerate this statue more than Mary or Christ? Yet her stance was neither devotional nor pleading. She was more idol herself than the image she stood before.

Quietly I moved towards the pair, wanting to be part of the moment. I looked closely at the nun. The aged wood had given her face the same leathery texture as the Indian woman. In places it had cracked, but the whole figure was carved from a single trunk. I stood spellbound, not knowing what I was witnessing, but unable to pull myself away.

There was only the graveyard left to see and as I walked among its huge mausoleum-like monuments, some of them like miniature basilicas, I was impressed and appalled. Impressed by the majesty of death, and appalled that it should be so worshipped. The sight of the Indian and the wooden woman was obviously yet to be resolved in me.

≡ ⫿⫿ ≡

We walk further out, passing a series of statues of a shepherd, a horse and a sheep in the middle of the wide boulevard. A plaque records that this fine piece was erected by one of Alfonso's Campos forebears.

We wander back into town via back streets, desolate and rutted, bleak in the grey light. Mangy-looking dogs follow us for a block or two before losing interest.

⋀⋀

That night we dined in a local restaurant with Alan, a young Englishman, one of our fellow travellers from the boat. As he relaxed into the wine he talked about his travels. He thought that the Chileans did not have the same sense of passion or love as he had found in other South American countries. But then Chile was economically far in advance of some of its neighbours. He had been reading books about the Pinochet and Allende years and was trying to understand what had happened. One woman he had been staying with had had her 21-year-old son 'disappeared'. He felt confused by her resignation and acceptance of her son's obvious murder. She spoke of that period as the 'evil years' and said that 'there was a time before'. As he continued to talk, I felt that here was a man more in search of the embrace of love than he was in search of great journeys. He was one of the misfits, roaming the continent but less a traveller than a soul searcher.

I wanted to talk about the Indian woman in the church but found I couldn't express myself as I wished. I could only say that perhaps some people understand love and passion differently. It wasn't as though they were instinctively or culturally less passionate.

'How then do you recognize love?' Alan asked poignantly.

'There can't be rules. You'll recognize it in its moment!' I replied.

The transfixed face of the Indian woman suddenly reappeared in my imagination, dispelling any ready-made answers I might have had.

Later that evening, I read Neruda's 'The More-Mother' and thought that maybe, just possibly, I had glimpsed something of the intense communication between the Indian woman and her nun.

> My more-mother comes by
> in her wooden shoes. Last night
> the wind blew from the pole, the roof tiles
> broke, and walls
> and bridges fell.
> The pumas of night howled all night long,
> and now, in the morning
> of icy sun, she comes,
> my more-mother, Dona
> Trinidad Marverde,
> soft as the tentative freshness
> of the sun in storm country,
> a frail lamp, self-effacing,
> lighting up
> to show others the way.
>
> Dear more-mother –
> I was never able
> to say stepmother! –
> at this moment
> my mouth trembles to define you,
> for hardly
> had I begun to understand
> than I saw goodness in poor dark clothes,
> a practical sanctity –
> goodness of water and flour,
> that's what you were. Life made you into bread,
> and there we fed on you,
> long winter to forlorn winter
> with raindrops leaking
> inside the house,

and you,
ever present in your humility,
sifting
the bitter
grain-seed of poverty
as if you were engaged in
sharing out
a river of diamonds.

Oh, mother, how could I
not go on remembering you
in every living minute?
Impossible. I carry
your Marverde in my blood,
surname
of the shared bread,
of those gentle hands
which shaped from a flour sack
my childhood clothes,
of the one who cooked, ironed, washed,
planted, soothed fevers.
And when everything was done
and I at last was able
to stand on my own sure feet,
she went off, fulfilled, dark,
off in her small coffin
where for once she was idle
under the hard rain of Temuco.

I reread the poem over and over. Never has a poet's work had such an effect on me. The place, the moment and the words, all burned into that long evening with a strange incandescence.

Chapter Twelve

≡Ⅲ≡

Next morning I walk down to look at the Straits of Magellan. Their notorious fierceness is quite absent and all is tranquil. Back at the hotel I meet Brian talking with the concierge who has tracked down a vehicle for us – an unfeasibly tall, four-wheel-drive Toyota Hi-Lux. I am elected driver.

We take possession of the car late and it is 6.30 in the evening before we head out of Punta Arenas. As the light thickens, I try to get used to the vehicle. The young man from the car-hire firm, named Ricardo and sporting a yellowing black eye behind wraparound sunglasses, had warned me that the height of the chassis made the truck unstable at any sort of speed. Not having absorbed this advice properly, I am cruising at a little over 50 m.p.h. when a moment's inattention has the nearside wheels moving off the tarmac on to the not-so-hard shoulder. Correcting the steering makes us rock scarily across both lanes of the road with a squeal of tyres. When my heart stops pounding and the vehicle is once more under control I settle down to a steady 40 m.p.h. Brian, stretched out in the back, raises his head to observe, 'That's much better. How am I meant to sleep with you careering all over the place?'

I look ahead confidently to reaching San Gregorio at about nine o'clock. A few miles out of Punta Arenas we take the right fork eastwards towards Argentina. Almost immediately the road becomes a single track, with priority given to the oncoming traffic. If someone approaches I have to pull off on to the gravel to the side.

The light fails and with it my nerve. I grit my teeth to endure the whole ride at 30 m.p.h. when Brian pops up in the back seat.

'Why don't you put on the other lights?'

'What, there are others?'

'Your man Ricardo pointed out another switch. Down there on the left.'

Suddenly I can see reasonably clearly and set off again with somewhat restored faith. But then the road falters as we weave around roadworks in terrain rutted and flooded like a scene from the Somme. We persevere.

We come up behind an overloaded truck that teeters and lurches around the potholes. I manage to overtake it, my mind full of memories of Henri-Georges Clouzot's film *The Wages of Fear* where a number of drivers, including Yves Montand, make a disastrous trek across some godforsaken Latin American landscape with a cargo of nitroglycerine. It all comes back to me. One by one they die. Except Montand who survives. Momentary relief, until I remember that, having delivered his deadly cargo, he too crashes and is killed.

Suddenly buildings loom out of the darkness. They all look deserted, derelict. Moonlight adds to the ghostliness of the scene. But there on one building are the words 'San Gregorio'. We have made it. Now to find the estancia. No lights anywhere: we drive on, confused by the lack of any sign of life. We know the farm is to our left. It has to be, as to our right, looking ominous in the moonbeams, the Magellan Straits shift soundlessly.

We go on, and on again.

'This can't be right. Surely the farm wouldn't be so far from the village,' I say after fifteen minutes. Brian is now up with me in the cab.

'Look there, ahead. There's a light!'

We stop and clamber over muddy earthworks to a little shack. As we come up to the door a pig scuttles off round the building. What is it about pigs appearing before me on troubled night drives? Looking in the window we are amazed. It is a bar! Here, in the back of nowhere, a lovely snug bar. We go in. Two young men play table football, and a smartly dressed couple are drinking at the counter. Where on earth had these people come from? I hardly dare look at Bri, the sense of fantasy is so great that I fear he will have dematerialized. But the people are real. They tell us we must go back three kilometres and cheerily wave us off into the night.

Back at the village we now see a light on the porch of a small house. Brian hops out and knocks on the door. A tall, elderly man appears who, after bending to listen to him, straightens and points up a track. The drive is long, maybe a mile before we arrive, cheering at the sight of a mansion glowing white in our headlights beyond elegant iron gates. Brian hops out again and stands fiddling, for an age it seems, trying to open this last obstacle.

'Can you believe it?' he says, coming up to my window. 'They're chained and padlocked! Honk the horn.'

After a few minutes a woman appears out of the darkness, happily shouting, '*Gringos importantes.*' The epic drive is at last over. It is nearly half past ten.

∿∿

The house was huge and not at all like the hacienda at Los Lingues. It looked vaguely like a palais de danse or one of those 1950s cinemas with would-be Roman names like the Lyceum. It was something of an anomaly in this barren landscape.

≡║║≡

We follow the woman's bustling form into a huge kitchen. This area seems strangely vast to modern eyes and speaks of a much busier household. The old range stands idle, perhaps just too big to move. Most of the business is done now in a former pantry where a modern cooker and fridge appear toylike in the high-ceilinged room. We walk through a number of passages lined with fading photographs of proud farmers standing beside rosetted sheep with fleeces of phenomenal proportions. An old hand-cranked telephone is fixed to a wall above a shelf of ultra-modern mobile phones.

The woman, who identifies herself as Maria and is clearly the maid, leads us into a large hall where there is a vast front door that obviously faces down the drive. It looks as though it has not been used for a long while. A staircase, eight feet wide, leads up to the next floor. Massive mahogany double doors lead off in various directions. Maria opens one pair and bids us wait in the vast reception room beyond. It is filled with antique furniture and portraits of ancestors. I open another door at the far end of this room and discover a conservatory that appears to run all down this side of the building. Within the pool of light coming from the room behind me I can make out the shapes of wicker furniture but beyond that there are just indistinguishable forms. Thinking of the wild empty spaces that come right up to the house I shiver slightly, half-expecting ghosts to come tapping at the windows. I close the door again and sit next to Brian on a sofa.

After a few minutes Isabel appears and greets us warmly, offering us pisco sours. She explains that Alfonso too is late but is expected any minute.

'He has been to the farm at Torres del Paine.'

'Ah,' I say, 'the dispute?'

'The dispute,' she confirms with her tired smile.

We talk a little about living in such a remote place and learn that with their three small children and Maria they live here in isolation at weekends but that she and the children move to Punta Arenas during the week for school. Isabel teaches in the city and also serves on the local council. When she says that she studied Chilean history at university, Brian seeks her view on Bernardo. It is not entirely favourable.

〰

It is always difficult to question the icons of a nation too closely, especially in one of the nation's repositories, which this house undoubtedly could lay claim to being. The whole atmosphere of San Gregorio was that of a museum, a place embalmed in time, stubbornly refusing to accept the imperatives of modernity.

But Isabel was a different creature. Her mind was more pragmatic and focused. She had based her master's thesis on Bernardo and I listened intently as she spoke. She had very fixed views on the man. He was not a democrat but an autocrat, she insisted, and lived at a great remove from those he governed. People hardly knew him, she said.

I couldn't understand Isabel's insistence on his autocracy or his supposed distance from 'the people'. Was she referring to the people who had betrayed him on the battlefield and those same people who had undermined him when he finally took possession of Chile? It was not my place to challenge. In any case I did not want to, for, although the portrait she was painting of Bernardo was on first consideration far removed from my own image of the man, it was also paradoxically affirming. When she explained that Bernardo consistently refused to make himself part of the aristocratic and governing class, I ceased my silent debate with her. Now she was coming close to the man who had travelled with me. And when she said that Bernardo refused to marry into the colonial establishment but kept a 'harem' of native women, my heart sang. I could not avoid declaring aloud, 'That's my boy, Bernardo!'

There was a moment's silence at my sudden remark, then relieved if nervous laughter. Bernardo had kept the faith! He had remained his own man, surrendering to the dictates of no one but his own experience, a rebel, a lover, an outsider to the end.

≡|||≡

The sound of tyres on gravel announces Alfonso's return. He joins us for a drink before we share a very late supper in the huge dining room. Mention of the problems with his other farm prompts a brief outburst against lawyers and the admission that he had been a lawyer himself in Santiago until six years ago when he came back south to rebuild the farm. He subsides into one of his reveries then abruptly perks up and looks at Brian.

'You said you liked Neruda?'

'Yes, certainly I do. A great poet!'

'I hated him. A useless man! Weak!'

'How so?' asks Bri, restraining himself.

'He was a lousy Stalinist. One day he praises Nobel Prize award to Pasternak. Next he changes the story, says Pasternak not worthy for it. Why?'

'I don't know,' says Brian.

'Because it is condemned by Stalin!' Alfonso goes quiet again for a while then looks up, grinning broadly. 'You know Neruda was sent to exile?' We both nod.

'By President Gabriel Gonzàlez Videla. He was my grandfather!' he announces proudly. There is another pause before he reiterates 'Lousy Stalinist!'

I listened intently. I was beginning to understand Alfonso's idiosyncratic dismissal of Neruda and Isabel's constant reference to Bernardo's denial of 'the people'. It all fitted with our young lawyer guide in the far north who did not want to discuss Allende's revolution and considered that Allende's regime would only have made Chile into another Cuba. There is a cultural crust on Chile that is not at first evident, but it is as permanent and thick as the salt flats of the Atacama.

I took in the huge room and the monstrous dining table at which we sat. The table could accommodate a dozen or more people with ease; as it was, the four of us were seated with several feet between us. I thought of the lavish dining room in Los Lingues. At one time San Gregorio would have been equally resplendent but now it reminded me of an old mirror whose ornate gold frame was broken and chipped. There was no reflection in it, for the silver that gave it this reflection was faded, and the looking-glass revealed only the woodwormed boards that held it in place. This was Miss Havisham's house and I was a naive Pip Pirrip entranced by its otherworldliness. While John chatted to our hosts, my thoughts wandered out of the room.

History had been rubbed out or reordered to fit the atrocious machinations of the Pinochet regime and its ghoulish backers in the White House in Washington. It was absurd for Isabel to state that Bernardo was not a democrat, absurd for Alfonso to decry Neruda as a Communist, and absurd for our young lawyer guide in Arica to compare Allende's government with Cuba. Such reordering of history necessarily carries with it the kind of contamination that limits vision. Visionaries are always considered heretics, apostates, despots, demi-gods, by those who sometimes unconsciously suffer from the very poison which they attribute to others. In such a world everything is absurd, and maybe there it is easier to believe lies than confront a horrible and insidious reality. In such a shadowy world, 'Stalinists' and 'dictators' might well hold hands in hell, sickly smiling at their bloody handiwork while accepting the adulation of closed minds.

A secret cable to the CIA station chief in Santiago, published in Washington in 1998, states: 'It is our firm and continuing policy that Allende be overthrown by a coup prior to October 24th 1970. But efforts in this regard will continue vigorously beyond this date. It is imperative that these actions be implemented clandestinely and securely so that the US government and American hand be well hidden.'

The operation of this clandestine world of covert intelligence cares nothing for people. It insidiously feeds the monster that created the death squads in Pinochet's Chile which were only another manifestation in another time and place of Stalin's purges, the pogroms of Nazi Germany, the gulags and internment camps, and the ethnic cleansing and tribal genocides of contemporary history. Both Pinochet and Stalin were the reverse faces of the same coin, blood money of the most evil perversion. Give me Bernardo and Neruda and let those who choose to bow and scrape at the feet of despots do so, for such minds have chosen the myopic comfort of slavery against the life-enhancing challenge of freedom.

After dinner, as Isabel and Alfonso showed us around the house, I noticed a small framed letter hanging obscurely on the wall. It was embossed with the crossed guns and anchor of the Chilean military and had an impressive and very regal seal on it. It was in Spanish, so I couldn't understand it – but it carried an equally impressive signature. Pinochet! Everything was falling into place and I almost felt as if Bernardo was smiling over my shoulder! Pinochet had done his job well – in true 'lousy Stalinist' fashion.

That evening extra blankets were left out in our rooms and we certainly needed them. Patagonia has no sympathy for the unprepared.

≡‖≡

We are up early and have breakfast in the kitchen.

'Well, Bri, here we are in Patagonia with a man with a large farm. I reckon it's time to ask about the great scheme.'

'Oh God! John, I don't know.'

Alfonso and Isabel look on, intrigued. Brian eats some bread, then slowly, obliquely, edges towards the question.

'Um, so um how much land do you need for each sheep?'

'Generally one sheep needs half hectare, one of your acres. Maybe a little more, in some places less. You want to farm sheep in Patagonia?'

'No. Well, no, not exactly,' Brian stumbles on. 'You see, I had an idea that maybe you could farm yaks here.'

'Yaks?' squeaks Alfonso. I start giggling.

'What are you laughing at, McCarthy? You thought it was a good idea too!'

᠂〜〜

Alfonso laughed and listened and then became intrigued. What facts and statistics we held about these animals, their habitat, diet and their quality of milk, leather and wool had our host in a stunned silence. We could see his mind was working overtime. Suddenly he interrupted.

'Did you know Chile is one of the few countries in the world to have an opposite land pole?' We were confused until he explained, 'You see, if it were possible to drill a hole from any country in the world down through the centre of the earth, it would be almost certain to emerge somewhere in the sea. Its opposite point would be in the ocean. But if you were to do the same in Chile, the point of our imaginary drill would emerge in China. I have studied this phenomenon and it's quite correct.'

Alfonso continued to elicit information from us. His serious demeanour was encouraging.

'But if it takes half a hectare to feed one sheep how can you feed an animal five times its size?' I asked.

'Sheep are not indigenous to Patagonia. But from what you say about the yak and Tibet, it would survive here much more easily than sheep.'

At first we thought Alfonso's curiosity was mere politeness. But when he told us that the Chilean government were offering subsidies to anyone developing new agricultural enterprises and that he might contact the Chinese embassy in Santiago, we realized how intrigued he was.

Before leaving, I wandered round this strange farmhouse standing in the middle of nowhere. It looked more and more like a set for a gothic fantasy film. The house was crammed with large bronze busts, Alfonso's stern-faced Victorian forebears. They were relatives and cousins, the rural aristocracy of a Chile that was fast disappearing. Among them was Don José Menendez, past president of Chile and another of Alfonso's uncles. Cracks were everywhere in the brickwork and large patches of plaster had long since fallen from the ceilings. But I could feel the command in those bronzes, that this house and all its history should not die. Alfonso had to pass them several times a day and I could imagine the intimidating effect of their gaze.

≡Ⅲ≡

We are due to meet a bus to take us north to Torres del Paine at noon. Alfonso is determined to show us his farm and works out that he can get us back to the main road, from where he can hitch a lift. He is anxious that we should witness the disaster that has befallen the farmers of the Magallanes. In a dreadful snowstorm forty thousand sheep were lost in one night; his farm alone lost four thousand. The catastrophe had been dubbed 'the White Earthquake' by the press.

First Alfonso drives our truck back down to the Magellan Straits where we had seen the group of buildings in last night's gloom. He shows us the massive shearing sheds full of bales of wool marked with Chinese characters, and points out the wooden buildings that had once housed workers, school and shops. On the beach lies the hulk of the *Amadeo*, a large coastal launch that the estate used in its heyday to take the wool to Punta Arenas. Estancia San Gregorio had once extended to 90,000 hectares (some 180,000 acres) but it had been expropriated and broken up in the Sixties and Seventies under the socialist governments.

'How did you get it back?' I asked Alfonso.

'With the dictatorship, some was given back to my family. But every member had a piece so for years I have been buying bits back, little by little.'

'So how big is it now?'

'It runs three kilometres along the strait and inland it goes forty kilometres. But it's still only one third of what it was before the socialists destroyed everything.'

He takes us to a little chapel, explaining that it was built on the spot where Magellan himself had first landed and held a service of thanksgiving when he discovered the channel. A simple building, peaceful and suffused with gentle light. I am surprised that it is in such good condition.

'You look after the chapel, Alfonso?'

'Yes, but it is sad, we have no services now.'

'Oh, I suppose there are not enough people?'

'No. People would come in from the farms if we had a priest.'

'Oh. Why no priest?'

'I am in dispute with the bishop!'

'Alfonso, you seem to be in dispute with everybody.'

Alfonso just laughs, a little wildly.

'Come, we have a long way to go.'

We head inland across the farm, racing on and on, bouncing over the rutted track and barrelling through puddles, the world instantly obliterated as the muddy water immerses the vehicle. Eventually we stop beside what is little more than a shed, hardly even a shack. One or two horses munch grass and give us a cursory once-over. A dog bounds out to greet us followed by a small man. His face is so sweet, wreathed in smiles at seeing Alfonso. His skin looks as soft as a baby's, not raw and lined as I would expect from a life outdoors in this wild climate. His excitement matches his dog's, his whole demeanour making me think of a happy puppy. He and Alfonso talk for a little while and then we roar off again.

Now we go off the beaten track, straight across the virgin land. We bounce and jolt wildly, desperately hanging on as the truck pitches and heaves over the mad terrain. Alfonso appears oblivious to the savage ride. I sit, or rather lie, in the front seat of the pick-up bracing myself with arms and legs, reminded with sur- prising fondness of Charlatán's relatively gentle camel-like gyrations as he laboured uphill and down. On this terrain being on horseback would be far more comfortable; but what can it be like to be a shepherd here, living in a tiny wooden house, maybe twenty miles or more from a neighbour?

·∧∧·

Meanwhile in the back Sancho Panza is musing between in- audible curses as he is flung willy-nilly like a storm-tossed bird. This place should have been named the Gulf of Pain. Alfonso is steering the jeep like a crazed Captain Ahab! He seems oblivious to the fact that if we seriously damage this vehicle it may take us days to walk out of this wilderness. Whenever we stop to get our bearings I think how much Alfonso's mind is like this landscape, excitedly bumbling and jolting from idea to idea. Then we are off again and I am flung every which way and backwards. I am glad Don John is up front as there is something dangerously Quixotic about Alfonso. They should get on well together! I make a mental note to write in my diary, 'Today we went pitching over Patagonia with a kamikaze sheepfarmer named Alfonso!' John insists on holding a conversation as we roll and flounder onwards. Obviously Quixotes One and Two are crazy as coots.

≡Ⅲ≡

'Do the shepherds live way out here permanently?' I ask Alfonso as he hunches over the wheel, gunning the truck through another fence of scrub like some demented Grand National jockey.

'They live here for a month at a time, with food supplied by the farm. Then they go into town with their money and maybe drink lots of beer and pisco.'

'What do you pay them?' asks Brian, who like me has pinned himself like a rigid starfish against the truck's motion.

'They get two hundred US dollars a month.'

Such a harsh life, it is difficult to imagine anyone starting it or staying with it for so little reward.

Under a slate-grey sky with wind-driven drizzle lashing at the car, Alfonso stops and points across a wide dip in the land. A fence runs along beside us. In the distance the ground is a grey colour. We move closer and start making out the shapes of sheep, thousands of them, laid out as far as the eye can see. It is horrific. So many animals lying there where they died. Some have already rotted, bones and skulls scattered in a tangled mess. Others are strangely intact, as if they are just lying down to sleep. One or two are still hanging from the fence and if you half close your eyes you can imagine them attempting to bound over the obstacle to safety. The area covered is so large and the carcasses so numerous that, now there is no snow, one cannot imagine a natural event causing such devastation; one's mind argues that it must have been done by a lunatic human. The air is filled with the stench of rotting flesh.

When I look at Alfonso with his thin body, pinched face and greying hair, he suddenly appears very frail. It is evident that this event, perhaps this land, had shocked him profoundly. We are all silent for a while. The engine still, the only noise is of the wind and rain.

'What happened, Alfonso?' Brian's voice is quiet from the back seat. There is a long silence before Alfonso answers in low, shaky tones.

'The snowstorm was very bad. Always the wind blows from there,' he says, pointing to the far side of the fence. 'The sheep know that. They shelter under the fence. This night—' He stops, swallowing hard. 'This night the wind comes from the wrong side, this side.' He stops again.

Brian and I remain silent.

'The snow was so thick, the wind so strong. They were buried there, alive, where they thought they were safe. Some try to escape and die on the fence.' He stops again, close to tears.

I study the profile of his face as he stares intently at this scene of devastation and realize that the tautness of his jaw, the agony in his eyes reflects no concern for the financial loss to his business. It is the loss of the animals for which he cared that troubles him; he imagines their suffering. The rain stops and the wind eases and as it does so Alfonso relaxes a little.

His face brightening, he asks in his usual high-pitched, excited tone, 'You want to walk closer, take photos?'

We get out of the car and walk to the carcass field. It is a horrible sight, the twisted, decaying faces of the sheep suggesting the terror and agony of their final hours.

'Were you able to save any?' I ask.

'Yes. With my men we saved those we could reach. But the work was so hard. It was so cold. After some time I collapsed.' He pauses and then goes on, his voice rising with a blend of shock and indignation, 'It took twenty hours to get to hospital. I almost died!'

We stay a few minutes more. Alfonso clearly wants us to take photographs, to record this awful event. I do so automatically but something keeps me from taking a picture of Alfonso, the driven, traumatized shepherd.

After a while Brian speaks.

'Alfonso. Why do you stay here? Why do the shepherds stay out here?'

'It is our home,' is the simple reply.

There is silence again for a while before Brian speaks again, his tone warm and gently teasing.

'So maybe your friend Neruda got something right. He called Chile "the harsh homeland"!'

Alfonso grins broadly. 'So maybe he got something right. Lousy Stalinist!'

∿∿

I was profoundly moved by Alfonso's response to this ghastly sight. All my unspoken thoughts about his eccentricity seemed trite and cheap. For a moment I walked away from Alfonso's anguish. Standing apart, looking at this hideous vision, I felt how Neruda's passionate romanticism could better capture this white death spreading out over the landscape like some hideous coverlet. His poetic emotion was, I convinced myself, very close to what Alfonso was now feeling. It was easy to forgive the man his intemperate dismissal of the poet. For I was sure if Neruda were standing beside me now he would have written Alfonso Campos into his *Canto General* as one of Chile's heroic figures.

He drove us around this scene which repeated itself for what seemed like miles. It was as if he didn't want to leave the sheep.

'What about the shepherds?' we asked.

It took Alfonso some minutes before he replied.

'One of them was snowed in for six weeks. He was crazy when we dug him out. He disappeared for many weeks . . . he is all right now.'

I could imagine the terrified shepherd and the terrified sheep buried alive and Alfonso's terrified, crazy desperation as he tried to save what was his whole world. It was enough. At last we left.

≡Ⅲ≡

We bounce on and on, increasingly worried that we will never meet the bus. The pampa rolls on relentlessly, our bodies battered by the mad lurches of the vehicle. After one stomach-wrenching bump, Brian's head appears between the front seats, his knuckles white as he holds on for grim death.

'Now I know what it's like inside a washing machine!'

Eventually we arrive at the main road. Alfonso gets out, reminds us where we should meet Ricardo the car-hire man and the bus for Torres del Paine, waves down a passing car and disappears into it, heading for home. A very unusual man; kind, full of emotion and great courage.

˄˄˄

Alfonso's sudden disappearance was odd. He was like a will-o'-the-wisp, that curious phenomenon that often happens in remote boggy land when the process of natural decomposition creates a phosphorescent gas that glows luminous in the half-light of dusk. Back home in Ireland these 'ghosts' are said to be the spirits of the dead returning to reclaim their land. Though Alfonso was no ghost, there was something luminous about him. This land was truly his, by something older than birthright. With all his eccentricity and enthusiasms, he somehow glowed here. This was his place. His roots were sunk deeper than history. When I think back on Alfonso I remember his face lighting up, almost fluorescent, like the bright yellow flower of the bog iris.

Chapter Thirteen

≡Ⅲ≡

We doze most of the way to Torres del Paine, tired after the battering of the earlier drive and now exhausted by the scenery. The mountains creep closer and closer as the light fails and the track begins winding through the foothills.

We are nearly there when the driver stops, hissing, 'Puma, puma!'

There, a hundred or so feet away on a small hill, are two puma. They, like us, are quite motionless, watching, their bodies facing away from us towards the crest of the hill. But their eyes, glinting yellow-green in the failing light, are fixed on our vehicle. We do not even think of photographs, our surprise is as great as theirs and we realize the encounter may last only a moment. In fact they remain looking at us for a few minutes before strolling off into the dusk. We are told later that to see one puma in a year of looking is lucky, but to see two, minutes after entering the park, is remarkable.

Once again Chile reduces us to what R. L. Stevenson called 'the virginity of senses' where words cannot match the impressions received.

⁘∿∿⁘

Patagonia is a word that has entered into the language as a metaphor for the ultimate, a point beyond which no one could go.

Some writers have dismissed it completely. Jorge Luis Borges once said, 'You will find nothing there, there is nothing in Patagonia.' Throughout the ages though, others have idealized it, among them Melville, Swift and Coleridge. W. D. Hudson, writing in the late nineteenth century, suggested that these literary stars were mistaken in their flights of fantasy, that instead it is a place full of intellectual rebuttal. The experience of Patagonia is a journey to a higher plane of existence, a kind of harmony with nature which precludes thought. It was for him the source of an animism bound to an intense love of the visible world.

Edgar Allan Poe adapted Wendell's book on Patagonia to write his own novel of a crazed self-destructive journey in *The Narrative of Arthur Gordon Pym*. In turn Dostoyevsky, Baudelaire and Rimbaud all took up ideas from Poe. So the literary reference library on this place is voluminous and diffuse, if somewhat esoteric. It would be pointless to argue who came nearer the truth. But the truth is only one's experience of it and whatever that truth may be, it must begin with a fascination.

Patagonia has sucked into itself a vast cross-section of the world's nationalities. Each, no doubt, had their own truth and their own fascination that brought them to these 'final capes of exile' as Bruce Chatwin called them. I wondered if I would find an answer or even a reason for my own fascination. These were, after all, our last few days in Chile and we were headed into the most mystically beautiful landscape imaginable.

It was already late when we arrived, and the darkness and silence outside had completely swallowed up our hotel, the Explora. Having at last reached the inner heart of Patagonia, we began to feel really exhausted. Thankfully we found the hotel was extremely plush and, after so much travelling, the luxury seemed well deserved.

When our driver called out boastfully to the rest of the staff about our encounter with the pumas, the significance of seeing them became clear. At first no one believed him. He had lived in the park for twenty-five years and this was his first sight-ing. Everyone was disbelieving that he should see two at once. I turned to John, bemused by the excitement.

'One for you, one for me, obviously.'

After a shower and change of clothes, we went to the bar to discuss plans for the next day. As luxurious as the hotel might be, people came here to do things! We decided, weather permitting, to take a boat across Lago Grey to the Grey Glacier at its head.

I went to bed thinking of the pumas who had come to welcome us, and thought of the poem I had written home to my wife. How long ago was that? It seemed like an infinity. We had been travelling harder than we thought. Though we had maps, timetables, compasses, tickets, schedules and all the other essentials of outward and onward travel, I was beginning to feel we had lost contact with our centre of gravity. The compass bearing to our point of departure had become buried under this urgency to reach the end of the earth. Now that we were practically there, now that we could sit back and relax, the call of home seemed to filter into my thoughts.

It wasn't home-sickness so much as a growing realization of the distance one had travelled in mind and time and an awareness of the emotional distance involved. Suddenly Patagonia slammed itself into me in a way I least expected. This was only a small episode in my life, yet, in these few weeks, Chile had consumed me utterly. It had infiltrated and taken possession of my every emotion. I had experienced joy, contentment, exhilaration. I had known fear and fascination in full and equal measure. I had had to deal with anger, resentment, boredom and exhaustion all trying to crush my sense of purpose. I had also had my challenges and disappointments. But now I was beginning to feel that I had lost contact with another part of my life, a vital and sustaining part. In the quiet splendour of Patagonia, here in these 'capes of exile', I was feeling desperately exiled myself.

I was beginning to wonder if this was the unconfessed impulse that drives travellers ever onward. All those echoing thoughts and feelings that centre them are perceived as a dead-weight to their expressed purpose. And when people talk of being more afraid of failure, as I myself have done, than having a purposeful sense of achievement, are they not voicing their fear of this siren-like attraction back to familiar places and the comfort of loved people and other things? If it is in man's nature to desire to possess everything he loves, then it is inevitable that it is beyond his capacity to achieve it.

My musings were beginning to send me into sentimental over-load. When we reach the point of our desired destination, we often feel that it is not the place of fulfilment we had imagined. Perhaps we carry that destination within us. It's always there, and everything else is a corollary or mirror image of it.

But reason and emotion are the poet's media. I was too tired for reason and too hungry for emotion to attempt to reconcile their wondrous opposition. But when a man is hungry he must feed himself. He must nourish his capacity for emotion. I prepared a swift fax to send home from the hotel before we departed into the wilderness once more.

Dear Sweetheart,

I have been reading Neruda's love sonnets today in the hope that I could crush away the distance between us. But instead their passion swept me away. They are a heady aroma of the heart's desire, and a perfume of loneliness lifts from every page.

I thought I would send the book to you but decided to keep it with me. It lets me hold you close, and I can smell your hair.

I am thinking of you always and love you with a depth that all the oceans and mountains that separate us cannot fill.

What do you think of SANTIAGO for a name!

Brian

The morning vista from my bedroom window stunned me for some moments. Like pillars holding up the morning clouds, the twin peaks of Cuernos del Paine and Torres del Paine ascended in stark contrast to the low, rounded foothills below. In scale and relief they were a visual paradigm of Patagonia and could be seen from virtually any point in this paradoxical landscape. I couldn't find the words to explain the sense of awe this vision prompted in me. Instead I lifted the phone and called John.

'Take a deep breath and look out your window, then take another one!' I said before replacing the receiver.

Our boat trip to the Grey Glacier had to be postponed. Powerful and sudden winds known locally as the 'williwaws' sent billowing clouds of spray clawing skyward as they streamed across the area's many lakes. The winds are constantly moving and circling the hills in this region like a pack of preying wolves. Suddenly they flow up and over the cordilleras, descending ravenously on the landscape below. Arising with little warning, their power and the immense volume of driving spray create conditions too treacherous for any kind of vessel.

I had seen something like this once before while walking along the famine road in the Doolough valley in Co. Mayo. An occasional pillar of spray like a miniature tornado was tossed up from the lough water by the crosswinds that had become snarled up in the valley. I remember thinking then how understandable it was that rural people were so religious. But this fierce ballet of wind and rain and rock drained me of such notions. I fell back on Hudson's words about an elemental animism that would not fit so neatly into the compartments of human reason. I thought of Moses questioning God, 'Who shall I tell them you are?' To which he received the reply, 'I am that I am.' Patagonia seemed similarly iconoclastic.

Denied the boat trip, John and I were hiking as close as we could to the glacier. In the distance the shimmering topaz of the vast expanse of frozen water confronted us. I had to remind myself how all the laws of physics were stood on their head here. This eternal wall of water had, after all, broken open granite mountains. Evidence of epochs of glacial sculpting was everywhere around us. Granite intrusions pressed into darker sedimentary rock and were then capped by even darker rock. In the early morning and evening light these rock formations seemed to take on their own inner Technicolor glow. Around us the small opalescent fragments of icebergs had broken free from the glacier wall and we stood watching their cumbersome movement. The sun was shining through the gnarled branches of ancient beech trees. The last red and yellow ragworts burned like sparks in the gold and green bushgrass. I felt again that we were standing in that symphonic paradox that this strange land threw up at you. In this intense place I felt all the power of Neruda's words.

I am surrounded
by a fortress
of most desolate moors.
The arriving wind
whistles in a thousand towers
and from the toothless cordilleras
falls the metallic water
in a swift thread
as if it were fleeing
from the abandoned sky.
All words die and everything dies
and all in silence and cold, stuff
of death and the sarcophagus.
In the full light shining, a river runs,
far from the stoniness,
and, hardened by gloom, the snow,
falling, takes itself off from dying
and dies as it falls
from the cruel heights
where it was sleeping;
yesterday, shrouded
today, lover of the wind.

Horse-riding jolted us out of this soporific intensity. McCarthy and I went sundancing across the golden pampas with exuberant yells and whoops. Our enthusiasm was unquenchable. We thought we could conquer the hills towering above us. We had, after all, conquered the Andes.

At the end of one day's ride, we watched a *huaso* bringing in a herd of horses. Some of them were straying from the main body of the herd and he was constantly forced to pursue and bring them back, only to have to repeat the task. Butch and Sundance set themselves up as outriders, preventing further strays. Herding these wild horses back to the corral was childishly exhilarating.

Our final Patagonian adventure was to be a long five-hour trek over the mountains to a high lake. Over dinner and drinks we talked about it with the excitement of fools.

≡ ⫴ ≡

During the night I wake with a feeling of unease. The wind has not ceased howling around our exposed lakeside hotel since our arrival. Such has been the noise that, even though we have separate rooms, I am still using my earplugs at night. As I come fully awake and cautiously sit up in bed I am aware of a soft light coming in around the curtains. I check my watch. It is 2.30. I take out the earplugs and then realize what is bothering me. It is completely quiet! Suddenly I remember people telling me of the night of the great storm that hit Britain while we were in Beirut. How the morning after there was an eerie calm that belied the devastation outside. With some trepidation I go to the window and pull the curtain open a little. Like a small child catching his first sight of a Christmas tree, I gaze in rapture at the vision before me.

The sky is clear and full of stars. The moonlight is so bright that I am dazzled by its reflection on the lake's still waters. Beyond and rising with fantastic clarity are the Torres. Until this moment I have only caught glimpses of them as the clouds raced past but now I see them in all their glory; massive buttresses rising to support the heavens. I stand for a while gazing and grinning then go back to bed laughing to think that our luck has come good once more. We will have fine weather for our expedition tomorrow.

〜〜

The day was bright and mild as we set out and, with a steady confident pace, we were soon in the foothills of the cordillera. Our guide, Moncho, eyed us with wry humour and suggested we take the quick way over the top rather than the long way around. We agreed, and Moncho had us all dismount. He needed to move the saddles forward and tighten the girths. With a final instruction to give our mounts a loose rein, we were on the way to stake our claim in the lake-clotted hills.

As the incline steepened, the horses' heads dipped perilously, and we leaned forward and clung tightly to the pommel of the

saddles. The climb seemed endless but when we turned to view
the sheer mountain, my confidence evaporated as quickly as the
weather in this place changed. I realized to my terrified astonishment that conquering the Andes had not conquered my fear of
heights. The path here was only about a foot wide, and many
hundreds of feet below us lay the valley we had galloped across.
My childish thrill of yesterday was now a distant memory.

My horse's name was Rabbit and I prayed furiously to every god
I believed in and others I didn't, that both me and the horse would
be transformed into such an animal so that we could scamper into
a hole somewhere. There was a big enough hole of absolute panic
opening up inside me. Moncho made precarious hairpin turns
around gullies so deep that had I fallen, I thought I would be
falling for ever. The lather on the horses' shoulders and hindquar-
ters was matched by the fear lathering up in me. Turning one of
the hairy bends and facing upward into an even more sheer climb,
Moncho stopped and nonchalantly lit a cigarette. For some minutes he puffed away while we lay on our mounts' necks dreading
that the horse in front would shy back and send us toppling into
oblivion. Butch and Sundance might still be galloping down on
the pampas below but up here two jellies were shivering on horseback. Finally Moncho moved on and we followed with some
enthusiasm. But it was primed by panic, not confidence. When
you confront something dangerous for the first time, anxiety is
compounded by fear of the unknown. But when you know from
experience how frightening something is, the second time you
encounter it, it is doubly terrifying. All through the climb I kept
remembering the old horse from San Pedro de Atacama who had
shown me the way. So I put my faith in Rabbit. With blind faith
tempering a yellow streak that skittered nervously up and down
my back, we finally made it to the top.

Soon we were cantering and galloping through the hilltop
glades and open spaces. The autumnal colours and the silence
around us acted like a kind of balm, broken only by a distant
boom.

'Avalanche,' said Moncho, pointing across to the far-off mountains. The resounding paradox of Patagonia was declaring itself
again.

We soon found our lake and enjoyed a picnic lunch washed down with fine Chilean wine named after the 120 patriots of Bernardo's Revolutionary Brigade. Even O'Higgins was in these hills with us.

We rode for several hours through the idyllic woodland. In the high, bright light everything shimmered as if a film of crystal had been gently blown across it. This was not colour you merely observed. This was colour which enveloped you. Sitting motion-less in the saddle with the horse moving beneath me was, I imagined, what it was like being an artist's brush moving gently from palette to canvas.

We were headed towards a high hill ranch where horses were broken and grazed for the summer months. As we emerged from the woodland and descended into the small valley bathed in mountain sunlight, I looked at John. He looked back at me and we both stared at the long, low, wooden ranch house and the horses grazing in the meadows beyond. This was it. This was our yak farm!

We rode into the place as if entering a dream. For me, every-thing seemed to be in slow motion. We dismounted and unsaddled our horses, then removed the bridles before shushing the animals on to the pastures surrounding the place. Everything was perfect, idyllic.

John and I investigated the farmstead separately. I would have loved to have spent the night there and to have seen it at first light, but it wasn't to be. We were due to leave our horses here and travel back by jeep. As I looked into the shed, stables and outhouses and poked about the skeletons of rusted machinery, I began to feel strangely sad. It was a passing thing, but I felt it powerfully. It was not just that this was the end of our Patagonian trek, it was also the end of the dream that had sustained us, even though like all dreams we knew it was an impossibility. But could it be? Here we were standing in the reality and the impossibility.

I walked around the place peering in every corner, taking in everything, smelling and looking and touching. My sadness was strangely adolescent. I didn't want the dream to end, though I felt I was standing in a place and a moment where dreams could come true. It was almost a post-coital kind of experience, full of urgent wonder that was too soon over. But memory is the great minder and I told myself that I could dream this dream again, because I knew it was real.

We left our horses with Moncho and travelled back to our hotel. On our way we witnessed a double rainbow, God's ancient promise. Everywhere abounded with animal life. Gorgeous pink flamingos frilled the water's edge. Further on, condors wheeled in search of food, and everywhere along the rough roadways, guanacos stood and eyed us imperiously. Perhaps they live only under the rainbow and are immune to the disturbing harshness of their homeland. There was no denying that this was Neruda's 'Bitter territory'.

The day we left our hotel, several of the staff told us that they too were about to go away for a while. When I asked why so many were leaving at one time, one of them asked me if I knew who was coming the next day. I did not and was very surprised to learn that the new guest was to be General Pinochet, which had caused much distress and anger among the hotel staff. The management had responded by saying that those who felt they could not stay during his visit could return home until he had left, and that their jobs would be waiting for them when they returned. I looked at the faces of the workers who were loading their luggage along with ours. There was anger, confusion, distaste and barely concealed hatred. Some of them spat as the general's name was mentioned.

I remember thinking as we set off, that although on the day we had arrived we had watched two pumas, an extremely rare sight, the day we were leaving we missed the biggest puma of all.

≡Ⅲ≡

We fly to Puerto Williams in a little twenty-seater plane whose pilots, in their leather jackets, look straight out of Biggles. Most of our fellow passengers seem to be locals. In the departure lounge we met a nice old fellow called Fichou, from Montreal. He seemed very happy to meet English-speakers, having been travelling alone around South America for two months, without any Spanish. He told us that he left his native Romania for Canada twenty-seven years ago. He has a high, piercing voice with a heavy mid-European accent and a big, hooked nose. His only luggage is a couple of plastic bags, one of which contains his video camera.

I can see him now talking to a woman in dark clothes, an occasional squeaky word reaching me over the roar of the engines. After some sign language they change seats so that he can point the camcorder down through the little porthole at Tierra del Fuego far below us. I cannot imagine he will capture much of the place.

The land is a vast expanse of pampa crossed by meandering rivers that often have formed ox-bow lakes. For mile after mile there is no sign of humanity save for one isolated farmstead to which there is apparently no track. There are wide swathes of red, perhaps heather, much grass, woods and areas of burned or decayed trees that look like spilled matchsticks. These are spooky and disconcerting; in some places the devastated acres, some bleached trunks still standing, others lying higgledy-piggledy on the ground, suggest the aftermath of some cataclysm, a disaster of awful power. I have that feeling, which I have had often in Chile, that while human beings can make efforts to control, tame and use this place, clearing forests, marking boundaries, their influence here is only transitory. As I think of this, I spot a squall of wind chasing across the surface of a small lake, like the whirlwind on the dune outside Iquique; a spirit hurrying with some mysterious purpose.

We descend and bump through cloud in among the peaks. There are boats in the channel below us.

'The Beagle Channel!' I call to Brian behind me. He nods and smiles and leans to look down when we bank and start bucking for the final approach to Puerto Williams.

In the small airport lounge, big heaters going full-bore warm the family reunions and prepare those waiting for the return flight to Punta Arenas and the heat that lies to the north.

The end of the world is far more welcoming than I had expected, a little like Scotland, with a bright blue sky framing black clouds over the mountains to the south. The town looks neat across the small bay; regimented rows of cream bungalows with blue and green roofs. The only discordant note is on the seafront, which is dominated by a large warship and two, quite black, fast patrol boats, mean-looking machines, and a fisheries patrol vessel.

Fichou is now filming everything madly with his camcorder, doing a running commentary in French. '*Maintenant je regarde la ville de Puerto Williams.*' He pans round: '*Ici mon ami Brian. Il est un Irlandais . . .*'

We share a taxi with Fichou to the Hosteria Wala, a large modern hotel that appears deserted but for the manager. Although they serve only breakfast we decide to stay here but Fichou, who is on a tight budget, elects to go to a cheaper establishment in town.

We return there and drop Fichou off, having arranged to meet the next day. We have some lunch in the one restaurant, Los Dientes de Navarino, named for some vicious-looking peaks to the south. The lunch is solid – soup of vegetables and spaghettini and a lump of fatty meat followed by the same meat with peas and spuds. All in all, rather reminiscent of Jihad fare. It is filling nonetheless.

There is a rough wooden dado around the restaurant/bar and the same big colour photographs of Viña and Valparaíso that you see on so many restaurant walls all over the country. A TV is on as always. Men with rugged, weathered, brown faces drift in for a drink. One man, who seems to be a permanent fixture, knocks back half-pints of wine.

The town square, little more than a dusty yard, has a tourist office (closed), a post office and offices for the rival phone companies, CTC and Entel. There are a few shops which all seem to stock the same limited choice of staid-looking clothes, tools, pharmacy items, toys and tourist knick-knacks. We take a short walk from the centre to the Plaza O'Higgins, a dirt track round-about with a few flowers.

We wander along the shore past the navy base and the yacht club, whose anchorage is dotted with many small sailing boats.

Back at the hotel, a young man appears to put sheets on our beds and I manage to talk with him a little. He tells me that there are more people here during the Chilean summer holidays which have just ended and that they get a few European tourists, though never many. The hotel is large and pretty smart, yet I cannot imagine it has ever been close to full. I gather that the navy owns the place and that sometimes military and governmental delegations descend and give the impression of life.

I join Brian for a beer in the bar, aimlessly watching television for a while before turning in. I read as Brian nods off and starts snoring. Then I too get my head down. Despite my earplugs, Bri's rumblings wake me a few times and I find myself getting angry with old, familiar resentments. My irritation takes an irrational turn as I begin to imagine his nasal sound effects are deliberate.

In fact I must have slept well as I wake refreshed, eager for the day. I go to breakfast ahead of Brian and find just the one table laid with toasted buns already cool on a plate. Looking through the picture window I see light and reflections on the river that comes up by the hotel and the masts of sailing boats further down towards the Beagle Channel. The dark river in the early morning mist looks jungle-like and I find myself daftly squinting through the brightening light for palm trees. I decide it is time for a cold shower.

Fichou is waiting for us in the town square with a young Israeli, Mordechai. Mordi is obsessed with getting his passport stamped with 'End of the World' and so we join him in a hunt for an office that might fulfil this desire. He has a contact, Ronaldo, who is a lawyer working for the regional government. Ronaldo advises us that the Chilean authorities do not stamp passports, only the Argentinians do – across the Beagle Channel at Ushuaia. Mordi is mortified but I can tell he remains determined for this trophy of his visit to Tierra del Fuego.

He has arranged to go on a sightseeing trip with a variety of acquaintances including Ronaldo's wife Patricia. For want of anything better to do, Bri and I decide to join the excursion.

Driving around in a massive, beat-up old pick-up, we get to know Mordi a little better. He is twenty-four years old and has recently completed his national service – in military intelligence apparently. He is obsessed with the price of things: our cameras, the flight here, everything. He is staying somewhere in town and is outraged at the cost of our hotel.

'Why you pay so much?'

'Because we can, Mordi. It's a good place.'

He is good-looking and eager to talk about his sexual conquests during his trip to South America. He explains that he was with a group but decided to go his own way. I cannot help thinking that maybe the decision was, at least, mutual but he does make an amusing foil for crazy Fichou. They tease each other a great deal, particularly about sexual appetites. When Mordi asks Patricia if there are any nightclubs on the island Fichou chips in, 'Ah! You young men, always thinking of the girls!'

'Don't tell me you don't, old man. You are the goat, eh!'

Fichou continues to film everything. The first time he starts his high-pitched, reedy French commentary for the film, the women jump with shock. It is hilarious. I would give a great deal of money to see his home movies, or at least watch his family and friends having to watch them. Most of the images would be hopelessly blurred, probably more dizzying than bucketing around on Alfonso's farm.

He speaks in broken and obscene English. Every now and then he starts a diatribe, which, as with Mordi, is usually on the subject of being ripped off. When we stop at one point he starts up.

'They people in the phone shop, they FUCK me!' he screeches. 'I ask them rate yesterday, they say 500 peso per minute for international, today they – FUCK – say 1,500 peso.'

Patricia, a pretty woman with short, salt-and-pepper hair, is Argentinian. Given the paranoid nature of the authorities down here and the proximity of Ushuaia, this leaves her rather exposed in spite of having a Chilean husband. She says her calls to friends and family at home are often bugged, sometimes cut off. When Brian asks why they are so paranoid she replies with a wry laugh, 'Seventy per cent of the population here is in the military, police, customs, navy, air force. They have to do something!'

Away from the settlement we follow a stony track through woods and small valleys, catching regular glimpses of the Beagle Channel and passing a few isolated farms rearing cattle, sheep and pigs. The forests show the same strange mix of decay and rebirth that I had seen flying over Tierra del Fuego. There is much fresh growth but also much dead wood. Some had been deliberately burned but the introduction of beaver has meant additional destruction. Trees everywhere are nibbled and great areas have been reduced to wasteland. The beaver take only the leaves and small upper branches so the trunks lie naked and grey. We stop to look down on a large beaver dam and, as I try to take a picture, Mordi's deep voice sounds close to my ear: 'How big is your zoom?'

We move on to look at the Indian cemetery, a very neat little place on the shores of the channel. The only noise is the lapping of water on the beach. Family graves are enclosed by little white fences, and a curious tepee of sticks and animal skins surround a shrine to the Virgin. There are some garish red plastic roses and, spookily, the skull of an animal – a sheep, I think.

'Why is the cemetery here,' I ask our source of local information, Maurice, 'so far from the Indian village on the other side of Puerto Williams?'

'The Indians used to live here but were forced to move by the military in 1960. In the old days they used to cross the channel to see their Ona cousins. But that meant they were visiting enemy Argentina so they were rehoused the other side of town where they could be watched. The last pure-blood Yaghan died in 1996.'

The neatness of the cemetery seems somehow ludicrous, pathetic in this beautifully wild spot.

'We have had a campaign to let them come and live here again,' continues Maurice, 'and now they can. We hope they can be happy here again. Patti helps them with their craftwork.'

'Is the future bright, given there are so few of them?'

'Mainly their life is as tourist attractions. It is sad. Many drink.'

We drive on along the shore of the channel, with Ushuaia gleaming in the sunlight as jumbo jets fly in and out. On our side the only thing in flight is the occasional upland goose. There are a few small fishing boats tied up in little coves and every once in a while a small abandoned dwelling. Brian, Mordi and Fichou spend much of the time snoozing, to the amusement of the ladies.

We stop off at one of the oldest farmsteads, Santa Rosa. Dogs and speckled pigs all rootle about the yard. There are a couple of large corrugated iron sheds and a fenced corral with cattle in it. Patti points to a bare, level piece of ground in the centre of the spread: 'There used to be a large house full of fine old furniture. Not so long ago it burned down. They had no insurance so the farmer and his family now live in that little shack on the hill over there. Before, it was for the farmhand.'

The farmer's wife comes over to talk to Patti and Maurice. She smiles a lot but her face is worn and deeply lined. There is no escape for her. Later we stop again when a strange creature of twelve or fourteen plods down to the road behind a train of horses. The horses wander off and the skinhead spectacle walks over to the truck to talk to Patti and beg a cigarette. It turns out that she is a girl. Patti explains that she is mentally handicapped. I cannot help thinking of the movie *Deliverance*.

At the western end of the island we stop, as the road does, at Puerto Navarino. There are only five buildings. Three of them are the deserted quarters and offices for the *carabineros*, although one is still occupied by the navy. The last is a farm. It is a rather eerie place. Bri and I wander into the empty police station but there is nothing of interest. We join our fellows for coffee and chocolate cake that Patricia has miraculously produced from the boot of the truck. We all pose for photographs as Mordi and Fichou continue their banter.

Back in Puerto Williams, we walk down to the Yacht Club, which is in an old boat owned by the navy. The club begins to fill with the members of a German sailing party just returned from the Antarctic, all obviously well pleased with their trip. One of their number is celebrating his birthday so we all join in singing 'Happy Birthday dear Dieter' and then have to do it again when one of his pals finally gets his camcorder working.

There are other European and American yachties, one awful youth from the States droning on about music with a dull Nordic lad. Later I spot Mordi in a corner negotiating with a charter skipper for a passage to Ushuaia so that he can get his passport stamped. A deal is obviously struck as he raises his can of lager to us across the crowded bar, looking very self-satisfied.

The noise and the heat are getting to me and I decide to walk home. It is wonderful. The woods are all dark against the moonlight glinting off the water. I feel a sense of peace and mystery all around. Bri gets back shortly after me, having cajoled Maurice into giving him a lift.

On waking it takes a moment or two before I remember where

I am. Last night I heard that one of the yacht charterers is an evangelical Christian. I imagine him hellfire and brimstoning it to his clients, 'The End of the World is nigh!' and them replying, 'Well, I should bloody well hope so too, matey, with the prices you're charging.'

After breakfast I decide to walk down to look at the Indian village on the far side of town. Brian elects to stay in bed.

'What are you going to see? They're not a freak show.'

On my way to town I stop near the Yacht Club. The dark clear waters here in the inlet from the channel could be the end of the mystic river far away in El Museo valley in the High Andes. I have a sense of being out of time, in a timeless place and I feel once more some of the magic of Neruda's 'harsh homeland'. These profound expressions of nature – the mountains, the deep rivers, the 'spirit' whirlwinds – perhaps they are all part of the rope that binds Chileans here even in such difficult conditions.

I see Mordi lugging the world's largest kitbag on to a yacht. He waves. I return the salute but, bound up in my thoughts, carry on.

I walk on along the shore past the town and sit looking across the channel to Argentina. Suddenly I feel sad, wishing there was someone here to share this place and these emotions with me. I realize that much as the country still moves me, the feelings it is now stirring are of a desire to be home among loved ones. We have been travelling a long while and after seeing so many new and remarkable sights, having been to places of such great isolation, I need the familiarity and comfort of home.

At my feet delicate little shells lie scattered and I realize that, for the time being, I have had enough of the world's grand scale. The landscapes of Patagonia and Tierra del Fuego have disturbed me. It is like meeting some glamorous and beautiful character whom you wish to befriend but you cannot think how to open a conversation. You feel his distance, sense his isolation and want to embrace him. Then suddenly he turns his face and it is pockmarked, ravaged and cankered. You shudder and want to run but know there is nowhere to hide. You are only hiding from yourself, your fear of lost opportunity. It is a strange confusion of emotions. 'At the end of my tether at the end of the world,' I say to myself.

High above me, stunning clouds dot the sky. Some are moving, others still. A small fishing boat chugs across towards the port, wavelets come lapping at my feet and gulls gather a little distance away on the shore. The water is all calm though one can imagine it raging in a storm. Maurice said that there are many sharks in these waters, dangers lurking beneath the surface.

As I near the Yaghan village, I find my steps slowing, having lost the appetite for yet another 'sight' and appreciating Brian's concerns of voyeurism. I turn back to the town square to meet him, following a winding path through a cool wood where the quiet and sweet scents restore my equilibrium.

I meet Fichou on a mission to post a great fistful of cards then join Bri for a final lunch in Los Dientes de Navarino. There is time only for a plate of chips and a beer. A party of American sailors sit at the next table talking loudly of the problems of marine insurance. A couple of local drunks prop up the bar. The 'half-pints of wine' man still lies slumped across the counter. When, occasionally, his head rises a few inches and his eyes flicker open, the barman roars in his ear *'Buenos noches'* and everyone falls about laughing. Another, worse for wear but still standing, is a young man. He has a fine physique and a broad, handsome Indian face. Brian, casually taking in the scene, suddenly stiffens.

'Look at that man, that's the face on the statue in Punta Arenas!'

'My God,' I reply, 'he could have been the model.'

In the sculpture he was bronze, wearing a loincloth, his eyes bright and alert. Now he is in jeans and weaving slightly, his eyes dilated. I feel sad, my mind spinning to faded black and white pictures of the last great North American Indian warrior Geronimo after his surrender. I wonder how you cope with being the last of your kind; how you bear the responsibility, even when you have no chance of victory, of leading your people to defeat.

I feel dog-tired but Bri is on great form, chatting away and making me laugh. It is a good thing to spend some time apart and have news to exchange. Perhaps we should have done this more often.

There are seats around the square and people gather to wait for the bus to the airport. We find an empty bench near the Entel phone company office. Fichou emerges from this building and sits with us, obviously seething. A woman comes out of the office and as she walks away he hisses, 'She FUCK me with zee rate.' He squirrels back in and we hear him shrieking, 'How much – how much?' I am sure his apparent madness must be a safer protection against potential robbers than the plastic bags in which he secretes his valuables.

Just before take-off, squalls of rain come gusting in and we are all slightly apprehensive. Safely off the ground we climb across the Beagle Channel and up among the high hills. The clouds floating below us look more like seaweed seen from the water's surface than massed vapour. The rain flies horizontally past the window until we meet dense grey cloud and enter Nowhere.

The last quarter of an hour of the flight to Punta Arenas has the little plane bucking furiously in the wind. I am reassured to see the co-pilot nonchalantly reading a newspaper. Brian is dozing across the aisle. My immediate neighbour nudges me: 'That one, he doan feel nuthin! Very good!'

The pilot wrestles with the controls before we touch down to a surprisingly smooth landing, for which he receives a generous round of applause.

On the bus out of town we catch our last sight of Fichou. Half hunched, his bags against a lamp-post, he is filming the exterior of the Braun Menendez Museum. His lips move and I imagine the commentary: '*Maintenant je regarde le Musée Braun Menendez, la maison de la famille* . . .' A kindly man, inspiring a mix of sadness at his solitude and admiration for his venturesome spirit.

We chug out towards the airport. These are our last terrestrial views of the flat pampa. The sky is a warm blue with light cloud and so very, very wide.

Epilogue

≡⫴≡

We sit eating sandwiches, facing each other on banquettes up-holstered in gold velvet. Like the rest of the train, our sleeping compartment on the overnight express from Temuco to Santiago has seen better days yet is still infused with the grace and charm of another era. The Pullman-style coaches were built in Germany in the 1930s and, although nearing decrepitude, are preserved in a state of elegant disrepair.

This trip will take no more than twelve hours, yet it seems appropriate that our transport for this, the last stage of our Chilean journey, should make us feel as though we are embarking on one of the great transcontinental railways: across Siberia, Australia or India. The age and rickety nature of the train add an element of risk too, heightening the sense of adventure. After an uneventful flight from Punta Arenas to Puerto Montt and an easy bus ride from there to Temuco it seems right to be rounding off the journey in a more antique mode of travelling.

᎐᭴᭴

Temuco was the place I had promised myself I would come back to. But this time it wasn't wholly by choice. The magnet of circumstance, predestination, call it what you will, brought us back here.

We had a few hours to kill before our dream ride into Santiago in a first-class overnight cabin on a train that was older than both of us. This was going to be the nightcap to our travels.

Our departure time allowed us several hours in the town. But there wasn't much to see. With little to offer in the way of architecture or cultural respite, it exists in its moment and shuts down quickly. I loved its blandness, knowing that that was only a cover.

We were able to stash our belongings in a baggage check and go prowling round Temuco's empty side streets. We were both dog-tired. A kind of claustrophobia surrounded our exchanges. Our mythic journey was over . . . almost, but we hadn't the words to share it. A submerged sense of elation was bubbling beneath the surface but we didn't know how to release that either.

Food is always a way of getting things moving, so we traipsed off round the seedy back streets of Temuco's railway station in search of sustenance for both the inner and the outer man. It was a Sunday and everything seemed to be closed. In the side streets that suckle from the station piazza, a few down-in-the-mouth bars and cafés were open, and mainly unoccupied. Had the sirens of Homer's *Odyssey* been singing there, I could not have been intrigued into them.

I was feeling an uneasy melancholy as we wandered half-heartedly from one back street to another. I didn't want to believe that this was Temuco's final testimony. It seemed shabby and not worth all that Neruda had promised me. I was dejected as we tramped nearer the centre of the city.

But then the promise came true! We chanced upon an indoor market, enclosed in an irregular octagonal square. Not knowing what it was, we would have walked past if we hadn't seen several groups of people emerge from it. We decided to chance our luck.

I never liked Santa or his grotto; I didn't believe in tooth fairies, black cats or broken mirrors . . . but I do believe in angels and spirit guides!

Inside the enclosure was a souk-like market filled with people, some selling, some buying, some browsing. Whole families were promenading through the most glorious pruck-house. I glanced at John. He rolled his eyes, as if to say, oh no, not again, only you could find a place like this. I smiled as he shrugged his shoulders and rolled his palms open in the typical Arab, 'so be it' manner.

We spent a few hours there, circulating through the alleyways as the market opened up. I had my saddle, but I knew that it wasn't by chance that we were back in Temuco. My perambulations confirmed that curious reasoning to me. This was an Indian market, and the overwhelming majority of faces and goods in the place were native. To another eye, it might be full of nothing more than cheap gee-gaws. But not for me: this was Neruda's emporium of words, images and people vivaciously enjoying themselves.

I wanted to buy several things at once but John's raised, chastening eye warned me off. Instead we had a great meal in one of the small cafés that were at the centre of the place. There was something wonderfully classless and cluttered about it. It was busy with life and not just commerce. We ate slowly and indulgently, sharing the place and the moment in a grateful silence.

We had about three quarters of an hour, allowing for our walk back to the station, collecting our bags and checking in for the train, but I still had things to do. I had earlier found a stall selling all kinds of bric-à-brac and so-called antiques. I dived back into it like a hungry horse into its nosebag. There was a plethora of wonderful things here: the remnants of beautiful harnesses, hand-worked in scrolled leather and silver, ancient stirrups and bridles embossed with figures out of a mythology I had no comprehension of; cooking pots and amulets that must have had their origin before Bernardo, Pablo or any of the prehistory of this country that we only half understood.

I hoked and poked with demented fascination while John quietly reminded me of the time. At last I found it. An ancient, broken clay figure of a llama. It was crudely formed, with its body worked to accommodate a small fat candle. A llama light, and I knew who had found it for me!

I remembered seeing examples of this simple artefact in the exposed graves of the desert mummies in San Pedro de Atacama's museum, and also in an exhibition of pre-Columbian art in Santiago. There were a few tiny examples containing burnt-out votive candles in the little church at Parinacota, reminding me even then of the primitive animism that underlies even the purest and simplest of faiths.

More significantly these creatures and their near cousins, the guanaco, had been everywhere in the extremes of this country that we had passed through. In the northern deserts, the High Andes and the Patagonian wilderness, they were watching over us. But my own little lamp had already become for me a keepsake and a symbol of Neruda's fabulous bestiary. The man's work and our travels had confirmed to me that 'you don't always find what you are looking for in the places you expect to, but you might find something else . . . and perhaps that is what you were really look-ing for!'

I also knew that when I was back home and lit my own votive candle in the recess of the clay figure, the hollow of its eyes would glow softly like the inscrutable stare of the living creature and I would know again the lure and pull of Patagonia.

'More pruck,' said John as we hurried back to catch Treno 10 to Santiago.

≡III≡

Exploring the train, we step nervously between the carriages where gaps open wide then slam closed with ear-splitting and potentially bone-crushing crunches. At times we bounce from wall to wall of the corridor, dodging bare wires that hang from light fittings and fuse boxes whose doors swing wildly. It is difficult to discern whether the train is being rewired or dis-mantled.

We make our way to the very back of the train to find we can stand out on an open platform. There is just a thin chain, with a dangling notice 'Treno 10', between us and the track that runs out beneath our feet. The orange glow of sunset lights up the scrub-lands we pass through. At times the vegetation of thick bushes and high grasses closes in about the track as if we are passing through a sea. At others the flora becomes sparse, with wide areas of dusty, flat pampas opening up and, in the distance, the Andes rising bright in the evening sun. Every now and then we go through a village and the engine, way off to the front, drones its hooter as children cry out a greeting. We wave to them, grinning.

'I've just realized that I've always wanted to do this!' I shout at Brian.

He shouts back an affirmative before his words are drowned out by another blast from the hooter. I lean closer to him.

'You'd probably never put it on a wish list, but when it happens it's so right – like an undreamed dream come true.'

As we run on into the darkening night I have the sensation of being taken into another dimension. It is as if the train is creating a vortex, a whirlwind mixing up the future into which it is ploughing, our present as we stand on this little platform and our past that we watch running out behind us on the tracks. The train rattles and thunders like a demented printing press frantically laying down our life stories between the tracks, too fast to read, in a script that is at once familiar yet indecipherable.

The dining car brings us back to the real world. At least back to the reality of this sweetly staid environment. Roof and walls are panelled in light oak and there are old gas lamps on elaborate wall brackets. Tonight illumination comes from more recent, though partial, strip lighting. The atmosphere, though slightly gloomy, is not at all depressing. We sit on free-standing dining chairs upholstered in faded brown corduroy; we admire the lace doilies on our table. The waiter cannot provide gin and tonic but kindly offers Campari and soda. In this curious time capsule even disappointments are resolved with something that is somehow more appropriate. We grin at each other as we sip our drinks, watching the cook and steward at work in the gloom of the smoke- and steam-filled galley at the far end of the carriage.

This train, with its blend of eras and cultures, sums up much of the Chile we have experienced. In any country the past is reviewed and redefined as the present unravels. Particular periods of history lose their distinctiveness and are blended into one saga. We came here with predetermined attitudes to Pinochet's regime and, while these have not changed, our growing understanding of Chile has brought a more subtle appreciation of how the 'military period' came about and how it is now being dealt with. Although I believe that the horrors of that time can only be laid to rest after a full investigation and acceptance of what happened, I have to ask myself whether we are stuck in Chile's past more than the Chileans and if we are wrong to let our preoccupations run apparently stronger than those of the locals. Our views, after all, are informed by our backgrounds, on the other side of the world, where another history has defined our present.

During our journey we have learned that anyone might have supported or opposed the dictatorship and that external appearances give nothing away. Looking now at our fellow passengers – a group of young people chatting noisily and an elderly couple – it is impossible to know what they are thinking and whether they were victims or abusers. The nation's motto *Par Razon o la Fuerza* – by reason or force – is a strong, combative one and perhaps explains the ambivalence to and the tacit acceptance of Pinochet. It speaks of a kind of laissez-faire that can condone anything in the name of the state. That sort of attitude must help the population to persevere in the face of their natural, brutal surroundings. We have witnessed the bitter wastes of the northern deserts, stood gazing in awe from the top of the Andes and with Alfonso shared the wonder and desolation of Patagonia. But we have only been passing through and observing. We do not have to stay and come to terms with this 'harsh homeland'. Perhaps the diversity of scales in the landscape, coupled with the mixture of bloodlines and names, explains the confusion over national identity.

The spine of my copy of *Isla Negra* was broken and its pages creased and covered in cryptic notes and heavily penned lines to mark significant stanzas. The author had also made this night journey to Santiago. Wearily I ran a crooked line under these words from his poem, 'Night Train' and felt the flush of kinship:

> Exhausted, I slept like wood,
> and when I woke
> I felt the agony of the rain.
> Something was separating me from my blood.

As I set the book down, I considered how I had brought eight thick notebooks in which to record this journey, yet I had used only two. Instead the three volumes of Neruda's poetry had replaced them and were now covered in a thick clutter of hastily written thoughts and observations.

I've always been a traveller in one way or another. The fascination of other places has been with me for as long as I can remember, and certainly since I took my first book from the library. I remember *Call of the Wild* by Jack London. Only a few years ago I had made a pilgrimage to Alaska to see for myself the author's cruel but heroic landscape. But when friends asked me of my impending trip, 'Why Chile of all places?', beyond John's and my dreams of it in captivity I could only answer that South America had always fascinated me. If they pursued me about why specifically Chile, I found I lacked the cosy reason and enthusiasm that my childhood memories of Jack London's wonderful story had locked away in my imagination.

Rolling through this Chilean nightscape which had insinuated itself under my skin more deeply now than any fantasy, I began to mull over what those reasons might be. In the dimness of the moving train, wrapped up in myself and trying to come to terms with the fact of our journey's end, I wanted to find again my own points of departure, so that I could, more fully, understand our odyssey.

I remembered many, many years ago, even before I opened London's book, sitting leafing through an ancient encyclopaedia. That sepia-tinted photograph of a group of South American Indians had remained with me unconsciously all these years. I could still see their questioning faces asking me if I had found whatever it was I came here looking for.

But an old photo re-emerging from my childhood could not be the only reason. As I accepted the memory of it, others came flooding back: the many evenings I would sit with my father watching all those nature programmes the early years of television brought into our tiny kitchen house; the wonderfully strange animals and birds and the magnificently huge landscape were all grist to my childhood imagination, and planted the seeds of my wanderlust.

Then all the other previously locked-away images and points of reference began to surface. During my student years, Pinochet and Allende were names constantly bandied about and the subject of much undergraduate debate.

But for me there was one character more important than either of these: Bernardo O'Higgins, my beloved Bernardo, my ghostly companion long before I came to his homeland to find him.

I laughed at the memory of Bernardo. For many months I had talked constantly of this character when John and I were incarcerated together. My knowledge was skimpy but my imagination was as big as the map of South America. What I didn't know, I fabricated, to McCarthy's confusion. Lebanon was suddenly back with me, as were those weeks and months John and I had spent travelling the continent of South America in our minds. But Bernardo would not leave me even now, with the train pushing towards his birthplace. I looked out of the window to try and catch a first glimpse. But the land was in blackout and only John's face caught in the yellowing light of the carriage was reflected out of the dark window. When he wasn't busy fingering his infernal Psion, he would pause and stare into the middle distance, caught up in his own rapture of reminiscence. My reflection was opposite his. We could have been ghosts ourselves. The idea made me study John's features more closely. I tried to imagine him as the young Bernardo, in the hope that I might get closer to his story before I left his Chile.

Bernardo was a reluctant soldier, yet the compulsive need to overcome the trauma of his father's rejection steeled some resolve in him. Love and hate are twin emotions and sit in symbolic relationship with each other. Perhaps Bernardo sought to gain his father's love by dreaming his dream, by recreating it and going beyond it. Even if it necessitated destroying the world his father had made.

Defeated and frustrated, O'Higgins spent three years hiding in the Andes and Argentina. Those three years in that desolation were formative for him: suspecting betrayal at every turn, haunted and taunted by his father's image, knowing his Irish peasant bloodlines were anathema to the Spanish in Chile. Feeling himself cheated and used by his father substitutes, Bernardo waged a private war within himself, battling with the fiercest of foes, the enemy within. With no advisers to counsel him, no embrace to reassure him, Bernardo was forced to dream his own dream of identity and purpose.

History has recorded Bernardo a hero. But wars, I think, do not make heroes. If anything they create accidental heroes or heroes made in the mind and the imagination. We need the reassurance that tells us we can overcome adversity. If courage is part of what heroism might be, then true courage has more to do with facing the frustrations, confusion, fear and loneliness in ourselves, and overcoming it by taking control and by fusing vision with will, creating ourselves anew, to achieve what is in us to achieve. There are in our history many heroes whom the textbooks will not record because ours is more than a history of events. It is rather a history of being and of becoming what is in us to be.

I laughed to myself as I thought of John, oblivious all the while to the metamorphosis I had imposed on him as a colonial revolutionary.

But Don John Harrison Ford Sundance Quixote McCarthy apart, there was something Bernardo-like about my companion. A hesitancy, a kind of reluctance to put himself forward. Neruda also had to struggle with such sensitivity in his own early career. For me, his bohemian later life was a cover-up, a way of dealing with the world. He writes:

> Shyness is a kink in the soul, a special category that opens out into solitude. Moreover it's inherent suffering as if we had two epidermises and the one underneath rebelled and shrank back from life. Of the things that make up a man, this quality, this damaging thing, is part of the alloy that lays the foundation in the long run, for the perpetuity of the self.

Coming to terms with that solitude within yourself, whether in the High Andes or the Patagonian wilderness, lets you run between extremes and come home with the knowledge that there are no finite edges to your self. I looked once more at John's reflection. Yes, I could see my Bernardo there.

≡Ⅲ≡

The train picks up speed again and the motion becomes wilder. If standing on the back of the train gave the sense of being in another dimension, sitting in the dining car is like being in a cartoon animation. The lurches of the train are so violent as it speeds on that I can be looking at Brian head to head across our table one instant then the next his head has moved three feet to one side. It hangs there, unnaturally stretched from his torso, for a couple of seconds during which my body is attacked by the demon animator and starts juddering as if I am operating a road-worker's compactor.

Then Brian's head is opposite mine once more and there is suddenly complete peace. We enter a realm of drifting tranquillity, where we seem to float in slow motion, smiling broadly as if in an ambrosial trance. Then a banshee wail from beyond the windows announces the arrival of another squall of disturbance and we try to get our drinks back on to the table as if pushing them down through a thick jelly. We do not talk much as we switch between concentrating on eating and laughing with a French couple across the way as forkfuls of food come dangerously close to being deposited in ears or up noses.

Brian decides to have a nightcap so I head back to the compartment. Trying to ready it for the night, I first do battle with the window which has just two positions: closed tight or open wide. Closed, the small room seems stuffy; open, the noise is deafening and the curtains flap alarmingly. I settle for the breeze. Next I rig up the lower berth and settle in comfortably, hoping that the rhythm of the train will rock me to sleep. Above me is a light fitting from the Thirties, a four-lamp candelabra of which only two bulbs are working, and in the corner there is a washbasin. Our luggage, including Brian's saddle, has stacked away surprisingly neatly. It is a cosy, safe little haven in this lower bunk; above me the varnished curve of Brian's closed, upper berth reminds me of a giant tortoise.

We are nearly at our journey's end and my thoughts turn to home. Travelling, while taking you to new places, emphasizes the value of having an emotional and physical base. T. S. Eliot said that 'the end of all our exploring/Will be to arrive where we started/And know the place for the first time'. This applies equally to an internal as well as an external environment and I feel that this trip has helped me see myself more clearly.

I have always hated rushing at things without thinking them through but at the same time I am highly biddable, so that often through life I have agreed to something that in my heart I have felt is a half-baked notion. At times I would throw up resistance to more determined natures but whether this was through caution or stubbornness I am not sure. There were, of course, moments of focus and calm – of being centred – then I would wheel off again into a world of uncertainty. Now I am less often so uncertain; over recent years I have gained confidence. Throughout our friendship Brian has had a great influence on this aspect of my character. Although at times I have felt irritated at his single-mindedness, his passionate adherence to his views is usually encouraging and a reassurance.

The perfect journey has become the journey to hell. It is nearing four in the morning, and a short while ago the guard and steward appeared at our door, jabbered something at me and left leaving the light on. Clearly something of importance is afoot. Brian is deep in sleep but after a few shakes he opens his eyes and listens to the news.

'I didn't do anything! Let's turn the lights out and get some more kip,' he says, determined that nothing untoward should happen.

I look out the window and see one of the noisy youths from the dining car standing on the platform with his bag. I go out into the corridor and meet a lady from the neighbouring compartment. Fortunately she speaks a little English and explains that an accident further up the line means we have to transfer to buses. This is only the second time we have ventured on to Chile's rail network and so far it has notched up a 100 per cent failure rate in delivering us to the expected destination. Last time we were marooned in Chillán. I have no idea where we are now.

Blearily we struggle into our clothes and I take out my bags to leave Bri more room for manoeuvre. A steward directs me to a bus so I load my bags and have a smoke while waiting for himself. After what seems an age the steward reappears with Brian's wheelie bag, loads it and chats to a colleague. The faces at the bus windows are pale in the neon light; everyone looks tired and confused. Suddenly heads turn back towards the station. Butch Cassidy lopes into view, hat down over his eyes, saddle thrown over his shoulder. Only his fellow gringo catches this tough hombre's muttered comment, 'I'm too tired for all this malarkey!' as we stagger on to the bus and find the only two unoccupied seats, at opposite ends.

Pulling out of the station yard I glimpse a sign – Chillán. My God, I think, the place must have a curse against us getting safely through it by rail! I swivel round to see if Brian has noticed the sign but cannot even locate him in the gloom and mass of bodies at the back of the bus.

I try to get some rest and, with the aid of earplugs and eye mask, am asleep when the bus stops at another station and we disembark to board another train. I feel that the lack of sleep and all the disruptions of this nightmare ride are causing me to hallucinate when I try to locate our bags in the pile that is emerging from underneath the bus. Struggling in the throng of people, I bend down to check a bag and realize there is a false leg beside it, with sock and shoe already on. Its owner, quite a young man, appears on crutches. My face must have reflected my confusion and shock as he stops and laughs, saying 'OK! OK!' as he sits on his bag to fix the leg. Catching up with myself I smile back and give him a thumbs-up, and go off in search of my own bag feeling humbled. In minutes we are ensconced in a new compartment, bags stashed, bunks set and heads down, dead to the world.

Next morning we dismantle the bunks and settle on the seats to watch the countryside roll by, wondering at the strange coincidence of failing to get through Chillán on the train for a second time.

'I blame your man Bernardo,' I tease Brian. 'Typical Irishman, putting a spanner in the works!'

'Don't forget that Neruda was born nearby too,' observes Brian, 'so maybe they were both talking to us, wanting us to wait a while, and feel something special.'

As we chat I am leafing through a small guidebook I'd picked up at the Hotel Explora and find a phrase I like:

'"The explicit purpose of the trip must be forgotten to allow the good side of the unexpected to appear." Maybe that was what was happening.'

'I like that,' says Brian, 'but humping a saddle around from train to bus and back again in the middle of the night is just a little too unexpected for my liking.'

'True enough.' I pause, reading another line from the book. 'But listen to this. "Almost every discovery is anticipated by a certain knowledge. Action begins the moment one thinks about it. The rest is only the consequence of the idea, or the dream." That could have been written for us sitting in Beirut! Except that our knowledge of yaks and Patagonia was a bit thin.'

'Yes, but we were right. We convinced Alfonso.'

It seems fitting that the inspiration for this journey was that scheme to farm yaks in Patagonia. Although we had developed that wild idea with Alfonso, it was really just the icing on the cake of the Chilean adventure. There had been no powerful emotional investment in the project, it was merely something that reflected the vital element of fantasy that we had used to bring us through the bad times. Yak farming was a symbol of our shared sense of humour, the determination to persevere and believe in a future beyond captivity. The exploration of the fantasy has been fun but, because it was a fantasy, we have been free to explore wider horizons both in Chile and in ourselves. This journey has held us together but, unlike our original 'holidays', this one has had all the freedoms included.

The profound need for mutual support we had in Beirut is not now so vital. Then we accepted that element of personal surrender: holding oneself in check to give the other room to breathe; affecting greater optimism than one really felt to carry the other through; frankly asking for help – 'I am frightened, don't let me go under.' These things are fainter now. Mutual responsibility, respect and love are still there. But without the spectre of mental and emotional collapse they do not command the old levels of selflessness. We are no longer in survival mode and recognize that relationships demand less when you can stand up and walk out of the door. This journey has reinforced our acceptance of this change and allowed us to enjoy the fact that we are no longer so responsible for each other.

I go down the corridor to take a last look from the back of the train. The door to the small platform is now cordoned off but I am not too disappointed – I have been there. Looking through the door's grimy window, I see that the printing press is still rolling away. On the way back I meet the guard who tells me we will be in Santiago in twenty minutes. In the compartment Bri is sitting looking out at the countryside as it begins to transform into suburbs. We share that sense of a secret, special, back-door arrival that you find reaching a place by boat or train. It is like looking over a garden fence and seeing the washing out to dry; here we go past ugly industrial sites, shanty areas and lorry parks. We pass old, rusting rolling stock, spot a man sleeping under a tatty bit of carpet and another, in a wide flat area of waste ground, covered in litter, looking neat and clean in trousers and shirt but wandering about looking lost.

'Oh well, back to Frank's flat for a shower and tidy up. Then off to the airport and home!' says Brian.

Sharing this view, it seems like a good moment to clear the air. In other times we voiced our frustrations immediately, realizing that if we did not, they would fester. Our circumstances may have changed, but the need to be open with each other has not.

'You know, you changing the plans and getting the key to Frank's place really annoyed me at the time.'

'I noticed. We were bound to get on each other's nerves. I was ready to strangle you and those bloody guidebooks.'

'Sorry about that.'

'I'm sorry too.'

Close friends know each other so well that much is communicated indirectly, the fingers on each other's pulse able to pick up every change of beat. But when your own emotional pulse is running erratically it is easy to presume to know what the other is feeling without seeking confirmation. Reactions are read incorrectly and misguide one's response. Such moments of failed communication can create unstated barriers and sometimes a wilful answer like that of a contrary child. This can escalate to cause moments of barely concealed hostility. I remember seething in La Serena over our efforts to hire a car. It seemed as if we both wanted to prove the other wrong and do our own thing, losing the facility to talk the situation through so that we could arrive at a decision happily and together. Eventually, on a practical level, all was fine and yet for some time I remained irritable, needlessly wasting emotional energy.

Yet the joy of true friendship is that there comes a point when bitchiness is suddenly thrown over; so deep is the relationship that much hurt can be put instantly behind you. A moment of confrontation when problems are aired leads to an affectionate toast, with wine, tea, water or a hug, which puts the world back on to a happier plane where the light is bright and the smiles broad. Happiness is profoundest when it is shared: an expression of love between friends is a wonderful human experience. That deep feeling of companionship envelops me now as we smile at each other then turn back to the view outside. I feel as I have so many times before: here is a man, a complex and kind being with a great spirit, whom I shall always cherish.

〰〰

As a hundred and one other thoughts and impressions were surfacing, I looked over our tiny cabin. It could not have been any bigger than our cells in Lebanon. I smiled at the notion. We had both been free now as long as we had been imprisoned and here we were thousands of miles from home and sharing a small room once more.

'Think I'll walk back to the tailgate again,' I said, getting up and opening the door. John nodded and I left him to himself.

I disregarded the notice not to pass. It was warm on the tailgate and I could see the small villages hurtling away from us. I wasn't feeling sad, just guilty. I was glad I was going home, but I wasn't sure why. There were lots of convenient explanations, but my thoughts were still with Neruda and Bernardo. Both men's early lives were formed by a significant absence or lack of relationship with their father. My wife was at home waiting to give birth to our first child and the train wasn't going fast enough for me. Maybe that was another reason why these ghosts had latched on to me so tightly, impressing on me the importance of my own fatherhood.

Was there more to my maudlin introspection than simple homesickness? The train was leaving behind the pungent odour of Neruda's woodlands. The scent of the early morning was becoming heady with the aroma of cornfields and fruit plantations as sunlight flooded the panorama before me.

I thought again of these 'fatherless' heroes of Chile's past and how this significant aspect of their intimate personal histories had played an enormous part in their own development as poet and politician. And indirectly how this had also played an important role in the development of Chile as a nation, and how that nation perceived itself.

I looked out on the drowsy villages we sped through and the small settlements on the hillside beyond. I wondered how many of the occupants of those adobe cabins were themselves fatherless sons and daughters of the 'disappeared'. It was as if the earth had subsumed the confusion, grief, anger and sense of loss which were the emotional foundations of my spirit guides. This orphaned nation had never known a natural father to give it confidence and assurance through which its own personality could flower. In desperation, it had floundered under colonial task-masters and economic exploitation. It had latterly suffered under a tyrant uncle who cared nothing for these children of the earth and whose vision of its destiny was steeped in blood and oppression.

Both Neruda and Bernardo were children of a great love hunger and in the shimmering, apple-scented morning, I knew it was there still, breathing up out of the earth and into every living thing.

Instinctively Chile's magical landscape had somehow resolved the urgent inclination in me to travel. It was, in its own paradoxical way, a kind of homecoming. I sensed that the only important journeys I would henceforth make would be journeys out of time and into mind. There was another landscape to be discovered and negotiated. The landscape of the heart, the emotions and the imagination had to be opened up and new route maps plotted.

Another Patagonian traveller whom I have begun reading since my return writes, 'We talked late into the night arguing whether or not we, too, have journeys mapped out in our central nervous systems; it seemed the only way to account for our insane restlessness.'

Both John and I know these conversations from our sojourn in Lebanon and perhaps Chile was somehow mapped out for us. Certainly the 'insane restlessness' that was our natural reaction to captivity needed to be relieved and fulfilled by exploring this place of our fantasies and we had had to go.

Text Acknowledgements

Extract from *The Royal Hunt of the Sun* by Peter Shaffer (Hamish Hamilton, 1964) copyright © Peter Shaffer 1964. Reproduced by permission of Penguin Books Ltd.

Poem on p. 284 from *Selected Poems* by Pablo Neruda (Jonathan Cape, 1970), translated by Anthony Kerrigan, edited by Nathaniel Tarn, reproduced by permission of Jonathan Cape.

Poems on pp. 48, 76, 99, 107, 168, 313 from *Canto General* by Pablo Neruda (University of California Press, 1991), translated by Jack Schmitt, reproduced by permission of University of California Press.

Poems on pp. 73, 243, 273, 292, 336 from *La Isla Negra* by Pablo Neruda (Souvenir Press, 1982), translated by Alastair Reid, reproduced by permission of Souvenir Press Ltd.